STUDIES IN RELIGION IN EARLY AMERICAN LITERATURE

Edwards, Poe, Channing, Emerson, Some Minor Transcendentalists, Hawthorne, and Thoreau

David Lyttle

Syracuse University

UNIVERSITY
PRESS OF
AMERICA

LANHAM • NEW YORK • LONDON

All University Press of America books are produced on acid-free
paper which exceeds the minimum standards set by the National
Historical Publications and Records Commission.

DEDICATION

I wish to thank Harrison T. Meserole for introducing me to Jonathan Edwards and for loyal support over the years; William Wasserstrom for liberal and wise council; E. S. Mills for endless and substantial understanding; and my wife, Eulene, for making this book possible. Most of all, I wish to dedicate this book to the memory of Charles H. Lyttle.

iii

ACKNOWLEDGEMENTS

An earlier version of "Jonathan Edwards and the Supernatural Light" appeared in the Church Quarterly Review (1966), published by The Society for Promoting Christian Knowledge. "Jonathan Edwards on Personal Identity" was published in Early American Literature (1972). Parts of the essay, "Hawthorne: Calvinistic Humanism" appeared in Studies in Short Fiction (1972). And parts of "Thoreau's Diamond Body" were published in the Thoreau Journal Quarterly (1975).

I am grateful to John C. Godbey, Neil Gerdes, and the Meadville Theological School for permission to print the sermon, "Father of Spirits," by William Ellery Channing, Sr.

I wish to thank Julie Riggall for her patient and careful preparation of this manuscript.

TABLE OF CONTENTS

INTRODUCTION

This book is a literary-philosophic study of the thought of Jonathan Edwards, Edgar Allan Poe, William Ellery Channing, Sr., Ralph Waldo Emerson, some of the minor Transcendentalists, Nathaniel Hawthorne, and Henry David Thoreau. Each essay treats the thought of a writer as it is exhibited by several of its salient features. These essays as a collection, therefore, are not held together by an explicit thematic bond. But they are implicitly and broadly related by such vast themes as the nature of God and man; and often in them the thought of one writer is compared explicitly with that of another writer. In other words, this collection of essays consists in a tapestry of themes.

The book starts with Edwards and proceeds through Poe, Channing, Emerson, the minor Transcendentalists, Hawthorne, and Thoreau. The fifth piece in the book is a sermon by Channing, published here for the first time. I include the essay on the minor Transcendentalists to clarify the originality of Emerson's thought and the evolution of liberal Transcendental-Unitarian thought into the twentieth century. The essay on Poe is perhaps the black sheep or raven of the collection. But because it may be that, it brings into relief, from another angle, the thought of the other writers.

None of these writers was a professional philosopher, with the possible exception of Edwards, the greatest theologian of our Colonial period and still one of our definitive personalities. One hundred years later, Emerson, breaking from Unitarianism, was a visionary who lived his few but important premises in terms of the theology of literature. He and Thoreau were less interested in developing an abstract explanation of experience than in finding a new way of perceiving the world. Hence the reader must learn to perceive the way they perceived before he can understand them fully and judge them accurately. Poe, on the other hand, prided himself on his ability to think philosophically, and devised an elaborate scheme of existence he called _Eureka_. But he designated this scheme a "poem;" and indeed its logic is so cryptic and its content the result of such profound sublimation that critics differ widely on what the work means. In contrast, Hawthorne, exposed to the increasing scepticism of the liberal religious movement, thought metaphysical speculation useless as a means to knowledge. The present study, then, chronologically begins with Edwards, the most professional philosopher of the writers considered, and ends with Hawthorne and Thoreau, the least convinced of these writers of the value of abstract speculation.

Edwards the Calvinist and Channing the Unitarian are the only orthodox theists of this group, excepting the minor Transcendentalists and possibly Hawthorne. Only they believed in a personal god and in the survival of personal identity after death. On the other hand, Poe thought that individual souls fused in heaven. Emerson and Thoreau denied the existence of a personal god and the notion of personal immortality. Emerson wrote that "Friendship, like the immortality of the soul, is too good to be believed" ("Friendship"). In his "existential" transcendentalism, he sought power of the infinite rather than relations with human finities.

Hawthorne made gestures of acceptance of orthodox religion, but he does not show conclusively in his work that he believed in a personal god and in personal immortality. But I do not wish to suggest that he denied the existence of a "higher world" of persons. One of my main problems in the essay on Hawthorne was to establish as exactly as possible the character of the "ideal" in his work. His "ideal" consists, at least in part, in ideological attitudes of contemporaneous liberal religion, stripped, as Theodore Parker would say, of the "transient." For example, he rejected, technically speaking, the Calvinistic doctrine of depravity, and gave priority to absolute moral value which, in turn, implies personal immortality and a personal god. Yet Hawthorne was very much a sceptic, vague, ambiguous, hard to pin down.

Since these writers do not agree among themselves about the efficacy of metaphysical speculation, about the existence of God and of personal immortality, not surprisingly they did not agree about how a person fulfills his identity. Edwards found his identity in glorifying God; Channing, in social relationships among members of a divine family that extended from earth, through death, to heaven. Hawthorne likewise found identity in relationships among people, even though that identity was sometimes, as in the case of Hester Prynne, developed largely in opposition to society. But Hawthorne did not have the confident faith of Channing in a god nor in a heavenly society; in a twilight world of pathetic souls, he sought human fulfillment in terms of love, compassion, and mercy. In contrast, Emerson, an individuated incarnation of the existent universal, stressed "self-culture," and achieved identity by himself, alone, in symbolic outer landscapes. In moments of spiritual awakening, he was flooded with power that made nature float before him, transparent as dawn. Poe also found his identity alone, by himself. A unique entity in a surrealistic landscape, he was torn by cosmic drives within, and clashed against by human entities without. In moments of illumination, he felt the horrendous suction of death, like the eye of an unusually aged person, drawing him toward the dream of supernal beauty.

Only Emerson among this group celebrated individuation of person. He argued that a person, to achieve his identity, must recognize his centrality in the universe and realize his uniqueness. Thoreau, although in practice more individualistic than Emerson, wrote little or nothing about the philosophic necessity for uniqueness. Poe, on the other hand, argued that individuation is a necessary characteristic of human existence, and prided himself on being a genius. But he found his uniqueness to be exquisite torment, and half-longed for extinction in primal unity. In contrast, Edwards, Channing, and Hawthorne, thought individuation of person irrelevant, even detrimental, to realization of identity, and stressed conformity to universals. Channing and Hawthorne, especially, were moralists.

Since the problem of moral in distinction to natural evil is intricately woven into that of personal identity, I treat at least implicitly the vision of evil in each of these writers. Edwards believed of course that people inherit depravity from Adam, and are forgiven, if at all, by God in his Mercy. Channing held that people do not inherit evil; that evil is due to wrong choice; and that people themselves can overcome evil when they freely choose to follow the voice of conscience, the revelations of the Bible, the lessons of nature, and open themselves to the Spirit of God. Poe believed that evil is the predestined condition of mankind, and that it is essentially manifested in the inner tension between the isolated ego and its mourning for lost unity of Beauty. Emerson and Thoreau held that moral and natural evils are the results of the failure of perception, of a lack of alignment with God and nature which are aspects of Being. Hawthorne was certain only that most human hearts have a mysterious inclination to "sin;" that God, if he exists, does not intervene in human affairs; and that therefore the only possible remedy for evil is compassion based on the universal need for love.

This book begins with a study of Edwards' Calvinistic doctrine of the Supernatural Light and draws to a close in Thoreau's Jungian moonlight. The ideological progression is from the Puritan stance that the source of life and revelation is supernatural conscious intelligence external to and different from man, to the Romantic stance that this source is within man, at one with man, and "unconscious." The progression of cosmic metaphors is from divine transcendence to divine immanence; from Edwards' excluding psychology to the including psychology of Thoreau. The Edwardsean cosmos is imaged as the blinding Light of God surrounded by the saints, like mirrors, while further out and downward is the deepening blackness of individuated sinners. The supernatural comes home in Thoreau for whom there is no other world and no external god: all men partake in all the elements of Being, in the sunshine of consciousness, in the fertile darkness of the unconscious, the dynamism of the creative "wild." Nature for Thoreau is not a battlefield filled with coded commands from the Comander-in-chief but a hut in the living woods, which he helped to build and on the walls of which are universal lyrical poems he helped to write.

From another perspective, Edwards may be seen as the forerunner of the manichean sensibility out of which grew our two Romantic sub-traditions.[1] Poe, Hawthorne, and Melville, carry on the tradition of his hell-fire sermons, of moral darkness, introspective guilt, and general preoccupation with evil. Channing, Emerson, Thoreau, and Whitman, further the affirmative tradition of Edwards' pastoral sermons and of the Supernatural Light. Emerson, for instance, argued that preoccupation with evil and guilt is sentimental, and that since God is Being, God, not evil or the absence of Being, should be stressed on principle in practice.

Of these writers, I feel closest to Emerson intellectually and to Thoreau emotionally. I am attracted to Edwards because he did not allow his theology to use him. He broke through its austere mask to speak authentically about the human condition; he remained alive to fundamental options and to essential mystery. His universe is more exciting than Edward Taylor's and indeed Franklin's, and more fragile than either. With Poe, I have little in common; yet I remain immensely impressed by his artistic genius. In regard to Hawthorne, I sympathize with his knowledge of existential solitude and with his sensitivity to the suffering of mankind, both of which are necessary to balance Emerson's and Thoreau's divine self-reliance; but I remain frustrated by the imprecision of his thought. Toward Channing, I am respectful but feel little rapport, except in so far as he was the forerunner of religious freedom and social enlightenment.

FOOTNOTE

[1]See Richard Chase, The American Novel and its Tradition (New York: Doubleday, 1957), especially page 11.

THE SUPERNATURAL LIGHT

> "I saw eternity the other night
> Like a great ring of pure and endless
>   light,
>   All calm as it was bright;
> And round beneath it, Time, in hours,
>   days, years,
>   Driven by the spheres,
> Like a vast shadow moved, in which the
>   world
> And all her train were hurled."
>
>   Henry Vaughan[1]

I

Jonathan Edwards, like Vaughan, made a sharp distinction between nature and supernature; the former is a shadow of divinity. He held, therefore, that divine inspiration or Supernatural Light, although it may enlighten this world is not of this world; that it is like the light of the sun but that it is not material light. When he walked alone in the fields and hills, he sometimes experienced an "inward sweetness," "a calm, sweet abstraction of soul from all the concerns of this world," a "divine glory, in almost every thing . . . in the sun, moon, and stars; in the clouds, and blue sky; in the grass, flowers, trees; in the water, and all nature."[2] These extraordinary experiences, according to Edwards, were grounded on Supernatural Light the origin of which is beyond comprehension.

Perry Miller, in his provocative book on Edwards, argues that Edwards was "the first and most radical, even though the most tragically misunderstood, of American empiricists."[3] Not surprisingly, however, other critics, such as Vincent Tomas, think that Edwards remained largely a medievalist.[4] Edwards, a creative, aggressive, and brilliant thinker fascinated by the philosophic thought of his day, wished to show how even that thought could be put to the service of Calvinism, and used empirical terminology to describe the Calvinistic concept of inspiration.

1

Much of the terminology Edwards used in discussing the Supernatural Light reminds one of John Locke, and we know that he read the Essay on Human Understanding when he was in college. No doubt Miller is correct in holding that Edwards may be put into the empirical tradition in regard to the epistemology of the natural world. The young Edwards held that sense experience provides us with the beginning of all our knowledge. In his Yale notebook he wrote that he planned to show "how the mind would be without ideas, except as suggested by the senses." He held, like Locke, that we have no knowledge of the physical world until our minds are activated by that world. But did he believe that sense-knowledge of this world gave us knowledge of the supernatural world?

Edwards frequently referred to Grace as a "new inward perception or sensation." He stated that Grace "is what some metaphysicians call a new simple idea."[5] Locke defined a simple idea as presenting to the mind "one uniform appearance, or conception not distinguishable into different ideas."[6] These simple ideas are not complex; they cannot be analyzed or broken down into components. They are, as it were, atoms of experience. They are utterly simple: "though the qualities that affect our senses are in the things themselves, so united and blended, that there is no separation, no distance between them; yet it is plain, the ideas they produce in the mind enter by the senses simple and unmixed."[7] Locke went on to say that "it is not in the power of the most exalted wit, or enlarged understanding, by any quickness or variety of thought, to invent, or frame one new simple idea in the mind."

A simple idea for Locke is then an unmixed element of experience. We have, consequently, one kind of simple idea, or simple experience, by each of the five senses, such as color by the sense of sight, sound by the sense of hearing, sweetness by the sense of taste, and so on. On the basic level of the physical senses, therefore, we have five completely different kinds of perceptions. We might call each of these senses a dimension, and say that according to Locke our basic experience consists in the five sense dimensions. We are imprisoned in a world of the five senses; there is absolutely no way for us to escape unless we have outside help. Furthermore, Locke pointed out, "the simple ideas whereof our complex ideas of substances are made up are, for the most part, such as carry with them, in their own nature, no _visible_ connection or inconsistency with any other simple ideas."[8] Not only are we imprisoned in the world of the five senses, but these sense-dimensions in which our world consists are completely different from each other. If these dimensions were not in some mysterious way unified into one continuum of experience, our world would be fractured, a crazy quilt of a world; hearing has nothing to do with seeing, nor seeing with tasting, nor tasting with touching.

Edwards' purpose in referring to the simple ideas of sense in respect to the Supernatural Light was as much for clarity of expression as it was for epistemological explication. That is, he was as keenly interested in making clear how radically different from each other the ideas we get from each sense-dimension as he was in propounding these senses as the ultimate origin of our ideas. In fact, Edwards' use of Lockean terms and his reference to sense experience in his descriptions of the Supernatural Light were in part efforts to express as clearly as he could the complete distinction between the Light and the experiences of natural man. He stated that this Light is a sensation "totally diverse from all that men have, or can have, in a state of nature;"[9] and that "all spiritual and gracious affections are attended with, and arise from some apprehension, idea or sensation of mind, which is in its whole nature different, yea exceeding different from all that is or can be in the mind of a natural man; and which the natural man discerns nothing of, and has no manner of idea of, and conceives of no more than a man without the sense of tasting can conceive of the sweet taste of honey."[10] Edwards' emphasis here is not on an identity of kind between the experience of the Supernatural Light and physical sense experience (an impression which Miller tends to give) but on the difference of kind between them. The experience of the Supernatural Light is, so to speak, a new dimension so basically different from our natural experiences that Edwards did not know how to talk about it precisely: "the spiritual perceptions which a sanctified and spiritual person has, are not

only diverse from all that natural men have, after
the manner that the ideas of perceptions of the same
sense may differ one from another, but rather as the
ideas and sensations of different senses do
differ."[11]   And in his sermon, "A Divine and
Supernatural Light," Edwards wrote "that there is
such a thing as a Spiritual and Divine Light,
immediately imparted to the soul by God, of a
different nature from any that is obtained by
natural means." Thus we experience the transcendental as fundamentally as we experience any of the
five dimensions of our senses, and we can no more
have this experience, if we are not saints, than a
man who has no power of taste can experience the
taste of honey. Like a simple idea, a revelatory
experience is "one uniform appearance, or conception
in the mind." When a saint experiences the Supernatural Light, he is as it were presented to a new
dimension so unique that he has no way, except by
analogy, to communicate his experience.

Now Edwards argued that this "new spiritual
sense, and the new dispositions that attend it, are
no new faculties, but are new principles of nature."
After the medieval tradition, he meant by faculties
the will and the understanding. He continued:

I use the word 'principles,' for want of a word
of more determined significance. By a principle of nature in this place, I mean that
foundation which is laid in nature, either old
or new, for any particular manner or kind of
exercise of the faculties of the soul; or a
natural habit or foundation for action, giving
a person ability and disposition to exert the
faculties in exercises of such a certain kind;
so that to exert the faculties in exercises,
may be said to be his nature. So this new
spiritual sense is not a new faculty of understanding, but it is a new foundation laid in
the nature of the soul, for a new kind of
exercises of the same faculty of understanding.
So that new holy disposition of heart that
attends this new sense, is not a new faculty of
will, but a foundation laid in the nature of
the soul, for a new kind of exercises of the
same faculty of will.[12]

Thus Edwards did not mean by the Supernatural Light
what Locke meant, for instance, by Reason. Locke
defined Reason as that which "perceives the
necessary (and probable) connection of all ideas or
proofs one to another, in each step of any demonstration that produces knowledge."[13] But again,
Edwards was clear in saying that the Supernatural
Light is not the ability to see new connections
among abstract ideas or reflection. It is not a
higher Intelligence Quotient, nor the ability to
have new logical knowledge. The Devil has these:
"The Devil has not only great speculative knowledge,
but he has a sense of many divine things which
deeply affect him, and is most deeply Impressed with
his heart."[14] Nor indeed did Locke equate Grace
or Revelation with Reason. Reason, he held, is the
God-given faculty of man abstractly to perceive the
coherency of experience, but Revelation is immediate
experience of Divine Being, the order of which Being
is too high and comprehensive for logic to grasp.
Even so Locke said, true inspiration never con-
tradicts Reason. In fact, inspiration is proved
inspiration only if such an experience passes the
ultimate test of universal Reason. In contrast,
Edwards held that inspiration is self-autheticating
and enlightening of Calvinistic doctrine. Inspiration, he said, has a "divine and godlike
beauty, a kind of intuitive and immediate evidence"
of its divine origin. It is a simple and unmixed
experience with the hallmark of God.

Thus Edwards believed that the difference
between a saint and a natural man is not in what
ideas are held in the mind, nor whether or not those
ideas are logically held. Both men can hold correctly all the ideas necessary for salvation. Nor
is the difference a matter of creaturely emotion.
The Devil, Edwards tells us, yearns probably more
deeply than most creatures for divine things.[15]
Fallen creatures simply do not have the right kind
of feeling; they live in a fallen world of limited
dimensions. The saint on the other hand is like a
blind man who suddenly at conversion experiences in
numinous color a world through which he has only
clumsily groped. The saint comprehends right ideas
in the depth of the Supernatural Light. He does not
have new ideas, nor new relationships among old
ideas; he has a new dimension of consciousness of
old familiar things.

Edwards was troubled about how he could convey to natural men his knowledge of supernatural Being. He concluded that "Because spiritual things being invisible, and not things that can be pointed forth with the finger, we are forced to borrow names from external and sensible objects to signify them by. Thus we call a clear apprehension of things spiritual by the name of light. . . . The Scripture itself abounds with such like figurative expressions."[16] Edwards could not speak directly of the experience of Revelation because he had no terms with which to do so; he had to speak metaphorically. Indeed, all his references to the senses when he spoke about the Supernatural Light are metaphorical. But what he meant to express literally by these metaphors, to repeat, is the absolute difference between Revelation and natural experience. We can appreciate Edwards' problem when we try to imagine how we would describe an experience totally unlike any experience we have ever had. But this is a traditional problem. History is filled with people who have tried to express in natural terms what they think is a supernatural experience. They use oxymorons such as "dazzling darkness," "darkness visible"--things which no creature with only five senses ever experienced nor, logically, could hope to experience. The Calvinist, for whom God was essentially inscrutable, simply used empirical terms to express the inexpressible.

Edwards was probably intensely interested in the following passage from Locke's treatment of simple ideas.

The domain of man, in this little world of his own understanding being much what the same as it is in the great world of visible things; wherein his power, however managed by art and skill, reaches no farther than to compound and divide the materials that are made to his hand; but can do nothing towards the making the least particle of new matter, or destroying one atom of what is already in being. The same inability will every one find in himself, who shall go about to fashion in his understanding one simple idea, not received in by his senses from external objects, or by reflection from the operations of his own mind about them. I would have any one try to fancy any taste which had never affected his palate; or frame the idea of a scent he had never smelt; and when he can do this, I will also conclude that a blind man hath ideas of colours, and a deaf man true distinct notions of sounds.

3. This is the reason why - though we cannot believe it impossible to God to make a creature with other organs, and more ways to convey into the understanding the notice of coporeal things than those five, as they are usually counted, which he has given to man - yet I think it is not possible for any man to imagine any other qualities in bodies, howsoever constituted, whereby they can be taken notice of, besides sounds, tastes, smells, visible and tangible qualities. And had mankind been made but with four senses, the qualities then which are the objects of the fifth sense had been as far from our notice, imagination, and conception, as now any belonging to a sixth, seventh, or eighth sense can possibly be; - which, whether yet some other creatures, in some other parts of this vast and stupendous universe, may not have, will be a great presumption to deny. He that will not set himself proudly at the top of all things, but will consider the immensity of this fabric, and the great variety that is to be found in this little and inconsiderable part of it which he has to do with, may be apt to think that, in other mansions of it, there may be other and different intelligent beings, of whose faculties he has as little knowledge or apprehension as a worm shut up in one drawer of a cabinet hath of the senses or understanding of a man; such variety and excellency being suitable to the wisdom and power of the Maker.[17]

Elsewhere Locke stated that "God, I own, cannot be denied to be able to enlighten the understanding by a ray darted into the mind immediately from the foundation of light: this they understand he has promised to do, and who then has so good a title to expect it as those who are his peculiar people, chosen by him, and depending on him."[18] These passages from Locke explain an immense amount of the philosophic Edwards. Here we have Locke dealing with simple ideas derived from sense experience, and referring to the senses of taste and color and sound, not to show their similarity but to stress their exceeding difference. Here we have Locke the modern empiricist stating that there may be creatures somewhere in the universe with senses totally different from our five. (Edwards, like many others of his time, was fascinated by the possibility of inhabitants in other worlds.) Here we have Locke the anti-Calvinist, the empiricist, speaking of the immensity of space (the shadow of God, for Edwards), and using a typical biblical metaphor to express the condition of man, "a worm." And last, in the quotation from the famous chapter on "Enthusiasm," we have Locke stating figuratively that God can send a supernatural ray of light into man--which Edwards would surely have seen could very well be experienced as the activator of one of those other "senses" of which Locke spoke. In Book IV of his Essays, in the chapter on "Faith and Reason," Locke wrote that "no man inspired by God can by any revelation communicate to others any new simple ideas which they had not before from sensation or reflection. For whatever impressions he himself may have from the immediate hand of God, this revelation, if it be of new simple ideas, cannot be conveyed to another, either by words or any other signs." Thus, here in these quotations from Locke, are many of the Lockean elements that Edwards transformed into his own Calvinistic theology. Here, very simply, is Edwards' basic outline for explaining, in contemporaneous philosophic terms, the relation of the supernatural to the natural; and for explaining how the supernatural is known by the saints, those chosen and peculiar people.[19]

In his early "Notes on the Mind" Edwards speculated:

> 31. Sensation. Whether all ideas, wherein the mind is merely passive, and which are received immediately without any dependence on Reflection, are not ideas of Sensation, or External ideas. Whether there be any difference between these? Whether it be possible for the Soul of man, in this manner, to be originally, and without dependence on Reflection, capable of receiving any other ideas than those of sensation, or something equivalent, and so some

external idea? And whether the first[20] ideas of the angels, must not be of such kind.

Edwards of course answered these questions in the affirmative. Yes, there is, as it were, a sixth sense, a supernatural sense, with which the saint, without dependence on Reflection, experiences the objective God who radically differs from natural objects.

Now Edwards is not an "empiricist" if one defines such a thinker as one who limits the origin of knowledge to the five senses of the natural world. For the sake of clarity and of tradition this limitation should be made. Thus Edwards is not an empiricist, at least in regard to Revelation. Miller writes that Edwards believed that the Super-natural Light "is[21] composed of nothing but what nature supplies;" and that conversion "is a perception, a form of apprehension, derived exactly as Locke said mankind gets all simple ideas, out of sensory experience."[22] But Edwards did not say that the saints receive the Light through the sensory experience of nature. He said that the saint knows the Light on a level just as funda-mental, just as non-intellectual, non-cognitive; but he did not say that the saint knows it in any natural way, in any way that has anything to do with the five natural senses. Edwards used empirical terms to describe the Light to emphasize the radical uniqueness of this experience, and to suggest--and here Miller is correct--that this experience is like (but is not) a vivid sense experience in that it is simple and irreducible. Edwards was simply using empirical terminology to express the orthodox Christian view that the knowledge of God is by supernatural means in which reason and natural sense experience play no fundamental part.

Consequently Edwards cannot be considered an "empirical nature mystic" for he does not hold that the saint receives the divine spirit through the medium of nature--presuming that this is the defin-ition of such a mystic. William Wordsworth, for example, wrote in "Tintern Abbey:"

> Well pleased to recognize
> In nature and the language of the sense

The anchor of my present thoughts, the nurse,
The guide, the guardian of my heart, and soul,
Of all my moral being.

But Edwards would never had said that the quality of
his spiritual life depended upon the quality of his
experience of nature. He said just the reverse:
the quality of his perception of nature, the shadow
of divinity, depended upon the quality of his
spiritual life. In his "Personal Narrative," in
passages that rival the best of their kind in the
English language, he described a transformation of
his perception of nature that took place in conjunction with, or subsequent to, his reading of
scripture and his reception of the divine spirit by
means of the supernatural sense. In "The Divine and
Supernatural Light," he insisted:

> This spiritual and divine light does not
> consist in any impression made upon the imagin-
> ation. . . . It is no imagination or idea of an
> outward light or glory, . . . or a visible
> lustre or brightness of any object. The
> imagination may be strongly impressed with such
> things; but this is not spiritual light.
> Indeed when the mind has a lively discovery of
> spiritual things, and is greatly affected by
> the power of divine light, it may, and probably
> very commonly doth, much affect the imagin-
> ation; so that impressions of an outward beauty
> or brightness may accompany those spiritual
> discoveries. But spiritual light is not that
> impression upon the imagination.

The Supernatural Light is not "an outward light or
glory." It is an inner light that floods the outer
world, providing the perceiver with a new perception
of nature. (In fact, Wordsworth himself, in spite
of the previous quotation, imposed upon David
Hartley's associationism "a Platonic principle of
mystical insight," "another gift of aspect more
sublime.")[23] Likewise, Ralph Waldo Emerson held
that an influx of Reason preceded alignment of inner
and outer worlds. Edwards, like Emerson, held that
there are two ways of knowing, and that the higher
way is not dependent upon the lower way; rather, the
higher way must guide the lower way.

Again, Edwards believed of course that "the system of nature and the system of revelation are both divine works, so both are in different senses a divine world."[24] But the Spirit always precedes the Word. Without the Spirit, nature and the Bible are flat, cold etchings: "A mind, not spiritually enlightened, beholds spiritual things faintly, like fainting, fading shadows that made no lively impression on his mind--like a man that beholds the trees and things abroad in the night . . . but he that sees by divine light is like a man that views the garden when the sunlight shines upon it."[25] Although the Bible is the divine word and "the beauty of the world is a communication of God's beauty," a person must have his natural perception sensitized by divine spirit to comprehend correctly the former and to appreciate the quality of the latter.[26] Both Edwards and Emerson held that ordinary consciousness is grounded on a greater reality; and each held that a deepening of ordinary consciousness is caused by power of that greater reality--not by sensitizing ordinary consciousness, by means of drugs, hypnosis, or by any other "natural" way.

What the natural senses and the spiritual sense have in common for Edwards is that they are passive, that the experiences men have as the result of each one are simple and unmixed, and that such experiences are non-cognitive. The significance of these characteristics of the Supernatural Light is this: that the experience of this Light is passive suggests that the source of spiritual knowledge, like that of natural knowledge, is not the will of the human creature but "outside" of him in God. That the spiritual experience is simple and unmixed suggests that it is utterly different from natural experiences, and that it is hardly deniable.

Alfred North Whitehead writes that the Reformation was a return to the contemplation of brute fact on the sense level; and Locke, that a man "has no greater assurance than that of his senses."[27] Thus the saint by means of the sixth sense experiences the self-authenticating brute fact of God. Since the Light is non-cognitive, it does not consist in universal and self-evident ideas, nor lead to a unique interpretation of doctrine. Edwards, like Locke, but for different reasons, saw no evidence for cognitive "innate" ideas; such ideas might allow salvation for all men and deny the necessity for a choosen ministry. Edwards, like Calvin, conceived of salvation as dependent upon the Spirit in conjunction with a trained understanding of the Word.

Edwards' stress on the non-cognitive, brute fact of the Light is doubly significant because, especially after 1741, he was forced by the circumstances of the Great Awakening to defend the "affections" against the growing rationalism and moralism of such "Old Light" Calvinists as Charles Chauncy who foreshadowed the nineteenth-century Unitarians. Edwards' perplexing problem in Religious Affections was to justify his position to the established church by devising tests of reason for his self-authenticating Light. In the next century, Emerson recognized the futility of trying to justify his revelation to the church; withdrew from the church; and justified his revelation in terms of the universal symbols of literature and of a serene self-reliance that passed all Understanding.

Thus the Supernatural Light for Edwards is known to the saint by a spiritual sixth sense. This sense is an innate, non-cognitive principle of perception; it is the recipient of the brute fact of God's Spirit. This is how the natural world of Edwards the empirical philosopher was not so much invaded by than exposed to the supernatural world of Edwards the medieval theologian. The supernatural sense is utterly different from the natural senses, but all are unified in the experience of the saint. The saint, like the rest of us, a depraved, light-exhausted creature, is, in the epiphanies of regeneration, filled with unearthly Light that makes numinous the impressions of nature.

II

Did Edwards believe that in his experience of the Supernatural Light he became one with God? Was he a mystic? The variety of definitions of the term "mysticism" defy a definitive answer to this question. What answer is given depends upon how one interprets Edwards' phrase "one with God." V. G. Allen thought that Edwards was a mystic and argued

that the "divine light is not the mere external
power of God: it is of God's inmost essence. . . .
This light within changes the nature of the soul,
assimulating it to the divine nature."[28] Although
Edwards protests against those who speak of being
"Godded with God," Allen continues, "the protests
. . . having been made, Edwards continues to use
language which conveys the same idea. And indeed,
that is his meaning, whether he owns it or not, -
the saint through an indwelling Spirit, which is the
highest, fullest essence of Deity, becomes as it
were one with God".[29]

But some contemporary theologians do not agree
with Allen. Conrad Cherry, for example, believes
that Edwards was committed always to the "object-
ivism" of Calvinism; that God was always in some
sense for Edwards a person who stands over against
man; and that he, Edwards, never lost his sense of
sin nor the feeling of being cut-off from and
opposed to God. Thus Edwards, although holding to
"union between the Spirit and the soul," did not
believe in "identity" between them. "God in his
Spirit communicates himself to the saint, but He
joins the saint as the saint's new principle or
foundation, and not as a human-absorbing divinity."[30] I am in favor of Cherry's view; but the
disagreement among critics about Edwards and
mysticism indicates that there are two tendencies in
Edwards, one toward identity of the creature with
God; and the other, toward their proximity but
separation. Even Cherry admits that there is
tension in Edwards between his "Neoplatonic metaphysics and his Calvinism."[31]

W. R. Inge believes that "the Unity of all
existence is a fundamental doctrine of Mysticism.
God is in all, and all is in God. . . . Mysticism is
always and necessarily pantheistic."[32] Expressions of the mystical and pantheistic tendencies in
Edwards are: 1) his beautiful passages in the
"Personal Narrative" in which he says that he
perceived, during his experiences of the Supernatural Light, divinity in all things, and that he
himself wished to be "swallowed up" in God; 2) his
doctrine of the totally sovereign Will of God (as
Dr. Channing and others pointed out);[33] 3) his
philosophic idealism in which he reduces all things
to one substance, "Mind;" 4) his definition of

13

personal identity which, as I try to show in the next essay, leaves the identity of the creature next to nothing; and 5) his statement in "Notes on the Mind," and others like it, that evil is the absence of Being (a characteristic position, according to Inge, of the philosophies of mysticism): "Disagreement of contrariety to Being, is evidently an approach to Nothing, or a degree of Nothing; which is nothing else but disagreement or contrariety of Being, and the greatest and only evil: and Entity is the greatest and only good."[34] There is little doubt that Edwards was in part inclined toward the affective and theoretic monism of the mystical tradition.

On the other hand, Edwards seems always to have retained a latent distinction between God and himself. As a sinner, he believed himself to be, and deserving to be, infinitely apart from God. Moreover, his great imprecatory sermons (intimate expressions of his personality that should not be swept aside in the interest of religious liberalism) counterbalance, in manichean fashion, his great affirmations of the Supernatural Light, and all but negate his abstract statements that evil is the absence of Being.[35] Above all, Edwards' stress on morality necessitates a philosophy based on relationships among persons, primarily between God and each creature. Since the reason for the creature's existence is to glorify God (not God _and_ man, as Emerson believed), the immortal created soul cannot be absorbed into deity but must retain its separate and distinct identity to some extent to act as a mirror or reflector of God's glory. Edwards wrote that the saints "have relation to God, as they have respect to him as their object. . . . God is the object of that love. . . . Here is both an <u>emanation</u> and <u>remanation</u>. The refulgence shines upon and into the creature, and is reflected back to the luminary. The beams of glory come from God, and are something of God, and are refunded back again to their original. So that the whole is <u>of</u> God, and <u>in</u> God, and <u>to</u> God, and God is the beginning, middle and end in this affair."[36] There is a give-and-take between God and the saint: God emanates his glory and the saint "remanates" or reflects that glory back to God. The identity of the saint consists in his ability not to become in essence one with God

14

but to reflect God. The saint, although not necessary to God, is within the total context of incandescent Being; as a mirror reflecting glory, he is always distinct from the center of Being. Analogous to the Son, in the doctrine of the Trinity, the created saint reflects the Father but, unlike the Son, is not one with the Father. The rational, intensely conscious tenor of Edwards' mind demanded not a homogenous whole but a whole consisting in balance and symmetry among its parts.

In short, Edwards' dismal evaluation of himself; his vision of the concreteness of evil; and his ethical or relational orientation toward God, restrain his pantheistic inclinations to fuse with the divine. There is a sense of "otherness" between God and the creature in Edwards that ultimately distinguishes him from the core of the mystical tradition and from an affective and theoretic pantheist, for instance, like Emerson.

In his vision of the ascension of the saints to God, Edwards further exhibits tension between the ideas of union and distinction of God and the creature. The last paragraphs in The Dissertation Concerning the End for which God Created the World (1755) are at once lyrical, theological statements that the saints will unite with God and refrain-like assurances that there will never come a time when it can be said that this union will take place:

It is no solid objection against God's aiming at an infinitely perfect union of the creature with himself, that the particular time will never come when it can be said, the union is now infinitely perfect. God aims at satisfying justice in the eternal damnation of sinners; which will be satisfied by their damnation, considered no otherwise than with regard to its eternal duration. But yet there never will come that particular moment, when it can be said, that now justice is satisfied. . . . God, in glorying the saints in heaven with eternal felicity, aims to satisfy his infinite grace or benevolence, by the bestowment of a good infinitely valuable, because eternal; and yet there never will come the moment, when it can be said, that now this infinitely valuable good has been actually bestowed.

15

Thus Edwards views creation for the saints as an infinite build-up to a climax that will never come (and for the sinners, in his fearful symmetry of heaven and hell, as an infinite let-down that will never end).[37] In the repeated phrase, "though the time will never come," Edwards the Calvinist protected himself against Edwards the Neoplatonist. In other places where he speaks of the ultimate God-saint relationship, he restrains pantheistic implications of his statement with the phrase, "as it were." For example, he wrote: "those elect creatures, which must be looked upon as the end of all the rest of creation . . . must be viewed as being, as it were, one with God. They were respected as brought home to him, united in him, centering most perfectly, and as it were, swallowed up in him; so that his respect to them finally coincides, and becomes one and the same with respect to himself."[38] The phrase, "as it were," guides the expression, "becomes one and the same with respect to himself," to mean unity, not identity.

Edwards said that out in the woods and fields he experienced the Supernatural Light which was the consuming presence of God. He wrote in the "Personal Narrative" that his heart "panted to lie low before God, as in the dust; that I might be nothing, and that God might be ALL, that I might become as a little child." But this was not to say that his Calvinistic head told him that he should or could be "Godded with God," obliterated in divinity. He was exquisitely happy to remain a special little child, a reflector of divine glory.

FOOTNOTES

[1] "The World."

[2] "Personal Narrative."

[3] Perry Miller, "Jonathan Edwards on the Sense of the Heart," *The Harvard Theological Review*, XL (April, 1948), p. 124. See for a discussion of Edwards' neoplatonism: Robert C. Whittemore, "Jonathan Edwards and the Theology of the Sixth Way," *Church History*, XXXV (March, 1966), 60-75.

[4] Vincent Tomas, "The Modernity of Jonathan Edwards," *New England Quarterly*, XXV (March, 1952), 60-80.

[5] *Religious Affections*, ed. John E. Smith (Cambridge: Yale University Press, 1959), p. 205.

[6] *An Essay Concerning Human Understanding*, ed. Alexander Campbell Fraser (New York: Dover, 1959), II, ii, 1.

[7] Fraser, II, ii, 1.

[8] Fraser, IV, iii, 10.

[9] *Religious Affections*, p. 214.

[10] *Religious Affections*, pp. 207-8.

[11] *Religious Affections*, p. 206.

[12] *Religious Affections*, p. 206.

[13] Fraser, IV, vii, 2.

[14] *Works*, ed. Sereno E. Dwight (New York, 1829-30), VIII, 10.

[15] Perhaps Edwards knew Milton's lines on Satan: "his griev'd look he fixes sad/Sometimes toward Heav'n and the full-blazing sun" (*Paradise Lost*, IV, 28-29).

[16] *Religious Affections*, p. 212.

[17] Fraser, II, ii, 2 and 3.

[18] Fraser, IV, xix, 5.

[19] See for a comparison of Edwards and Locke on the Supernatural Light: David Laurence, "Jonathan Edwards, John Locke and the Canon of Experience," Early American Literature XV (Fall, 1980), 107-23.

[20] Works, I, 666.

[21] Perry Miller, Jonathan Edwards (New York: Meridian, 1959), p. 276.

[22] Miller, p. 139.

[23] Samuel C. Chew, in A Literary History of England, ed. Albert C. Baugh (New York: Appleton-Century-Crofts, 1948), p. 1141.

[24] Quoted in The Philosophy of Jonathan Edwards, ed. Harvey G. Townsend (Oregon: University of Oregon Press, 1955), p. 233.

[25] Townsend, pp. 249-50. Compare Edwards with Thoreau at the end of "Walking:" "So we saunter toward the Holy Land, till one day the sun shall shine more brightly than ever he has done, shall perchance shine into our minds and hearts, and light up our whole lives with a great awakening light, as warm and serene and golden as on a bankside in autumn." In revelation, nature does not precede spirit for either Edwards or Thoreau. Thoreau's "Holy Land" is not material; and his sun is a symbol of spiritual power originating not in nature nor in his empirical ego. It is a power that fills him, as ego, and illuminates his perception of nature. In this case, doctrine, not experience, separates these men.

[26] Townsend, p. 260.

[27] Science and the Modern World (New York: Macmillen, 1944), p. 12.

[28] Jonathan Edwards (Boston, 1889), pp. 70-1.

[29] Allen, p. 224.

30 Conrad Cherry, The Theology of Jonathan Edwards (New York: Doubleday, 1966), pp. 85-88. See for a defense of Edwards as mystic, Douglas J. Elwood, The Philosophical Theology of Jonathan Edwards (New York: Columbia University Press, 1960).

31 If Edwards is designated as a mystic, he might be classified as an "extrovertive mystic." W. T. Stace defines two kinds of mystics: "The introvertive mystic, getting rid of sensations, images, and thought content, comes at last to find within himself the pure self which becomes, or is, unified with the Universal Self or God." Such an experience, we are told, is ineffable. In contrast, the extrovertive mystics see "the world around them, the grass, the trees, the animals, and sometimes 'inanimate' objects such as rocks and mountains, as God-impregnated, or as shining from within with the light of life which is one and the same life flowing through all things" (Mysticism and Philosophy [Philadelphia: Lippincott, 1960], pp. 218-220). Stace believes that the experience of the introvertive mystic is the profounder of the two.

32 Christian Mysticism (New York: World Publishing Col, 1956), p. 28.

33 See the following essay, "Channing and Emerson on Personal Identity."

34 Quoted in Jonathan Edwards: Representative Selections, ed. Clarence H. Faust and Thomas J. Johnson (1935; revised ed. New York: Hill & Wang, 1962), pp. 33-4.

35 Edwards states that God is no more the author of evil than the sun is the cause of darkness when it "descends below the horizon;" the sun is merely "the occasion of darkness and frost." Edwards continues: "If the sun were the proper cause of cold and darkness, it would be the fountain of these things . . . then something might be argued from the nature of cold and darkness, to a likeness of nature in the sun; and it might be justly inferred, that the sun itself is dark and cold, and that his beams are black and frosty" (Freedom of the Will, ed. Paul Ramsey [New Haven: Yale University Press, 1957], p. 404). The imaginative power of

19

this metaphor emotionally seems to negate the purpose of its logic.

36 Faust, p. 344.

37 There is in Edwards a negative mysticism:

> God also is everywhere present with His all-seeing eye. He is in heaven and in hell, and in and through every part of His creation. He is where every devil is, and where every damned soul is: He is present by His power and by His essence. He not only knows as well as those in heaven who see at a distance, but he knows as perfectly as those who feel the misery. He seeth into the inmost recesses of the hearts of those miserable spirits, for He upholds them in being (Works [1808], IV, 169; also quoted in Allen, p. 123].

The identity of sinner and saint alike, in Edwards' vision, is almost totally sacrificed to the grand design of the Whole. Evil in his system is the dark consciousness of God that intensifies the joy and happiness of God with Himself (and the saints). William Ellery Channing wrote in "Likeness to God" that "the idea of God, sublime and awful as it is, is the idea of human nature, purified and enlarged to infinity."

38 Works, III, 26.

JONATHAN EDWARDS ON PERSONAL IDENTITY

> "Is it not better, that the good and evil which
> happens in God's world, should be ordered,
> regulated, bounded and determined by the good
> pleasure of an infinitely wise Being . . . than
> to leave these things to fall out by chance?"
>
> Jonathan Edwards[1]

I

In "The Mind" and in The Great Doctrine of
Original Sin Defended, Jonathan Edwards examined the
problem of identity. He was certain that men were
created miserable and that he himself labored under
infinite guilt. Human beings, Edwards thought,
suffered for some crime that they were not conscious
of having committed, but, as he put it, "there is no
reason to be brought, why one man's sin cannot be
justly reckoned to another's account, who was not
then in being, in the whole of it."[2] Edwards
utilized Lockean terminology in defining how men are
punished for a crime of which they are not aware,
but his use of this terminology, like his use of it
in his definition of the Supernatural Light, is a
mere facade of a medieval structure. Edwards could
not hold at the same time Locke's position on
identity and the Calvinistic doctrine of Original
Sin.

John Locke was the first philosopher to raise
the question of personal identity. He did so
because of his opposition to the philosophy of
Descartes, who held that "the indivisibility of the
self or thinking substance is a self-evident
truth."[3] Since for Locke the mind is not given
"clear and distinct ideas of [its own] substance,"
it "can have no certain knowledge" of its identity
nor of its immortality.[4] Locke did not deny
immaterial substance, however; he simply held it to
be unknowable, a "we now not what."[5]

If Locke's opposition to Descartes brought the
problem of identity to his attention, "it was the
recognition of its ethical significance which forced
him to provide a solution." Locke assumed that
"personal identity is the ultimate source of all the

21

right and justice of reward and punishment." But if we can have no clear and distinct ideas of immaterial substance, and if we are to have certain "means of determining the limits of personal responsibility," then personal identity must be defined in terms other than substance.[6]

Locke held that personal identity consists in "same consciousness." "For, since consciousness always accompanies thinking, and it is that which makes every one to be what he calls self, and thereby distinguishes himself from all other thinking things, in this alone consists personal identity . . . and as far as this consciousness can be extended backwards to any past action or thought, so far reaches the identity of that person."[7] Since personal identity does not extend beyond continuity of idea, a person should not be punished for any crime which he is not conscious of committing. Locke commented that "supposing a man punished now for what he had done in another life, whereof he be made to have no consciousness at all, what difference is there between that punishment and being created miserable?"[8] Moreover, Locke argued that since personal identity is separate from immaterial substance, "a person," a continuity of idea or same consciousness, could trade immaterial substance with other persons and remain the same person. "If the same consciousness . . . can be transferred from one thinking substance to another, it will be possible that two thinking substances may make but one person. For the same consciousness being preserved, whether in the same or different substances, the personal identity is preserved."[9] For Locke, then, personal identity and moral responsibility were limited to continuity of idea.

In the earliest passage about identity in "The Mind," Jonathan Edwards accepted this position of Locke and enlarged upon it. "Well might Mr. Locke say, that, Identity of person consisted in identity of consciousness; for he might have said that identity of spirit, too, consisted in the same consciousness; for a mind or spirit is nothing else but consciousness, and what is included in it. The same consciousness is, to all intents and purposes, individually the very same spirit, or substance; as much as the same particle of matter can be the same with itself, at different times."[10] Edwards made gestures towards concurring with Locke, but at the same time added the presupposition of "substance" to the idea of personal identity. "A person," according to the preceding passage, consists in continuity of idea <u>and</u> in an immaterial thinking substance. On the one hand, Edwards wished to establish personal identity with empirical certainty, but on the other hand, he could not hold that continuity of idea is fundamental to identity, hence to moral worth, for the obvious reason that a person here and now cannot remember committing Adam's crime. Identity, therefore, must consist in more than continuity of idea if it is the source of moral worth; it must consist fundamentally in immaterial substance, the nature of which differs from the phenomenal content of consciousness.

In regard to moral worth, Edwards approvingly quoted "Stapferus, an eminent divine of Zurich:" "We should distinguish here between the <u>physical act</u> itself which Adam committed, and the <u>morality</u> of the action, and consent to it. If we have respect only to the external act, to be sure it must be confessed that Adam's posterity did not put forth their hands to the forbidden fruit."[11] But Adam's posterity "are to be looked upon as consenting to" that intent, and therefore to be as guilty as Adam. Like Adam, a person today, even though he cannot recall committing the original disobedient act, intends to "kill" God, and is thereby damned--although through meditation, preaching, and other means of salvation, he may be made humble and open to salvation by being kept aware of his Adamic desire. In Edwards' world, a man is defined by his intent toward God. In Locke's world, identity and moral worth are defined by action, by turning intents into spatial events that are frozen in the past. If a person cannot remember himself doing an act of evil, he should not be punished for it. On Judgment Day, Locke wrote, "no one shall be made to answer for what he knows nothing of."[12]

Locke defined personal identity in terms of individuation as continuity of idea: "it is that which makes every one to be what he calls self, and thereby distinguishes himself from all other thinking things." This was Locke's fundamental point: no two persons can have the same continuity of idea; each person consists in a unique sequence of ideas, and only he is responsible in terms of that sequence. But for Edwards, the "ultimate source" of moral worth for each person is not a unique sequence of ideas grounded in remembered experience, but generic human mind. Locke, therefore, sought a principle of individuation in his quest for a definition of identity as the source of moral worth; Edwards sought a principle of oneness that is manifested neither as individuation nor as generalness, but as identical multiple units of generic consciousness. For this reason, Edwards could hold that the content of a person's consciousness is fundamentally inconsequential to his identity, and that indeed that content can be duplicated without one's significant identity being lost. In "The Mind," he wrote:

> Identity of person is what seems never yet to have been explained. It is a mistake, that it consists in sameness, or identity, of consciousness-if, by sameness of consciousness, be meant, having the same ideas hereafter, that I have now. . . . It is possible without doubt, in the nature of things, for God to annihilate me, and after my annihilation to create another being that shall have the same ideas in his mind that I have, and with the like apprehension that he had had them before, in like manner as a person has by memory; and yet I be in no way concerned in it, having no reason to fear that that being shall suffer, or to hope for what he shall enjoy. . . . Yea, there seems to be nothing of impossibility in the Nature of things, but that the Most High could, if he saw fit, cause there to be another being, who should begin to exist in some distant part of the universe, with the ideas I now have, after the manner of memory; and should henceforward co-exist with me.[13]

Whereas Locke argued that a person's identity--the unique sequence of ideas in which a person essentially consists--may be grounded on two or more (unknowable) immaterial substances, without destroying that person's identity, Edwards held that that sequence of ideas may be duplicated without destroying that identity. For Edwards, the essence of "a person," therefore, is not uniqueness or individuation but a generic thinking substance; he

24

sacrifices a person's individuality to his (inherited) moral worth.

Edwards, in contrast to Locke, held that immaterial substance is necessary for personal identity. But was his principle of individuation based on created thinking substance in which ideas are grounded? He was ambiguous. In fact, he was reluctant to admit that created immaterial substance, individuated or not, exists at all. In the "Miscellanies," he commented: "The mere exertion of a new thought is certain proof of a God. For certainly there is something that immediately produces and upholds that thought. Here is a new thing, and there is a necessity of a cause. It is not in antecedent thoughts, for they are vanished and gone; they are past, and what is past is not. But if we say 'tis the substance of the soul, if we meant that there is some substance besides that thought that brings that thought forth, if it be God, I acknowledge it."[14] Therefore "God is not only the universal mind which constitutes the substance of the external world, but He is also the essence which lies behind the phenomena of consciousness or mind."[15] Not created substance but the universal mind of God is the ground of the creature's consciousness. God is before and aft, above and below: he is the ground of experience, and of the soul. The creature, in this perspective, seems to be merely a thin unit of generic mind, a frail oneness anchored nowhere in nature, but hovering precariously upon the Will of God.

In contrast to this striking exclusion of created immaterial substance in his "Miscellanies," Edwards pointedly included it in his discussion on personal identity in Original Sin Defended. But even here, he relegated it to a minor role in his definition of a person. "So the derivation of the pollution and guilt of past sins in the same person, depends on an arbitrary divine constitution; and this, even though we should allow the same consciousness not to be the only thing which constitutes oneness of person, but should, besides that, suppose sameness of substance requisite."[16] Behind Edwards' ambiguous position on created immaterial substance was a dilemma. If he did not posit such substance, he paid respect to his consuming vision of the utterly absolute God, but he ran the danger of pantheism and raised the old problem (as did Locke) of the immortality of the soul.[17] On the other hand, if he did posit created immaterial substance, he met the dangers of the last two points, but reduced the absoluteness of God. Edwards' ambiguity toward immaterial substance, therefore, is another example of the tension in his thought between the ideas of monism and dualism of Creator and created.[18] For Edwards, the phrase "same substance" in his discussion of identity in Original Sin Defended parallels the phrase "the time will never come" when the eternally ascending saint will be united with God, in his Dissertation Concerning the End for which God Created the World. In both cases, Edwards guarded himself against pantheism. Moreover, mere substantiality of soul is not a principle of individuation.

In sum, Edwards taught that a person's identity consists essentially in a created generic unit of light-exhausted thinking substance, and that a person's inherited moral worth, which is overwhelmingly more important than his individuation, resides in his generic nature. This is not to say that Edwards did not believe in personal immortality but that his idea of "a person" disregarded, if it did not negate, the value of individuation. Although he held that the soul of each person is "immediately and directly" from God, he did not consider significant uniqueness of each soul.

II

In Original Sin Defended, Edwards once again took up the question of identity. He tried to explain the continuity of discrete units of consciousness; to explain, in other words, how all men through time and space are one with Adam. To elucidate this unity by analogy was the general purpose of the selection on wholes and identity in Original Sin Defended. This method is not the "metaphysical analogy" of the early Church Fathers, but is rather a clear-cut and systematic effort to learn something about the unknown from careful observation of the known."[19] Edwards assumed, as did many divines, that the laws of nature were analogous to the laws of spirit. He wrote that even Dr. Turnbull, his opponent, "says of the laws of

26

nature, as cited from Sir Issac Newton," "It is the will of the mind that is the first cause, that gives substance and efficacy to all those laws, who is the efficient cause that produces the phenomena, which appear in analogy, harmony and agreement, according to these laws." "And 'the same principles must take place in things pertaining to moral, as well as natural philosophy'."[20] Thus Edwards attempted to demonstrate by the following analogies the principle by which mankind remains a moral whole while persons, the ultimate constituents of mankind, are constantly changing. "A tree, grown great, and a hundred years old, is one plant with the little sprout," even though it is different in form, and has not "one atom the very same" as it had in the beginning. "So the body of a man at forty years of age, is one with the infant-body . . . though now constituted of different substance, and the great part of the substance probably changing scores (if not hundreds) of times." "Again the body and soul of a man . . . considered in themselves . . . are exceeding different beings . . . and yet, by a very peculiar divine constitution, or law of nature, which God has been pleased to establish, they are strongly united, and become one . . . so that both become different parts of the same man."[21] Edwards tries to show by analogy how mankind remains one, although its respective parts change. These specific analogies, and this method of using "Analogical arguments of continuance," were not original with Edwards but were used by Locke, Berkeley, Butler, "Strapferus" whom Edwards himself quotes, and others, to demonstrate different kinds of "wholes" or identities. Although Perry Miller suggests that these analogies may be called "organic," their purpose was not to show development but how one whole can have distinctly different parts.[22] Edwards was interested in Being, not Becoming.

Also in this section of Original Sin Defended, Edwards used a radically different kind of analogy to express not changing wholes characteristic of nature, but how "God's upholding of created substance, or causing it existence in each successive moment, is altogether equivalent to an immediate production out of nothing, at each moment." This analogy consisted in "images of things in a glass:" "The image that exists this moment [in a mirror], is not at all _derived_ from the image that existed the last preceding moment: for, if the sucession of new _rays_ be intercepted by something interposed between the object and the glass, the image immediately ceases: the _past existence_ of the image has no influence to uphold it, so much as for one moment."[23] This metaphor was particularly appropriate for Edwards' thought, because it expressed at once his notion of the complete dependency of the creature on God, and his philosophic idealism. He had used the metaphor at least once before in his essay on "The Mind" where he argued, similar to Berkeley, that the sense of seeing, in distinction to that of feeling, leads us to conclude that the objects of the visible world "are merely mental existence" as "in a looking glass, where all will acknowledge they exist only mentally."[24] At any rate, Edwards, in his work on original sin, juxtaposed to his "organic" metaphors which suggest self-sustained continuity in nature, a Calvinistic-Platonic metaphor which negates natural continuance. To the modern mind these two kinds of metaphor can do no more than lie contiguously, one under the other, as it were; they are not even "metaphysical" in the manner of some seventeenth-century poetry, e.g. John Donne's, for although they are juxtaposed, they are essentially expressive of radical disunity not of aesthetic harmony. But of course their relation is appropriately expressive of Edwards' stress on the Will of God, and they do suggest a wholeness in the sense that "the _body_ and _soul_ of a man are _one_." Thus with his double, or rather, split, vision, Edwards gave us both worlds, one of nature, one of divine establishment, just as in The Nature of True Virtue he argued for a natural principle of self-love and a supernatural one of benevolence; and in _Freedom of the Will_, for "free-will" and for predestination. Edwards was in the world but not of the world.

Furthermore, the mirror image vividly establishes Edwards' idea that mankind inherited Adam's guilt not by way of organic transmission, not through the "blood" or nature, but by way of created generic spirit, that is, by consciousness which, in distinction to matter, was "substantial reality" for Edwards. Our moral inheritance is given to us like a category of the mind. The guilt of Adam is suffused like a black dye through our consciousnesses, tinting the greenness of our perceptions.

28

Thus God sustains each person, that is, each unit of consciousness, as an image is sustained in a mirror by its original. And the ideas or images within each unit of consciousness, are impressions of nature, which in turn constitute other ideas in the mind of God; and the ideas or images retained in the memory of each unit, are sustained each instant not by inherent ability of the unit (for it has no such ability), but by God. Hence each unit of consciousness, and the images of present consciousness and the images of memory contained in that unit, are ideas of God. Whether or not each unit of consciousness is grounded on a unit of created substance which is separate from God, Edwards did not decisively inform us; we have examined his dilemma in this matter. But certainly, individuation of person played a small role, if any, in his view of moral worth. Perry Miller puts it well in saying that Edwards "assumed that no person could be an end in himself because he was unique."[25]

Edwards probably only faintly suspected that Locke's definition of personal identity as continuity of idea meant that the Englishman had broken with the traditional notion of fixed human nature. Consciousness was given, but the content of each unit of consciousness, that is, the continuity of idea in which moral worth resides, was determined by the concrete and changing world, not by supernatural imposition. If the impressions of the world upon the blank tablet of the mind governed personal identity and hence pleasure and pain, persons by experimenting with facts, not abstractions, might be able to achieve identities and create a world in harmony. Locke was a man of the world; he marks the moment Englishmen went on the offensive against the Fate of innate depravity, when men could help determine the kind of cosmos they lived in. A person believes in himself and in freedom to the degree that he is confident that he can control his environment. But Edwards, raised in physical, psychological, and spiritual surroundings that dominated the creature, never was able to open his mind to such frightening autonomy. Moral worth, personal identity, and destiny, were forever guaranteed.

[1] *Freedom of the Will*, ed. Paul Ramsey (New Haven: Yale University Press, 1957), p. 405.

[2] *Works*, ed. Sereno E. Dwight (New York, 1829-30), II, 562.

[3] Henry E. Allison, "Locke's Theory of Personal Identity: A Re-Examination," *Journal of the History of Ideas*, XXVII (1966), 24. My discussion owes much to Allison's study.

[4] The brackets are mine; Locke held of course that the mind cannot have clear and distinct ideas of either immaterial or material substance.

[5] *An Essay Concerning Human Understanding*, ed. A. C. Fraser (New York: Dover, 1959), I, 107.

[6] Allison, p. 43.

[7] Locke, I, 449.

[8] Locke, I, 468.

[9] Locke, I, 454.

[10] *Works*, I, 680. The last statement in this quotation is subsumed under the problem of "wholes" which I consider later: one's identity remains the same although his ideas change.

[11] *Works*, I, 680.

[12] Locke, II, xxvii, 22. Hawthorne, a spiritual part-descendant of Edwards, states in his tale "Fancy's Show Box," that "it is a point of vast interest whether the soul may contact [guilt] from deeds which may have been plotted and resolved upon, but which, physically, have never had existence." He concludes that "In truth, there is no such thing in man's nature as a settled and full resolve, either for good or evil, except at the very moment of execution." Yet Hawthorne characteristically modifies his conclusion by speculating that no person shall enter heaven with unclean thoughts. Thus Locke the empiricist held that a person's

essential worth is decided by his conscious acts, and Edwards, that that worth is pre-determined by one's total inclination, that is, by his "habits and dispositions of the heart, and moral motives and inducements." William Ellery Channing, following Locke, argued in "The Moral Argument Against Calvinism" (1820) that the Calvinistic assumption that a man deserves eternal punishment for doing evil which he is incapable of not doing, is morally and rationally absurd. Now evil resulting from conscious acts is not a theologic problem, but evil outside the human will, originating either in the unconscious or in nature, is a problem. Edwards grounded the latter type of evil on the Wisdom of God, and hence made it meaningful--in distinction to Naturalism, e.g. Freud, that held it to be purposeless. Hawthorne, an ethical humanist, agreed with Channing that mankind is not innately depraved, and that men do not deserve eternal punishment for doing evil that they cannot help doing. But Hawthorne saw through the glass of his temperment darkly, and gave less credit than Channing to the ability of men to control their actions, and had less hope than Channing that there is a god who can help to save mankind.

[13] The Philosophy of Jonathan Edwards, ed. H.G. Townsend (Eugene: University of Oregon, 1955), p. 68.

[14] Townsend, p. 78.

[15] Alexander V. G. Allen, Jonathan Edwards (Boston, 1889), p. 309.

[16] Works, II, 551.

[17] Edwards' position may be likened to that of Malebranche whom he may have read or heard of, and whose theologic idealism is similar to his, e.g. "the universe exists only in the mind of God." Morris Ginsberg believes that Malebranche never discarded immateriality, that "the real motive of Malebranche's teaching . . . was his fear of a pantheistic notion of the soul. . . . If we have an idea of ourselves, i.e., if we knew ourselves as in the mind of God, the conclusion that our individual existence is an illusion, that finite souls are but particular modifications of the divine or universal mind, could hardly be resisted" (Nicholas

Malebranche, *Dialogues* on *Metaphysics* and on *Religion*, trans. Morris Ginsberg [London, 1923], p. 32).

[18] William Morris states that Edwards "denies any substantival ego or persistent soul, but allows such a soul in normal speech" (*The Young Jonathan Edwards: A Re-Construction* [University of Chicago dissertation, 1955], p. 752).

[19] Ernest Campbell Mossner, *Bishop Butler and the Age of Reason* (New York: Macmillan, 1936), p. 82.

[20] *Works*, II, 551.

[21] *Works*, II, 549-50.

[22] Perry Miller, *Jonathan Edwards* (New York: Meridian, 1949), p. 281.

[23] *Works*, II, 555. Sacvan Bercovitch writes: "It has become fashionable to link the production of mirrors during the Renaissance with the growth of modern individualism. This may hold true for the humanist Renaissance. For Baxter, Bell, and Richard Mather, the mirror radiated the divine image. They never sought their own reflection in it, as did Montaigne and his literary descendants through Rousseau. . . . The Puritans felt that the less one saw of oneself in the mirror, the better; and best of all was to cast no reflection at all" (*The Puritan Origin of the American Self* [New Haven: Yale University Press, 1975], p. 14).

[24] *Works*, I, 668.

[25] Miller, p. 47. Compare Edwards' thought here with Emerson's, in the subsequent essay, "Channing and Emerson on Personal Identity."

EDGAR ALLAN POE'S ELECTRICAL WILL

"If God should open a window in the heart, so that we might look into it, it would be the most loathsome spectacle that ever was set before our eyes."

Jonathan Edwards[1]

"No man dare write" "a very little book" entitled "My Heart Laid Bare." "No man could write it, even if he dared. The paper would shrivel and blaze at every touch of the fiery pen."

Edgar Allan Poe[2]

I

Poe's exquisite identity may have been the empirical ground of his poetic philosophy. It 'may have been' because recent criticism of him as a writer of hoax raises the possibility that he was not committed fully to anything he wrote.[3] He may have been in his tales merely taking advantage of "the extravagant gullibility of the age," hinting at everything, asserting nothing.[4] Or he himself may have written from the stance of hoax because he wished to shield himself from a charge of guillibility in believing what his enemies thought sheer nonsense, not because he disbelieved what he said. But one finds hard to believe that Poe, although an actor of sorts, was fundamentally uncommitted to his philosophic vision. Let it be assumed, at least for the duration of this essay, that Poe tried seriously to structure his vision in Eureka and in certain parts of other "philosophic" works; that this structure can be perceived; and that, once perceived, it can help us to clarify some of the themes of his tales and of his life. He wrote his Aunt Maria Clemm that "It is no use to reason with me now; I must die. I have no desire to live since I have done Eureka."[5]

Poe's fundamental philosophic premise in Eureka is that "Unity . . . is a truth--I feel it. Diffusion is a truth--I see it;"[6] and that "All

Things and All Thoughts of Things, with all their
ineffable Multiplicity of Relation, sprang at once
from the primordial and irrelative One" (514). He
arrived at these conclusions, presumably, by observing that the universe consists in 1) discrete
objects, animate and inanimate; 2) a force between
objects that draws objects toward each other,
manifested as gravity, love, beauty, (and death);
and 3) another force between objects that repulses
objects from each other, manifested as electricity,
ego-centricity, consciousness. On these observations he based his entire "poetic" philosophy.[7]

In _Eureka_ Poe began his argument for his cosmic
vision by stating that we can know nothing about God
unless we are God ourselves, and concluded the work
by claiming that "This Heart Divine--what is it? It
is our own" (587).[8] He held in effect that by
means of intuition of self-existence, not by logical
nor empirical methods, we can know, since we are
God, as much about God as we can know about ourselves. However, since intuitive messages cannot be
communicated in cognitive terms, the essence of God
and hence of ourselves remains a mystery to the
rational mind.

In the beginning, Poe said, God "the Incomprehensible . . . assuming him as a Spirit--that is to
say, as not Matter . . . created, or made out of
Nothing, by dint of his Volition" (501) "Matter
which . . . he first made from his Spirit, or from
Nihility" (502). (In "Mesmeric Revelation" Poe
defined God as "the perfection of matter," but
admits that "the matter of which I speak is, in all
respects, the very 'mind' or 'spirit' of the
schools." Later, in _Eureka_, he dropped this
sophistry and defined God in the above way.) The
transportation of the above quotation into conventional terms drains it of complete absurdity.
The propositions that the essence of God is incomprehensible (but not necessarily irrational) and
that God created the world out of Nothing (otherwise
the world would be divine) belong to orthodox
supernaturalism. But Poe makes a novel departure by
equating the divine Spirit with "Nihility." Thus he
asserts at once, perhaps with tongue in cheek, that
God, by creating Matter out of Nothing, created it
out of his own Spirit. He supports a solemn statement of pantheism with verbal agreement with con-

34

vention. This strange beginning foreshadows a
cosmos of painful abnormality.

Poe did not hold that the divine Spirit,
although Nihility or No Thing, was ontological zero.
In his creation theory he seems to have been mani-
pulating the motif of subject and object, dear to
the hearts of idealistic thinkers, such as Fichte,
Schelling, and notably Coleridge with whose work he
was well acquainted; indeed, dear to the heart of
the intellectual reader of the day, for he advised
in "How to Write a Blackwood Article" that "the tone
metaphysical is also a good one. If you know any
big words this is your chance for them. . . . Say
something about objectivity and subjectivity."
Coleridge wrote in Biographia Literaria that "the
ground of creation is neither subject nor object but
an identity of both; that is, the subject originally
contained unconsciously within itself the object."
The essence of Spirit, according to Coleridge, is
self-consciousness or self-representation. "The
Spirit (originally the identity of object and
subject) must in some sense dissolve$_9$ this identity,
in order to be conscious of it."[9] This dissolution "implies an act. . . . The self-conscious
spirit therefore is a will; and freedom must be
assumed as a ground of philosophy, and can never be
deduced from it" (Thesis VII). Coleridge continued:
"Whatever in its origin is objective, is likewise as
such necessarily finite. Therefore, since the
spirit is not originally an object, and as the
subject exists in antithesis to an object, the
spirit cannot originally be finite. But neither can
it be a subject without becoming an object, and, as
it is originally the identity of both, it can be
conceived neither as infinite nor finite exclusively, but as the most original union of both"
(Thesis VIII).[10] Poe could have been thinking
about Coleridge when he wrote, in Eureka, about
creation out of Nothing and about the Volition of
God as the incomprehensible ground of the Universe.

Let us surmise then that Poe, remembering
Coleridge and wanting (as always) to be "novel,"

conceived that a primal unity of absolute subject and object existed in the beginning (a unity which, because neither a subject nor an object can exist except in anti-thesis to the other, did not "exist," that is, was not [self-] conscious); that this unity, by an unintelligible (unconscious) act of volition, dissolved itself; created a finite and simple object; established the principle of disunity; and initiated self-consciousness and creation. Thus "ex nihilo nihil fit" (490), Poe claimed, is false. The universe is "created, or made out of Nothing, by dint of his Volition" (501). That is to say, the universe or consciousness consisting in the antithesis of subject and object, comes from Nothing or unconsciousness, the original unity of subject and object. This unity is split into subject and object by divine volition which, by definition, is beyond cognitive comprehension.

The incomprehensible Will of God, immanent in divine unity, manifests itself in disunity of subject and object, and proceeds (since the principle of disunity is established) to express itself by further diffusion of the Godhead. "The Divine Being," Poe held, "passes his Eternity in perpetual variation of Concentrated Self and almost Infinite Self-Diffusion (589). . . . Those inconceivable numerous things which you designate as his creatures . . . are really but infinite individualizations of Himself" (590). Poe believed that the universe is "a poetic or artistic creation, a 'plot of God' [that] has come about through God's breaking-up His original unity and His self-radiation into space."[11] Thus Spirit and Matter are (mathematically) radiated throughout the "utmost conceivable expanse" of space in terms of innumerable finite spirits in material bodies. This phase of creation, therefore, consists in the diffusion of primal unity into an almost infinite number of heterogeneous, conscious, willful entities, some of which are human creatures.

But the diffusion of the Godhead is determinant: just as volition is immanent in original unity, a counter-impulse of unity is immanent in disunity. As diffusion reaches its maximum, volition toward heterogeneity diminishes, and the reconstruction of unity begins. On the physical level, "The Newtonian Law of Gravity" is the most obvious manifestation of reconstruction. "So long as diffusion lasts," Poe assured us, "reaction could not take place; but gravitation has taken place; therefore the act of Creation has ceased" (549). Hence the many finite entities who are the radiated Godhead slowly regather, in stages of increasingly universal agglomerations, into the original unity of God.

Of the final regathering, Poe wrote: "While undergoing consolidation, the clusters themselves, with a speed prodigiously accumulative, have been rushing towards their own general center--and now, with a thousandfold electrical velocity . . . and with the spiritual passion of their appetite for oneness, the majestic remnants of the tribe of Stars flash, at length, into common embrace. The inevitable catastrophe is at hand" (585). This "catastrophe" is that "the absolute consolidated globe of globes would be objectless" (585-6). "Matter is no more. In sinking into Unity, it will sink at once into that Nothingness which, to all Finite Perception, Unity must be--into that Material Nihility from which we can conceive it to have been evoked-to have been created by the Volition of God" (587). That is to say (keeping Coleridge in mind), as entities rush together, they consolidate until there is left, just before the end, one Subject and one Object (each of which is metaphysical) which then collapse into the primal Nihility of each other's arms. Or, just before the end, there exists one huge antithetical Entity consisting in one Subject and one Object, an entity composed of the almost infinite number of finite entities which, as they have streamed back to primal unity, have fused with each other into increasingly greater entities. What remains after the collapse of the Object into the Subject is "Nothing," an apparent Humian negation of "no matter, never mind." What is left, however, is a "non-existent" positive Unity of Subject-Object (perhaps an all-potential whiteness, like that at the end of A. Gordon Pym) that will once again, by an incomprehensible act of Volition, construct itself objectively to itself and radiate itself through the void as innumerable divine entities.

Poe termed "creative" the phase of radiation, and concluded that it is finished, and that we who

now live on earth "can no more expect, then, to
observe the primary processes of Creation" (549).
The present universe is in the state of regathering
or "collapse" back to original unity. The collapse,
Poe informs us, cannot be instantaneous, for this
would defeat the divine purpose of creation (of
which more will be said). To retard the impulse of
collapse, therefore, something like the original
impulse of diffusion lingers in each entity in terms
of a non-creative volition that fights defensively,
even desperately, against the now dominant impulse
toward unity. There is, Poe said, "the necessity
for a repulsion of limited capacity . . . which, on
withdrawal of the diffusive Volition, shall at the
same time allow the approach, and forbid the
junction of the atoms; suffering them infinitely to
approximate, while denying them positive contact
. . . up to a certain epoch when the finite entities
shall fuse into primal unity" (505).[12] At the
withdrawal of divine Volition, "Repulsion (Electricity) must have commenced" (533). The epoch we
humans live in now, consequently, has two immanent
cosmic forces opposing each other, that of regathering or homogeneity and that of radiation or heterogeneity. "Unity . . . is a truth--I feel it.
Diffusion is a truth, I see it." We know now
Attraction and Repulsion. Gravity and Matter are
physical manifestations of these opposing forces.
Gravity, although the desire of Matter to return to
Unity, does not belong to the essence of Matter:
"the gravitating principle appertains to Matter
temporarily," only during the process of regathering
(579). Matter, in distinction to Gravity, manifests
the principle of heterogeneity and is the agent, we
are informed at the end of Eureka, through which
spirit is individualized. Hence the final archetypal globe of Matter on the verge of collapsing
into the arms of the Subject, is self-contradictory:
it consists at once in the principle of Unity
(Gravity) and dis-unity (Matter), or in the two
forces of attraction and repulsion; it glares with
inner tension just before it falls into the metaphysical subject.

The tension between Matter and Gravity, in the
physical context, corresponds to the tension between
Will and Love, in the spiritual. Matter and Will
are divisive principles, seeking individuation and
intense consciousness; Gravity and Love (and Art)

are principles of fusion and beauty. More specifically, we living entities know the drive for unity as
Gravity, as Love, as dreams of Supernal Beauty; and
we know the drive for disunity as material forms, as
"electricity, heat, light, magneticism" (505), and
as "vitality, consciousness, and thought" (508,
545). Although Poe wrote that "The Body and Soul
walk hand in hand" (533), the reader of his tales
often gets the impression that this stroll, as it
were, is not happy. Rather, we are torn between the
forces of attraction and repulsion. At once we flee
from discrete materiality toward love and beauty,
toward the death of individuation; and struggle for
intensity of consciousness, the thrilling individuation of life.

Poe, in his search for love and beauty, sought
escape from sharp specificity of things; his body,
electrifying space, was not a medium for love.[13]
"Indeed, indeed, Annie," he wrote, "there is <u>nothing</u>
in this world worth living for except love . . .
love . . . so pure--so unworldly."[14] Although
Beauty and Love for Poe were the only things worth
living for in this world, they were not of the
electric materiality of this world. They were
supernal realities, attributes of primal unity,
manifested in this world only in glimpses and
reflections, and particularly in a beautiful dead
lady who has lost the will for aggressive individuation.[15]

"<u>Electricity</u>, with its involute phenomena,
heat, light, magnetism, is to be understood as
proceeding as condensation proceeds" (542). Thus,
since earth is now in the process of regathering or
condensation, "we shall find indications of re-
silient luminosity in <u>all</u> the stellar bodies" (543).
"Our moon is strongly self-luminous," Poe said,
mistaking the sunlight reflecting off the earth onto
the moon for self-luminosity of the moon (543). And
our earth in its "feebly-continued condensation" has
"a certain appearance of luminosity" (543). Hence,
the environs of the House of Usher, as the disciner-
grating Usher consciousness collapses or implodes
into the supernatural, glow "in the unnatural light
of a faintly luminous and distinctly visible gaseous
exhalation which hung about and enshrouded the
mansion" and "all vegetable things" have a strange
"sentience."

Now the ultimate design of the universe, according to Poe, calls for maximum heterogeneity of the divine particles. Strangely, he believed that the climax of heterogeneity comes during the phase of universal collapse. An almost infinite variety of "vitalic development" occurs "during the period in which all things were effecting their return to Unity" (571). The reason for this, apparently, is that, although discrete entities achieve in theory their acme of heterogeneity at the furthest point of diffusion, their identity, in the phase of regathering, is exquisitely intensified as it is torn between the drive toward unity and the "repulsive spirit" or retardative impulse toward individuation. Indeed, electrical vitality or consciousness increases in direct ratio to condensation: "the importance of the development of the terrestial vitality proceeds equally with the terrestial condensation" (544). Hence, as earth ages and condenses, greater and greater heterogeneity of its entities occurs: "As it proceeds in its condensation, superior and still superior races have appeared" (544). With "these successive elevations of vitalic character," superior individuals develop. Thus for Poe the more unique or individuated a person is, the more that person exemplifies condensation toward Supernal Beauty, and the greater the artistic genius he is. This paradox is typical of the Romantic Spirit, and is found also in Emerson and others.[16]

At any rate, the consolidating entities gradually reconstruct the Godhead, and the moment fusion occurs, Matter gravitates into a titanic globe that in a flash vanishes into Subject-Object Nihility. The flash, we may assume, is the last of the residual Will to diffusion that retarded the impulse to Unity. It is the anti-type of the "faintly luminous" and "electrical phenomena" that, throughout Poe, signals imminence of the end, as in "The City in the Sea," "The Fall of the House of Usher," and "The Conversation of Eiros and Charmion."

II

Poe believed that at death many entities pass through the dark valley and shadow of death to a higher and more universal realm, but that some, like the narrators in "The Black Cat" and "The Tell-Tale Heart," due to crime, may wonder where they will go. The narrator of "The Imp of the Perverse" cries out, "Today I . . . am here! To-Morrow I shall be fetterless! But where?" However, for Poe, since souls are self-existent and free-will negligible, there is no supernatural hell, and all matter and spirit return eventually to primal unity. Thus, once again, there is no ontological zero, even in the grave. The narrator in "The Pit and the Pendulum" refers to "the state of seeming nothingness into which my soul had lapsed;" and assures us that "I had swooned, but still will not say that all of consciousness was lost. What of it there remained I will not attempt to define, or even to describe; yet all was not lost. In the deepest slumber--no! In delirium--no! In a swoon--no! In death--no! Even in the grave all is not lost. Else there is no immortality for man. Arousing from the most profound of slumbers, we break the gossamer of some dream."[17] The narrator in "Berenice" speaks of awaking "from the long night of what seemed, but was not, nonentity." Bedloe of the Ragged Mountains states that "my sole feeling--was that of darkness and non-entity, with the consciousness of death." He continues to be conscious although his consciousness seems to be of void, objectless. In short, Poe believed that consciousness is self-existent and cannot be destroyed.[18]

Poe's apprehension of death, therefore, was less of ontological zero than of consciousness of nothingness, that is, of seeming to be a subject without an object, a living dead, as it were; 'seeming to be' because a subject cannot exist without an object. The narrator in "The Pit and the Pendulum" "grew aghast least there should be nothing to see." The "Man of the Crowd" "stalked backward and forward, without apparent object." Possessed by the Imp of the Perverse, "we act without comprehensible object"--(an act, by the way, that is "a radical, primitive impulse--elementary," like the first "abnormal" act of creation; creation for Poe may be the result of an act of perversity). Roderick, after he has entombed the living Madeline, "roamed from chamber to chamber with hurried, unequal, and objectless step." The Usher consciousness is collapsing into pure subjectivity. The

41

subject, over generations, has grown so narcissistic and dominant that the object has become its mere reflection or twin, and is about to be destroyed by the subject in the ultimate act of introversion. In contradictory gestures, Roderick summons the narrator from the outside, and tries to suppress Madeline or the object completely. His eyes are lusterless; he gazes "upon vacancy for long hours;" he roams the House like a zombie. The letter he has sent the narrator is a desperate plea of a dying psyche in the grip of obsessive subjectivity. But the presence of the narrator, instead of bringing sanity or balance between the two poles of consciousness, is traumatic. The narrator's arrival at the house, the location of his chamber above the vault, and the death and resurrection of Madeline, are not coincidental. The shock of outsideness induces catalepsy and then frenzy. In related, parallel patterns, Roderick enters the narrator's room as Ethelred breaks in and kills the dragon and Madeline breaks out and falls upon the subject with the vengeance of objectivity scorned. There is no loving reciprocity between subject and object; no harmony, as Emerson would say, between the Me and the Not Me. Roderick is a ruined god. Ultimately, the Usher psyche as a whole splits in two parts and vanishes in the black tarn of the Where? of nothingness. What happens after that to Roderick and Madeline we are not told, but it is hard to imagine that they achieve "the majestic novelty of the Life Eternal" mentioned in "The Colloquy of Monos and Una."[19]

Even a successful passage through the valley of Death is terrifying, according to Poe, because the soul suffers diminution of consciousness and verges upon ontological zero. The soul moves in periods of "terrible darkness," in "stupor," with "wild sickness." In "Mesmeric Revelation," Poe used the conventional image of a worm changing into a butterfly to illustrate the "painful metamorphosis." "The Colloquy of Monos and Una" is about the experience of Monos of the various stages of his journey through the grave and of his rebirth in heaven where Una eventually joins him. In the grave, he knows at first the synesthesiac disintegration of his earthly senses and then the deep dormancy of consciousness when he had no sense of form, of thought, had no feeling, no soul, no matter; when "the grave was

42

home." He was in a state of entity approximating ontological zero, a state with only enough consciousness to remember faintly how his senses fell apart. Although Monos concludes his narrative while he is still in the grave, his experience of the sixth sense "all perfect" "Of which no words could convey to the merely human intelligence even an indistinct conception," which he earlier described, foreshadows his rebirth in heaven where in fact he is located when he tells his tale. Unlike Roderick and Madeline, Monos and Una achieve Supernal Beauty.

Poe held that the "other world" is totally different from this world, and utterly inconceivable by any natural means. On earth, an entity is confined within the dimensions of the five senses: "To rudimental beings, organs are the cages necessary to confine them until fledged," he wrote in "Mersmeric Revelation."[20] In the journey through the grave, an entity loses his five idiosyncratic earthly senses and then, on becoming a new being in heaven, possesses an almost infinite number of new senses in "the nearly unlimited perception of the unlimited life." But although the supernatural is unknowable in terms of earthly sensation, mankind has a sixth sense whereby men on earth can experience hints of the supernatural as "weird," "strange," "novel," "sublime."[21] This sixth sense is activated by love, by art, by experiences of terror, and is the ground of the Poetic Sentiment Poe mentioned in "The Poetic Principle." In terms of the sixth sense, one experiences neither "the excitement of the heart" nor moral value nor a factual world, but the supernal "novelty of Beauty" (Charmion to Eiros).

There is for Poe no personal immortality. At last, he wrote in Eureka the "myriads of individual Intelligences [will] become blended . . . individual identity will be gradually merged in the general consciousness" (590). Beyond earth, regathering is the process by which particulars become increasingly universal. One critic complains that the speakers in "The Conversation of Eiros and Charmion," "The Colloquy of Monos and Una," and "The Power of Words," "are not differentiated; not one is individualized."[22] But these speakers are in a stage of regathering above the earth; Monos and Una, for instance, like the flowers around them, are "prototypes" of earthly entities. Monos' narrative is about his sense-experience in his translation into a more universalized state of being. He experiences the decay of his five earthly senses; the loss of even the idea of contact; and the development of a new consciousness of pure entity and duration. He loses, in the journey through the valley of the Shadow, his specific personal identity so that he can fuse with Una in heaven. Monos and Una (as their names imply) are two beings of earthly origin, who, through love, fuse at death into a prototypical entity.[23]

In distinction to "The Colloquy of Monos and Una," the tale "Morella" is about the failure of two entities to fuse. It concerns Romantic mysticism and Lockean empiricism, and exhibits Poe's advice in "How to Write a Blackwood Article" to "be sure and abuse a man called Locke." The narrator, marrying Morella because of some feeling he cannot define, is a rational empiricist who is at once intrigued and repelled by Morella, the embodiment of mystical intuition. Morella, with the hope of converting the narrator to her philosophy and hence to an immortal fusion of souls (the destruction of single personal identity), presents him with a collection of "mystical writings" which at first seem to be "the mere dross of the early German literature." But gradually these writings begin to fascinate and to terrify him with their wild pantheistic implications of fusion of souls beyond the grave. The narrator, pondering the possibility of such fusion, recalls Locke who, denying clear and distinct ideas of substance, defines personal identity in terms merely of memory, and hence provides grounds for doubting personal immortality.[24] Faced with Morella's intuitions of fusion and Locke's scepticism, the narrator develops an hysterical hatred for Morella who appropriately sickens and dies. But as she dies, she gives birth to Morella II, the off-spring of herself and the narrator. The narrator now goes with Morella II into the "rigorous seclusion" of fantasy. Morella II therefore is Morella I come back in the form of fantasy to haunt the narrator. She is his longing for what he could have had but now cannot, his once repressed but now dominant hunger for mystical fusion of two individuated souls in the hereafter. Thus the narrator, at Morella

44

II's death and at his discovery of Morella I's empty tomb, is left completely alone with his single empirical self, laughing bitterly. Morella I's statement that "joy is not gathered twice in life" is proved true; her prophecy that the narrator's life will be one of sorrow after her death, is fulfilled; and the quotation from Plato at the beginning of the tale, "Itself, by itself, solely, one, ever-lasting, and single," is explained.

III

Poe's creation is not a divine work of art nor a "plot of God" in the sense that it does not exhibit variety within unity but variety and unity exclusive of each other. Poe speaks of "the design of variety out of unity--diversity out of sameness--heterogeneity out of homogeneity--complexity out of simplicity--in a word, the utmost possible multiplicity of relation out of the emphatically irrelative One" (503-4). He held that God, once primal Unity, exists now only in terms of an almost infinite variety of finite entities. We are told in Eureka that "each soul is, in part, its own God--its own Creator:--in a world, that God--the material and spiritual God--now exists solely in the diffused Matter and Spirit of the Universe; and . . . the regathering of this diffused Matter and Spirit will be but the reconstitution of the purely Spiritual and Individual God" (589). Since God as original unity does not now exist, our dreams of Supernal Beauty or Unity have no existent objective referent. They are only "ever present Memories of a Destiny more vast" (588), of what we once were, of what we hope to be again, and of what we should dream to realize. A person, therefore, has no absolute foundation nor sustenance. He has nothing to fall back upon for comfort but himself and his memories. By positing a diffused God, Poe expressed his terrible orphanage in an atomistic or monadic world. He and other divine entities were scattered throughout space, shining in divine isolated individuation. He was one of many lost atoms of primal stuff with an appetite for unity with the "lost parent" (513). His universe is a projection of his arrogancy, of his loneliness, of his failure to achieve rapport with others. He had the "Impenetra-

45

bility of matter" and sought to shed through death the shell of particularity so as to be reborn in the white fusion of the womb.

The ultimate design of the universe for Poe, as we have seen, involves "that of the utmost possible relation" (505) attained by the greatest possible heterogeneity of the divine particles. The purpose of this design is "to extend, by actual increase, the joy of [God's] existence" (589). Unfortunately for us who are God on the human level, divine joy is found only among beings of higher realms of creation. We are told in "Mesmeric Revelation" (and there seems no reason to question Poe's seriousness on this issue in this tale) that "The pain of the primitive life of Earth is the sole basis of the bliss of the ultimate life of Heaven." Hence in "The Colloquy of Monos and Una," the "wild sobs" of Una as Monos dies, conveyed to Monos "no intimation of the sorrows which gave them birth." On the contrary, Una's "large and constant tears" fell on Monos and "thrilled every fibre" of his "frame with ecstasy alone." Our exquisite pain on earth is the foundation of the bliss in heaven.

Poe's metaphysical relativism of pleasure and pain is reminiscent of the implicit balance of heaven and hell in Jonathan Edwards. "An Equality, or Likeness of Ratios" is a fundamental principle in the latter's cosmic vision.[25] Each man, struggling to control and to justify the latent chaos in his emotional life, compulsively sought the rationale of symmetry in the realms of Truth, Beauty, and Goodness. Near the end of Eureka, Poe stated that once we comprehend that we who are divine particles were once God who planned the design of the universe, we will be able to endure sorrow; we will realize that "we ourselves have imposed [sorrow and evil] upon ourselves, in furtherance of our own purposes--with a view--if even with a futile view-- to the extension of our own Joy" (589). Thus we on earth who are God are in predetermined hell, impotent to halt our martyrdom until death.

"Unity . . . is a truth--I feel it. Diffusion is a truth--I see it." The agony of Poe originated in the tension to be at once one with humanity and to be individuated. He felt compelled by the mechanism of residual will to be alone in the superiority of genius. In _Eureka_ he stated strikingly several times that the condition of the Many is "abnormal," that the original act of divine volition was that of "forcing the normal into the abnormal--of impelling that whose originality and therefore whose rightful condition, was One, to take upon itself the wrongful condition of the Many" (548). "Wrongfulness," furthermore, "implies relation" (524). He believed that the dominant desire of finite entity is to "return from the condition of as it is and ought not to be into the condition of as it was, originally, and therefore ought to be" (524). And in "Mesmeric Revelation" he wrote: "In the organic life, as well as in the inorganic matter generally, there is nothing to impede the action of one simple unique law--the Divine Volition. With the view of producing impediment, the organic life and matter (complex, substantial, and law-encumbered) were contrived." Pain of distinct personal identity, horror of the abnormality of a person being a single human digit, of simply existing on the human level, binds like wire the heart of Poe's metaphysics. Singleness of existence is a contrived "impediment" against happiness; the creative phase of the universe, the phase or radiation or diffusion, is simply "abnormal." Poe's intuition of omnipotent will to heterogeneity is excruciating. "No one soul is inferior to another--each soul is, in part, its own God--its own Creator" (589) because each soul is a particle of God who, as God or primal Unity, predetermined the cosmic design which includes pain of human identity. Poe's "Democracy," like Hawthorne's, is a democracy of suffering. It is no wonder that Poe said that "I have no faith in human perfectibility."[26]

Further, Poe argued (as we have seen) that heterogeneity, manifested as vitality, consciousness, thought, intensifies as the dominant impulse of regathering accelerates and is resisted by the residual impulse of diffusion. He did not believe, once more, as one might expect, that most intense variety occurs at the maximum point of diffusion or creation. The fulfillment of genius was not for him, as it was for Emerson, a happy result of creativity. He wrote of "The fate of an individual gifted, or rather accursed, with intellect very far superior to that of his race."[27] He spoke of rare moments when the soul abandons matter, "separates itself from its own idiosyncrasy, or individuality, and considers its own being, not as appertaining solely to itself, but as a portion of the universal Ens;" and concludes that "it is our sense of self which debases, and which keeps us debased."[26] Only Poe among the Romantics in America designated individuation of person as tortuous, the variety of the Many as abnormal. He lacked self-reliance grounded on an existent universal, on God. Genius for him was extreme abnormality, the reductive result, during the collapse of the universe, of cosmic war between the electric will to individuate and the aesthetic longing for anonymity in maternal arms, between the drive for Diffusion, and the drive for Unity. Poe was exquisitely self-conscious of aberrant egotism that burns bright under pressure to conform, like a spark whipped alive by dark wind. Eureka is above al his attempt to build a metaphysic on the basis of his acute sensitivity to the opposing forces of egotism and love, individuality and loss of self.

Thus for Poe each human entity manifests at once the contrary impulses toward individuation and toward cosmic unity. The man of the crowd, for example, rushes frantically to and fro seeking, on the one hand, to lose himself in a crowd and, on the other, to maintain his single, self-absorbed, Leibnitzean identity. He desperately seeks other people but shudders when he is touched by any one of them. His crime, which cannot be told, is simply the crime of all human beings of the crowd, that of being a single monad--an abnormality predetermined by God of whom he is now a diffused particle. The tale moves from a description of the general down to that of the particular. And the description of the paradoxical qualities of this particular man indicate that he represents the essence of the crowd, that he is Everyman (including Poe himself, for the man manifests signs of Southern genteel poverty). And Everyman, Poe says, is a monad who at once intuits proximity of other monads and cannot intimately relate to any one of them. Indeed, the man of the crowd looks through the narrator at the end: "He noticed me not"--just as earlier, he has "stalked backward and forward without apparent object." He seeks proximity but denies reciprocity. The narrator, in turn, examines Everyman incognito,

with a handkerchief around his mouth and with "a
pair of caoutchouc over shoes" in which he "could
move around in perfect silence." They are alter
egos, at once desiring fusion and remaining separate, monads whose retardative wills suffer them
"infinitely to approximate, while denying them
positive contact" (505). The tale is about the
narrator recovering from an illness who perceives
humanity divided into two major groups, those who
blend with others and those who are isolated "on
account of the very denseness of the company
around;" and who, in a moment of acute self-awareness, perceives himself torn between unity and
disunity. The tale exhibits urban loneliness, and
is very modern.

"Ligeia," a Poe-vision of complex archetypal
simplicity, is about the conflict between Entity
gravitating toward primal Beauty and gigantic
Volition for individuated life.[29] Ligeia herself
comes from the Rhine, the homeland of German Romanticism, and is played-off against the mundane Rowena
from empirical England. Her beauty, first emphasized, is like that "strange" beauty Poe speaks
about in "The Poetic Principle." "It is found in a
chrysalis, a stream of running water . . . in the
falling of a meteor . . . in the glances of unusually aged people" In "the intense scrutiny of
Ligeia's eyes" the narrator is "upon the very verge
of remembrance" of her origin which can be only "of
a Destiny" that is "more vast--very distant in the
by-gone time, and infinitely awful" of supernal
unity (588). But as the tale unfolds, we learn that
it is appropriately preceded by the (supposed)
Glanville quotation concerning the will "which dieth
not," "the mysteries of the will, with its vigor."
Ligeia represents not only supernal beauty; she
embodies divine volition, and is "the most violently
a prey to the tumultuous vultures of stern passion."
Her eyes both delight and appal the child-like
narrator, and the "placidity of her very low voice"
is offset by the "fierce energy" with which she
utters "wild words." She cannot lead the narrator
"gently back to Beauty" ("Monos and Una"); she is a
practitioner of "World Reason " (588), with immense
cognitive knowledge, who seeks "the tree of knowledge . . . not meet for man in the infant condition
of his soul" ("Monos and Una"). Indeed, the tale
turns out to be primarily about the "principle of

her longing," not for beauty but "for life--but for life." Her vehement desire to be alive, to come back to individuated being, makes "ill-omened" from the beginning a marriage or fusion of souls between her and the narrator. But then, she is not an actual woman but the projection of the artistic narrator's schizophrenia that is indigenous to the human condition. Torn between the Glanvillian will to live and the desire to be absorbed in Beauty, Ligeia fights back out of the grave for individuation, and nearly succeeds, but cannot: creation is on the wane.[30] She is an archetype of the darkness of human experience, of the gigantic drive of a human being to exist as a unique one at the expense of longing for Unity. Her will-power overshadows her qualities of supernal beauty. But stronger even than she is the destiny of all entities to return to primal unity in the phase of regathering. In (the watercloset tales) "Ms. Found in a Bottle" and "A Descent into the Maelstrom" the revelatory power of regathering is imaged by whirlpools of "prodigious suction," and the narrator is made aware of how paltry "a consideration [is] my own individual life." But opposing the vortex of regathering in the Poe cosmos is the towering Ligeian principle on which is grounded exquisite individuation.

The disturbing discrepancy in Poe between the idea of death as return to supernal beauty and the dramatization of death as terrifying disintegration is understandable in view of these opposing forces in his cosmos. Like many other thinkers, he was torn between the theoretic absolute and concrete experience, two worlds which at different times accommodated and negated each other, but neither of which alone represents the "real" Poe. Death, from the relative view, is the annhilation of personal identity, and from the absolute view, the return of individuals to desired unity. Poe wrote that "The pain of the consideration that we shall lose our individual identity ceases at once when we further reflect that the process . . . is, neither more or less than that of absorption, by each individual intelligence, of all other intelligences (that is, of the Universe) into its own."[31] The narrator in "The Pit and the Pendulum," after recovering from his first swoon, asks the critical question of the relative view: "And that gulf is--what? How at

50

least shall we distinguish its shadows from those of the tomb?" Since the impulse of heterogeneity acts as a retardative force to the now dominant thrust of regathering, the individual, who is the arena of these forces, is torn with agony and confusion between them. We live in an imploding universe, in the heated phase of withdrawal (that is necessary for the bliss of heaven), a terrible time of conflicting forces, when the will is frustrated and non-creative, when the impulse to beauty is often known negatively as suicidal drive, when the final regathering is called, as Poe himself called it, a "Catastrophe" (585).

IV

In sum, the motif of cosmic pulsation is common in the history of metaphysics, but what is unusual in Poe is the negative values he assigns to the creative phase, and the place he assigns this world in the phase of regathering. The ultimate ontological terms for him are Beauty and Will: "Unity . . . is a truth--I feel it. Diffusion is a truth--I see it." Possibly I over-stress the tension and pain in Poe. But it should always be remembered that "the Volition of God" which is "the truly ultimate Principle" (527) created the Universe which is "abnormal" and during the earthly epoch, painful; and that we are particles of diffused, incomprehensible (and perhaps mad) deity. Furthermore, excepting such "unimpeded visions" as "The Domain of Arnheim" and "The Island of the Fay," and such poems as "Annabel Lee" and "To One in Paradise," (if one assumes that these works express the opposite of pain) there is not much else in Poe but pain and mournfulness.[32] Poe tells us in "The Poetic Principle" that "the Human Aspiration for Supernal Beauty" is manifested as "an elevating excitement of the Soul." This "excitement" is not the "calm, sweet cast, or appearance of divine glory" as it is in Edwards and others, but more like terror that turns a man's hair prematurely white.[33] Poe's apocalyptic visions are deadly. The phase of regathering is not an idyllic ascent to Beauty but an exquisite conflict of immanent cosmic forces. Life and death are at once feared and sought. Concrete nature and personal identity are phased out

and so profoundly sublimated in internal fantasy
that there is almost nowhere in Poe, in his poetry
or prose, a real person and a real outside world.
Yet death, though not in theory, is in fact ap-
prehended as defeat, as a black pit, as a whirlpool
of nothingness. Society, instead of being a harmony
of persons moving back toward Primal Unity, is a
fatal chaos of heterogeneous identities. People,
backlashing against each other, like knives, facing
apparent nihility in death, have no one to turn to
for salvation; they themselves are God, particles of
Deity. But indeed this conflict is built into Poe's
system. His intuition of subjectivity, not like
Edwards' and Emerson's, rendered no essence of an
existent universal to unify particulars, only an
electric asceticism of mournful void. We live, for
all practical purposes, in a decaying, phosphorescent world collapsing into a catastrophe of Beauty,
a world of which Poe, with his curious psychology,
may have enjoyed being the center and the
victim.[34]

FOOTNOTES

[1] _Works_, ed. Sereno E. Dwight (New York, 1829-30), VIII, 10.

[2] Quoted in _Introduction to Poe_, ed. Eric W. Carlson (New York: Scott, Foresman, 1967), p. 543.

[3] One recent critic who treats Poe extensively as a writer of hoax is George P. Thompson in _Poe's Fiction: Romantic Irony in the Gothic Tales_ (Madison: University of Wisconsin Press, 1973).

[4] "The Angel of the Odd" and "How to Write a Blackwood Article."

[5] Quoted by Hervey Allen in _Israfel_ (New York: Rinehart, 1949), pp. 650-51.

[6] From _Edgar Allen Poe: Selected Prose, Poetry, and Eureka_, edited and with introduction by W. H. Auden (New York: Holt, Rinehart and Winston, 1950), p. 520. Hereafter all references to _Eureka_ are to this edition, and the page or pages of each reference are given in parentheses.

[7] Poe thought _Eureka_ "a Poem" because he thought the universe which _Eureka_ is about, poetic. The key term in Poe's metaphysical aesthetics is symmetry. In "human constructiveness," we are told, "a particular intention brings to pass a particular object; but this is all; we see no reciprocity. The effect does not re-act upon the cause; the interaction does not change relations with the object. In Divine Constructions the object is either design or object as we choose to regard it--and we may take at any time a cause for an effect, or the converse" (571). Elsewhere in _Eureka_ Poe speaks of the "analogical, symmetrical or poetical instinct of man" (581), and gives as his first "general proposition": "In the Original Unity of the First Thing lies the Secondary Cause of All Things, with the Germ of their Inevitable Annhilation" (485). In other words, Poe's universe like Edwards' has no loose ends in space or time; its movement is cyclical, not linear and open-ended. It is self-contained, self-existent. The universe is for the

universe's sake, just as a poem is for the poem's sake. That is to say, Poe wrote, the universe is "a plot of God" (580).

[8] See the following selected items particularly for explications of Eureka: Margaret Alterton, "Origin of Poe's Critical Theory," University of Iowa Humanistic Studies, II no. 3; Richard P. Benton, "Cross-Lights on Poe's Eureka," American Transcendental Quarterly (Spring, 1974); Introduction to Poe, ed. Eric. W. Carlson (New York: Scott, Foresman, 1967); Richard D. Finhold, "The Vision at the Brink of the Abyss: 'A Descent into the Maelstrom' in the Light of Poe's Cosmology," Georgia Review, VII, 356-66; Daniel Hoffman, Poe, Poe, Poe, Poe, Poe, Poe, Poe (New York: Doubleday, 1972); Robert P. Jacobs, Poe: Journalist & Critic (Baton Rouge: Louisiana State University Press, 1969); John F. Lynen, The Design of the Present (New Haven: Yale University Press, 1969); Sidney P. Moss, "Poe's Apocalyptic Vision," Papers on Poe, ed. Richard P. Veler (Wittenberg University, 1972), 369-78; Geoffrey Rans, Edgar Allan Poe (Edinburg and London, 1965); Charles W. Schaeger, "Poe's Eureka: The Macrocosmic Analogue," Journal of Aesthetics and Art Criticism, XXIX, 353-65; and Philip P. Weiner, "Poe's Logic and Metaphysics," The Personalist, XIV, 268-74.

[9] Frederick Copleston, in discussing post-Kantian idealism, writes that "the ultimate principle is, considered in itself, without object. It grounds the subject-object relationship and, in itself, transcends the relationship. It is subject and object in identity, the infinite activity from which both proceed," A History of Philosophy (New York: Doubleday, 1965), VII, part 1, 18-19.

[10] Biographia Literaria, chapter twelve. Coleridge continues: "self-consciousness may be the modification of a higher form of being, perhaps of a higher consciousness . . . that self-consciousness may be itself something explicable into something which must lie beyond the possibility of our knowledge." For a more comprehensive and less speculative treatment of Coleridge's influence on Poe than mine, see Floyd Stovall, Edgar Poe the Poet (Charlottesville, University of Virginia, 1969), chapter five.

[11] Richard Wilbur in _Major Writers of America_ (New York: Harcourt, Brace, 1962), p. 373.

[12] In comparing the respective definitions of "Imagination" by Coleridge and Poe, Stovall points out Poe's early apparent variance from Coleridge, but concludes that Poe eventually "agreed with Coleridge in every respect" (Stovall, p. 161). However, the fact that Poe conceived that the creative phase of the cosmos is now over, and that the process, the energies, of the cosmos are pre-determined, makes one hesitate to accept fully the conclusions of Stovall's excellent discussion. For instance, would Poe have identified, as did Coleridge, even have believed analogous, imagination and the creative power of God? In Poe's terms, since "the primary process of Creation" is now over, the phase of regathering, of which art is a manifestation, is not creative. Creativity, as we humans know it, is a remembering of Primal Unity. Poetry, for instance, is "the rhythmical creation of Beauty" based on "Memories of a Destiny more vast" (588). Poe does not in _Eureka_ designate "creative" the phase of the return to Supernal Beauty. Alterton writes that Poe denied that man's imagination truly could create (pp. 117-18).

[13] See Lynen, pp. 217-18.

[14] Hervey Allen, p. 626.

[15] Poe wrote in "The Philosophy of Composition," "the death then, of a beautiful woman is, unquestionably, the most poetical topic in the world."

[16] See the following essay, "Channing and Emerson on Personal Identity."

[17] Poe had read Leibnitz and Dugald Stewart. The latter wrote that Leibnitz held, "in opposition to Locke" "that the soul never ceases to think, even in sleep or in deliquium," nor that there is "such a thing as death" (_Collected Works of Dugald Stewart_, ed. Sir William Hamilton [Edinburgh, 1877], I, 276). See Alterton for information on Poe and Stewart, p. 1.

[18] I press the point that for Poe neither God nor death is ontological zero. I agree with Carlson

who writes that for Poe "God does not . . . equal zero" (Introduction to Poe, p. XXIV). But for different views, see Thompson and Robert Adams, NIL (New York: Oxford University Press, 1966), both passim. David Halliburton holds that for Poe "consciousness and identity are by definition that which cannot be lost" (Edgar Allan Poe: A Phenomenological View [New Jersey: Princeton University Press, 1973], p. 381). Poe writes: "In proportion to the dreamlessness of the sleep . . . would be the degree of the soul's liability to annihilation" (Carlson, p. 529). Poe, like the other thinkers treated in this book, opposed Humean scepticism about the soul or self consisting in substance. Hume wrote:

> When I enter most intimately into what I call myself, I always stumble on some particular perception or other of heat or cold, light or shade, love or hatred, pain or pleasure. I never can catch myself at any time without a perception, and never can observe anything but the perception. When my perceptions are removed for any time, as by sound sleep, so long am I insensible of myself, and may truly be said not to exist. And were all my perceptions removed by death, and could I neither think, nor feel, nor see, nor love, nor hate after the dissolution of my body, I should be entirely annihilated, nor do I conceive what is farther requisite to make me a perfect nonentity" (A Treatise of Human Nature, Book I, part IV, section VI, "Of Personal Identity").

19   Another tale in which the term "objectless" is used is "William Wilson." When William I looks into the bed of William II, his "whole spirit became possessed with an objectless yet intolerable horror." William I may have seen the moral Dorian Gray essence of himself, or literally nothing at all. William II is the unconscious projection of William I's conscience or social objectivity. At the end, William I, by murder, internalizes William II and feels guilt. This is why he is guilt-ridden at the beginning of the tale. Perhaps the scene in the bedroom foreshadows the end: William I sees no object in the bed because he has momentarily internalizes William II, and has an awful twinge of conscience, of self-revelation, at what kind of

creature he himself really is; he immediately leaves the school.

20 Poe's concept of the body as a cage was common place. William Ellery Channing, Sr. wrote in the _Treatise_ on Man: "sensations have their fountain in the Soul itself" (8); nature is the occasion not the cause of sensation; the "soul is essentially active" (11). "It is an unbounded force . . . and if left to itself, it would break out into a chaos of sensation, thought, affection and will" (12). But the soul "does not need excitement but (repression) restraint. It needs restraints to determine the order of its development, and to give it the possibility of moral self-control. The body I apprehend is ordained by God as this restraining, regulating power" (12). "In a higher life the mind will probably cease to be passive and dependent as regards its sensations, or will be able to waken them at pleasure" (7).

There are for Channing five classes of sensation (14). "A new organ would give us a new class as different from the present as sight from sound. The spirit is probably susceptible of infinity of sensations, as well as of thoughts" (15). These quotations are found in Morton deCorcy Nachlas, _A Study and Transcription of William Ellery Channing's Unfinished Treatise on Man_, Dissertation (Chicago: The Meadville Theological School, June, 1942); page numbers are given in parentheses.

21 The notion of a sixth sense was also commonplace. See the first essay in this book.

22 N. Bryllion Fagin, _The Histrionic Mr. Poe_ (Baltimore: John Hopkins Press, 1949), p. 72.

23 Halliburton believes that Monos and Una have "no intersubjective relations;" that they are "but a single subjectivity housed in a plural pronoun" (p. 381). Hawthorne, more interested than Poe (and Emerson) in preserving the integrity of the individual soul, but still interested in greater communication among souls, wrote (probably facetiously, however) to Sophia: "When we shall be endowed with spiritual bodies, I think they will be so constituted that we may send thoughts and feelings any distance, in no time at all, and transfuse them warm and fresh into the consciousness

of those we love" (quoted in Julian Hawthorne, Nathaniel Hawthorne and His Wife [Boston, 1885], I, 223).

[24] Alterton observes correctly that in "Morella" Poe "clearly copies from the Essay, the outstanding points in Locke's presentation of the subject" (p. 100).

[25] In "Notes on the Mind."

[26] Quoted in Carlson, P. 549.

[27] Quoted in Carlson, p. 526.

[28] From "A Chapter of Suggestions." In "Experience" Emerson wrote that "the discovery we have made that we exist . . . is called the Fall of Man." But Emerson is bewailing not individuation as such but the momentum of the analytical Understanding to sever spirit and matter, the Me and the Not Me.

[29] I concur with Richard Wilbur that Ligeia is the embodiment of the sentiment of the beautiful (Major American Writers I, 375-77); but I concur more with D. H. Lawrence that "Ligeia" "is a ghastly story of the assertion of the human will" (Studies in Classic American Literature [1923; rpt., New York, Doubleday, 1951], p. 85). My point is that she represents the terrific tension in human beings between the two, Beauty (Unity) and Will (Disunity).

[30] Poe wrote: "I should have intimated that the Will did not perfect its intention--there should have been a relapse--a final one--and Ligeia . . . should be at length entombed as Rowena--the bodily alterations having gradually faded away" (The Complete Works of Edgar Allan Poe, ed. James A. Harrison [New York, AMS Press, 1965], p. 52).

[31] Quoted in Jacobs, p. 403. In regard to this quotation: Poe defined space, not as "infinite" for that term would imply a non-cyclical system, but as "a sphere of which," in Pascal's words, "the centre is everywhere, the circumference nowhere" (500-1). Since, according to Poe, all physical entities attract each other by gravitation, there can be no general material center to which

these entities are regathering. The ultimate center turns out to be the Primal One, the universal Subject. But this Spirit has been diffused at the beginning of creation by Volition. Hence each particle of that Spirit, each finite soul, each of us, is the center to which all matter is regathering. These souls or particles of subjectivity are themselves, simultaneously with material particles, returning to Unity. This Unity, the ultimate center, will be eventually the universal Subject, the result of the fusion of all finite soul-particles. Into this Subjectivity, the final globe of Matter will be absorbed. Each one of us, as subject or spirit, out of Time and out of Space, therefore, is the center to which the almost infinite universe of Matter is regathering. Allen Tate writes: for Poe "Every man [is] the non-spatial center into which the universe . . . will contract, as into its annihilation" ("The Angelic Imagination," in The Recognition of Edgar Allan Poe, ed. Eric. W. Carlson [Ann Arbor: University of Michigan Press, 1966], p. 252).

32 The description "unimpeded visions" belongs to Stuart and Susan Levine, in The Short Fiction of Edgar Allan Poe (Indianapolis: Bobbs-Merrill, 1976), p. vii and passim.

33 Edwards, "The Personal Narrative."

34 Walt Whitman dreamed of a ship in a storm "flying uncontrolled with torn sails and broken spars through the wild sleet and winds and waves of the night. On deck was a slender, slight, beautiful figure, a dim man, apparently enjoying all the terror, the murk, and the dislocation of which he was the centre and the victim. That figure [was] Edgar Poe" (quoted in Fagin, p. 237.)

> "For Marius . . . those eternal doubts as
> to the <u>criteria</u> of truth reduced themselves to
> a skepticism almost drily practical . . . the
> possibility, if an outward world does really
> exist, of some faultiness in our apprehension
> of it--the doctrine, in short, of what is
> termed 'the subjectivity of knowledge'. That
> is a consideration, indeed, which lies as an
> element of weakness, like some admitted fault
> or flaw, at the very foundation of every
> philosophical account of the universe; . . .
> with which none have really dealt conclusively,
> some perhaps not quite sincerely; which those
> who are not philosophers dissipate by 'common',
> but unphilosophical sense, or by religious
> faith."

Walter Pater

I

William Ellery Channing's praise of man foreshadowed Emerson's glorification of him, but
Channing's persistent definition of man and God in
terms of "person" kept him ultimately from concurring with Emerson. Elizabeth Peabody reported
that Channing thought Henry Ware was "fighting a
shadow" when contending against Emerson's denial of
the personality of God.[1] But Channing must have
known that his sweet temper of reconciliation could
not deal adequately with the issues between him and
Emerson. Emerson, in turn, although admiring the
older man for his character and for being an early
crusader against conservative theology, knew beyond
doubt that he and Channing could never agree on the
metaphysical image of man.[2] Channing, a
traditional theist, held that God and men are
"persons" or spiritual units who are separate and
distinct from each other; and Emerson thought
Channing's position essentially materialistic.

Channing defined God and man, throughout his
writings, in terms of "person," and imaged a created
person as a spiritual "germ" or seed part of which
is conscious and rational and part, sub-conscious,
turbid and divine. In his unpublished <u>Treatise</u>

60

on Man he devoted an entire chapter to the definition of the "Idea of the I or Self." He stated that
"The 'I' cannot be analyzed. There is nothing more
simple into which it can be resolved."[3] "The I .
. . that which thinks, acts, feels" is "a simple
unity" which cannot be the object of thought; it is
distinct and "separate from all other beings."[4]
Further, the soul or person is a germ of self-
determining spiritual energy the destiny of which is
the development or unfolding of its potential
attributes on occasions of experience. The fulfillment of a soul, since there is not sufficient time
on earth, takes place in eternity. The soul is
self-determining; it only is responsible for actual-
ization of its potential. "I am not to ask God,"
Channing said, "to determine my mind. That is my
proper work."[5] In short, a person for Channing is
a unit of spirit, separate and distinct from all
other such units; it alone is responsible for its
essence which is moral and social.

Consequently Channing opposed any philosophy
that sought dissolution of persons. In respect to
Calvinism, he wrote that "The doctrine that God is
the only Substance, which is Pantheism, differs
little from the doctrine that God is the only active
power in the universe. For what is substance
without power?"[6] Concerning the Transcendental
movement, he claimed, "Their vague generalities do
not satisfy me. They seem to overlook the actual
moral condition of the human race. . . . At this
moment most of the 'true spiritualists' are in
danger of losing their faith in immortality through
their Pantheistic notions of the soul and its
absorption in the only substance, - Deity. These
notions threaten all sense of moral responsibility
and moral freedom."[7] He sternly declared that "a
mind, rapt, absorbed in God and other beings, so as
to forget itself, never to recur to itself, hardly
seems sane."[8]

Although God in quality, for Channing, immensely excels human beings, he and they belong to
the same ontological category. A man is "a recipient, a partaker" of God's nature, and shares with
God such divine attributes as reason, free-will, and
knowledge of the good. The thrust of Channing's
phrase "likeness to God" was at once toward the
affirmation of man and against the Calvinistic

61

notion of God as unintelligible.[9] This phrase,
however, does not express precisely the relation
between God and man Channing had in mind; this
relation, he thought, is more than analogical.[10]
In his sermon "Likeness to God," he stated that "the
idea of God, sublime and awful as it is, is the idea
of human nature, purified and enlarged into infinity. In ourselves are the elements of Divinity.
God, then, does not sustain a figurative resemblance
to man. It is the resemblance of a parent to a
child, the likeness of a kindred nature." Men
partake in the nature of God in the same way children partake in that of their parents; they are
literally the children of God. God is the great
Parent of mankind, of whom, furthermore, men can
have "some clear ideas."

Thus Channing held that there is an eternal
family each member of which, including God, is a
separate spiritual unit whose essence, since it
consists in his relation with all other units, is
realized by his moral will which is free from all
other wills.[11] Channing wrote in perhaps one of
his more pantheistic moments, "How near to me is my
Creator! I am not merely surrounded by his influence, as by this air which I breathe. I am
pervaded by his agency. He quickens my whole being.
Through him am I this instant thinking, feeling, and
speaking."[12] But he did not mean that God and he
were one in essence or subject; all souls, including
God, are separate and distinct from each other.
Within this eternal family, each created soul passes
from this kindergarten world to the next world where
each will mature as a citizen in heavenly society.
Our education, Channing felt, "is going on perpetually" under our Parent; "we are through ages on
ages to form closer and purer friendships throughout
the vast family of souls, and to diffuse our sympa-
thies through ever-widening spheres; . . . we are to
approach God forever by a brighter vision, an
intenser love, a freer communion, and a larger
participation of his spirit and his life!"[13]

Channing was interested also in that part of
himself which was not immediately evident to consciousness. His interest in his "depths" as a
source of fundamental knowledge helps place him in
the ranks of early American Romantics. Unlike
Emerson, however, he was (as were other

Unitarians) influenced positively and strongly by Locke's rational tradition modified by the Scottish School of philosophy. Thus, although he held that the soul provides the greatest evidence for God, when he explored his depths he moved with extreme caution. "If there springs up within you," he wrote in "Self-Culture," "any view of God's word or universe, any sentiment of aspiration which seems to you of a higher order than what you meet abroad . . . Do not trust it blindly, for it may be an illusion; but it may be the Divinity moving within you, a new revelation, not supernatural, but still most precious." Channing gazed into his rich and turbid depths with curiosity, trepidation, and awe. He found there, he stated in the Treatise on Man, that part of the "inward world is dark, confused, ever tossing ocean," filled with "volcano[es] of passion." Since "even reflecting men understand little of what passes within themselves," "one of the most [important] parts of mental illumination consists in bringing into light, in turning into distinct perceptions, the cloudy, dim, twilight impressions which long experience has given birth." When Channing did this (we are told) he began not only to gain knowledge of and control over the negative forces within his depths, but to discover "what endless ages are to unfold," "a fountain of Power" that is "the creative nature of God." "By looking within," by reflection (not intuition), he gained "the feeling of a deeper mystery in himself than in outward nature." He continued:

> This power of introspection is of inexpressible dignity. By this we become acquainted with spiritual existence, - we enter the spiritual world. This glorious universe, of which material nature is the dim expression and semblance, is first revealed to us in our own spirits. We enter it through the portal of our own souls. Even God is manifested within us. The infinite Mind has impressed his image in ours, and through these alone we know him. Intelligence, wisdom, power, love, beauty, joy, these are intelligible to us through the dawning within ourselves. By looking within, we find in the confused mass of our thoughts, the elements of the Grand thought of God.

Channing held, therefore, that the soul is at once the main source of man's hopes and a place of imperfection, of uncontrolled, even chaotic, forces. The inner world could not be implicitly trusted. The contents of our depths, like those of other areas of experience, must be analyzed and judged by reason and the moral sense.

Channing's vision in which persons are conceived as bounded units is extraordinarily pictorial, familial, and filled with moral vigor, a vision eminently suited to a preacher wishing to communicate. Channing, far more than Emerson, moreover, contributed to the genteel tradition of moral and social orthodoxy that denied "the unknown god" of Calvinism. He preached "We Ought" and Emerson essayed "I Am."[14]

II

Emerson, living apart in Concord, wrote in his Journal in 1838 (the year of the "Divinity School Address" and the year that marked the beginning of the furor over "personality"), "What shall I answer to these friendly youths who ask of me an account of Theism, and think the views I have expressed of the impersonality of God desolating and ghastly? I say, that I cannot find, when I explore my own consciousness, any truth in saying that God is a person, but the reverse."[15] Emerson found that positing persons as separate units, of whom God was one, prohibited him from attaining what he sought. And what he sought above all, Stephen Whicher observes, was "What Edwards, what New Englanders, had always wanted an assured salvation, not simply moral capacity."[16] Emerson found this salvation not in prayer to nor in glorification of another person, but (as W. R. Inge phrases it in another context) in "something much closer than an ethical harmony of two mutually exclusive wills."[17]

Many critics are reluctant to grant that Emerson believed in an identity of God and man. Lawrence Buell, for example, thinks that a passage in the "Divinity School Address" which seems to suggest such identity in fact does not, but "dwells between metaphor and metaphysics," and that Emerson "prefers to make a striking general impression rather than to be exact."[18] Rather, Emerson hesitated, for obvious reasons, to make an explicit claim to identity with God in his public utterances. He blurred the issue to diffuse criticism of egotheism--and thereby gained, incidentally, a reputation for imprecision of thought. But the claim is there. For example he stated outright in his Journal: "In certain moments I have known that I existed directly from God, and am, as it were, his organ, and in my ultimate consciousness am He."[19]

But "identity" may be a misleading term to describe what he meant. He did not mean that he was the universal; he believed that there is no separation between the universal and the particular ego. "There is no bar or wall in the soul. Where man, the effect, ceases, and God, the cause, begins" ("The-Over-Soul"). His problem, Caponigri states, was in theory "to relate the individual directly to absolute Being, while preserving the individuality, the separateness intact."[20] This problem Emerson may not have solved in logical terms. But he claimed experience of this identity, and he recorded this experience in metaphoric terms: "the consciousness in each man is a sliding scale, which identifies him now with the First Cause, and now with the flesh of his body" ("Experience"). In his Journal he said almost the same thing: "Every consciousness repeats mine and is a sliding scale from Deity to Dust" (VI, 220). Thus God and ego are not the same: the ego is God but God is more than the ego. If "man" is defined as ego, he is less than God. As ego, Emerson was fallible and mortal; as God, he was self-existent, uncreated, eternal.

Emerson had four arguments to support his belief in man's identity with God: subjective idealism, centrality of self, individuation of person, and sympathy. In regard to his idealism, he wrote his Aunt Mary Moody: "I know that I exist, but the age and the Universe are alike abstractions of my own mind, and have no pretensions to the same definitive certainty."[21] Emerson's extreme idealism developed out of his search for assured salvation. He sought God, but the only thing that he knew, and indeed was ever to know, with "definitive certainty," was himself. He experienced "the age and the Universe" but questioned the status of their reality: although they were more real than dreams of sleep and images of day-dreaming, they

65

were not, he was forced to admit, as real as he; they did not have substantial reality.

A sane man, however, Emerson could not hold that he was the Creator of the world. The world was always there when he opened his eyes, and always acted as though it had been there even when he had had his eyes shut. Furthermore, it was always the same world, whether or not he wanted it to be, with its own natural laws and moral principles that he could not violate if he and the world were to endure. He was in the peculiar position, he realized, of being like a god who could choose to have or not to have a world (by living or dying) but who if he chose to have a world was unable to chose the world he wanted. Alas, he was a god in ruin; if the age and the universe were a dream, they were not his dream but the effect of a power greater than his ego-will. He confessed with common sense humility that "I am constrained every moment to acknowledge a higher origin for events than the will I call mine" ("The Over-Soul").

Yet Emerson refused to grant that this power that created and sustained the universe was separate from himself. He insisted that whatever could save him had to be able to be verified in terms of which he could not doubt, and that those terms must coincide with himself because he was that-only which he could not doubt. Consequently he concluded that the power that created and to a large extent controlled his experience, although other than his limited will, was not other than he; and that, since it was not other than he, it was, paradoxically, himself. Or rather, he concluded that he and his will were greater than he had at first believed. Emerson, for salvation, looked far within himself to contact the hidden, universal power that projected and sustained the world he experienced. He had to become God to believe in God.

Like Channing, therefore, Emerson held that the relation between God and man is closer than analogy allows. But whereas Channing argued that God and man are separate and distinct persons belonging to the same category of Being, Emerson held that there is no relation at all between God and man. This meant, for one thing, that he knew what God knew, a claim totally opposed to the Calvinistic doctrine of the inscrutibility of the divine. He made the extraordinary claim in Nature that "Undoubtedly we have no questions to ask which are unanswerable." Believing that he had entire access to the mind of the creator, Emerson represents the climax of the liberal religious movement of the nineteenth century toward conceiving the divine immanent in man, except that he reversed the equation to read: man in God.

This hidden, universal power of which his conscious will was a part, Emerson called the "Unconscious" that is "ever the act of God himself" (III, 325). Later, when the definition of "Unconscious" was challenged, he explained that "the unconsciousness we speak of was merely relative to us; we speak, we act from we know not what higher principle, and we describe its circumabient quality by confessing the subjection of our perception to it. . . . But in saying this, we predicate nothing of its consciousness or unconsciousness in relation to itself, we see at once that we have no language subtle enough for distinction in that inaccessible region. . . . We cannot say, God is self-conscious, or not self-conscious," (VII, 344). But whether God is "conscious" or "unconscious," and although "inaccessible" to the Understanding, Emerson held that he and God were not separate units or centers of consciousness. Emerson's desire for monism overrode all considerations of duality. When he said that "the consciousness in each man . . . identifies him now with the First Cause," he meant that the consciousness in each man is the consciousness of God.[22] The terms "God" and "man" are simply two poles, one universal, the other, particular, of One Mind or Being.

Thus God for Emerson is universal subjectivity, an inner, not an outer God. In "Thoughts on Modern Literature," he distinguished this subjectivity from privateness: "There is a pernicious ambiguity in the use of the term subjective. We may say . . . that the single soul feels its right to be no longer confounded with numbers, but itself to sit in judgment on history and literature, and to summon all facts and parties before its tribunal. And in this sense the age is subjective." According to Emerson, when the pronoun "I" is used to refer to the particular ego, it designates privateness, a single digit. When it is used to refer to the universal soul with which the particular ego is fused, of which the ego is an incarnation, it designates the universal subject:

> A man may say I, and never refer to himself as an individual; and a man may recite passages of his life with no feeling of egotism. . . . The criterion which discriminates these two habits in the poet's mind is the tendency of his composition; namely, whether it leads to Nature, or to the person of the writer. The great always introduce us to facts; small men introduce us always to themselves. The great man, even whilst he relates a private fact personal to him, is really leading us away from him to an universal experience.

Emerson's subjective idealism, in positing mind over matter, and in giving priority to the perspective of "from within" over that of "from without," was one step in his argument for a bipolar monism of mind, in which there was a unity of the universal and the particular. It is the peculiar property of mind, he thought, to be at once One and Many.

Hence unlike Channing who, in self-reflection, studied critically with reason the voices of his unconscious to determine whether or not they were messages from God who was another person, Emerson accepted without question his intuition as the voice of his Greater Being. His seemingly irresponsible claim in "Self-Reliance" that he would follow those voices even though they were from the devil was of course rhetorical and audacious. He assumed that they were voices of universal laws of Being that were ultimately on the side of life. He trusted, like Thoreau, what he could put his hands on in the dark.

III

In addition to his idealism, Emerson was convinced that the perspective of centrality of self and the fact of individuation of person evidenced his divinity and assured salvation. He was particularly sensitive to the perspective of centrality

68

that seemed to permeate like a lyric each moment of his life. The universe, he observed, is structured around each person; each person is the axel around which revolve the stars, the cities, the people. He was not alone in the sensitivity to this view. Thoreau wrote in A Week on the Concord and Merrimack Rivers, "Let us wander where we will, the universe is built around us, and we are central still. If we look into the heavens they are concave, and if we were to look into a gulf as bottomless, it would be concave also" ("Thursday"). Charles Anderson writes that "Thoreau, like other Transcendentalists [but only Emerson and Whitman], stuck to the pre-Newtonian conviction that the spectator is central."[23] But this statement neglects the traditions of Descartean dualism, of Lockean empiricism, of Berkeleian idealism, that came between medieval and Transcendental thought, and inevitably led to the idealization and internalization of perception. Emerson, Thoreau, and Whitman were, if you will, post-Lockean, "Ptolemaic" subjective idealists: the soul or self as subject (not as an object of God's attention) is the center of the universe because it is divine. In "Song of Myself," Whitman exclaims, "I know I am solid and sound,/To me the converging objects of the universe perpetually flow,/All are written to me, and I must get what the writing means" (Section 20). These writers believed that were a person not divine but ontologically equal or inferior to nature, he would not be at the center of the universe.[24]

The idea of centrality began to develop for Emerson as early as 1820. He noted that "It is a singular fact that we cannot present to the imagination a longer space than just so much of the world as is bounded by the visible horizon. . . . stern necessity bounds us to a little extent of a few miles only" (I, 5). Thus by the time he was seventeen, Emerson had developed a rudimentary motif that had two opposing aspects: he was at the center of the world, and the world was a limited world. Both this sense of centrality and this sense of limitation were to play increasingly important roles in his life. The creative power of centrality will augment his religious awakening, and then the sense of limitation or Fate will move to the foreground. However, neither pole will at any time entirely overcome the other. When he feels the world closing

69

in upon him, he will find compensatory strength in the central perspective.

Later, in 1829, Emerson wrote in his _Journal_ the first version of a passage that he used in the sermon "Solitude and Society." He spoke of centrality with easy freedom, aware of its solipsistic danger: "When I look at the rainbow I find myself the centre of its arch. But so are you; & so is the man that sees it a mile from both of us. So also the globe is round & every man therefore stands on the top" (III, 168).[25] And in 1834, in the sermon "The Miracle of our Being," he asked the congregation to "See how cunningly constructed are all things in such a manner as to make each being the centre of the Creation. . . . Thus is each man placed at the heart of the world."[26] This sermon, written after his resignation from the church and after he had met the great Romantics abroad, is a last step toward "Self-Reliance" and contains, as a major idea, centrality of self.

Centrality can be a dangerous idea. Emerson did not impose it upon his audience after he was attacked for solipsism and egotheism, but it is implicit throughout his later work. In the late thirties and early forties, when he was debating problems of social action, he moved away from the perspective, but kept attached to it by a thread so that he could always return to it when issues became apparently insoluble. Indeed, this central perspective, a corollary to his subjective idealism, is his native posture, his religious stance, of being in the world but not of the world.

In the First Series of essays (1841), the poet speaks "from within" and "stands on the centre;" a self-reliant man "belongs to no other time or place, but is the centre of things;" when a man has "found his centre, the Deity will shine through him." The "eye is the first circle; the horizon it forms is the second." The center of the circle, to which the circle necessarily refers, is not the physical eye but the "i", the perceiver (the center of the world) that is in essence the "I" or Oversoul, "the energizing spirit," that creates circles that are the world. Being is a process of creating increasingly greater circles. Although the center always has logical priority over the circle, the ego can become fixated on the circle, drift off-center, and lose power; cut-off from its roots in universal subjectivity, it views itself as object, an imperial self.[27] The remedy for off-centeredness is the central perspective, with its radical inspiration, and its reduction of nature to second-class reality. The perfect posture, Emerson says in "Circles," is at the center, with consciousness plugged into "the central generator" of circles, becoming greater Being, a deeper center of wider circles.

In the Second Series (1844), in "Experience," the Lords of Life appear to force us off-center, but "the act looks very different on the inside." From within, "the eye makes the horizon," and we "possess our axis more firmly. . . . In the solitude to which every man is always returning, he has sanity and revelations." Hence we must be loyal to our center, in spite of the danger of privateness, of scandalous egotheism, because only there, in that perspective, is the foundation of awareness of our priority over multiplicity; only there do we gain confidence to generate circles of Being great enough to circumscribe or at least to mitigate the tragic, the absence of Being.

In The Conduct of Life (1860), in "Fate," the circle of "tyrannical Circumstance" tightens, and we need the morale of the central vision to attack the alien horizon. From the view of the center, the circle of the horizon walls nothing out; it is merely the boundary of our Being, of all there is. The cause of Fate is therefore in ourselves, and we must negate the illusion that the outside has priority over the inside. Victory depends upon tactics. "Fate has its lord . . . is different seen from above and from below, from within and from without." See from within, from the perspective of centrality, "thought dissolves the material universe;" creates a "pictorial view;" abolishes dominance of the object; and makes irrelevant the logically insoluble problem of determinism and free-will. Yet the aging Emerson, like many others, found that the power of the central position could not command circumstances as easily as he had at first believed. No enlargement of circles could retard age or bring back those he had lost. One must reside more at the center, closer to the light, less on the circumference.

71

In _Society and Solitude_ (1870) and in _Letters and Social Aims_ (1875), Emerson intensifies, particularly in the latter, the motif of centrality. In "Old Age" he writes: "That which does not decay is so central and controlling in us, that, as long as one is alone by himself, he is not sensible of the inroads of time, which always begin at the surface." In this striking observation, he affirms centrality, denies essential relevance of phenomena, and claims immortality (but not personal immortality).

The ego remained for Emerson always the middle term in the sequence of God-man-nature. The Over-Soul does not build up nature around us but projects it through each one of us who is the center of the world. In _Nature_ he wrote that "Nature is a great shadow pointing always to the sun behind us." Although the terms "up" and "down," "in" and "out" are relative in Emerson, the order of the creative sequence is always light-lens-picture. To prove that he at sometime rejected his subjective idealism, one must demonstrate disorder in this sequence of priority. This cannot be done. At different times in his life, Emerson placed different emphases on the various components of the sequence, but he never disrupted the sequence.

For example, Stephen Whicher argues that Emerson, in the late thirties and early forties, "moved from a subjective toward an objective idealism," and that "the cause of this shift was not so much the collapse of his dream of Self-Reliance, as it was the entrance into his thought of a new way of conceiving nature, the general idea of evolution." "Originally, he thought of the Soul as within the self; nature was an exteriorization of this aboriginal Self, was even in a transcendental sense man's creation. Now, rather, he thought of the Soul within nature, and of man as her late, if supreme, product." Even so, Whicher observes, Emerson "continues to insist on the centrality of man in nature."[28]

Within the context of Emerson's doctrine of centrality, man cannot be at once the ground of nature and its "product" (Whicher's term, not Emerson's). If man is conceived to be an evolutionary product of the Soul in nature, Emerson's psychological monism is torn apart; and furthermore,

72

history is introduced as a part of fundamental reality. But his thought never underwent such a drastic change. He lost neither the perspective of centrality (which is not at all the same thing as the conception of man as the supreme product of nature), nor the assured salvation of the Eternal Now. Whicher's thesis is not supported by "The Method of Nature" nor "Nature" (1844), two essays that he keys on to prove his point. Emerson writes in the former: "I conceive a man as always spoken to from behind, and unable to turn his head to see the speaker;" of man being "the channel through which heaven flows to earth;" and in "Nature," that "we feel that the soul of the Workman streams through us;" that "we traverse the whole scale of being, from the centre to the poles of nature." These quotations do not contradict but support the metaphor in "Experience" of the sliding scale of consciousness from the First Cause to "the flesh of his body," the motif of light-lens-picture.

That Emerson used the theory of evolution, as Whicher says, to account for the imperfection of nature and to provide hope for the future, is certainly feasible. But how he incorporated the theory into his psychological monism, with his concomitant belief in immediate revelation, is a problem outside the main concern of this essay. My contention is simply that Emerson, however he tried to incorporate the theory of evolution, indeed, the theme of time in general, into his theology, and however disheartened he became with the contingencies of the Not Me, never abandoned his psychological pantheism with its central perspective and its assured salvation.

Critics have repeatedly documented Emerson's doctrine of centrality with smiles of disbelief. They forget that he taught a new perspective that must be lived at least with the suspension of disbelief before it can be adequately comprehended. Seeking assured salvation, Emerson held the central perspective to be real, not illusory; taught revision of vision, to view creation with the eyes of God. Viewed "from within," he found centrality to be a fact. He never wavered from this position; from his early sermons to his last essays, "really the soul is _near_ things, because it is the centre of the universe. . . . There is no quality in nature's

73

vast magazine he cannot touch; no truth in science he cannot see; no act in will he cannot verify; --there where he stands" (XI, 12). His commitment to the central perspective marks the beginning and extends to the end of his great career.

In his essays Emerson's usual strategy, as we have often been told, is to talk about the world of the Understanding as though it were first-class reality, and then to turn for final answers to general statements abut the sacred poverty of the central position. Although he wrote in "Nominalist and Realist" that he "liked everything by turns and nothing long; that I loved the centre, but doted on the superfices," he went back and back again to the center to receive the nourishment of perspective. This perspective was not for him a psychological gimmick; it was true vision that established the priority of the ego over matter, and prepared the ego for upsurge of the First Cause.

IV

Whereas Locke sought a principle of individuation on which to ground moral worth, Emerson sought such a principle on which to ground the divinity and self-reliance of man. The theme of "the perfect unfolding of our individual nature" runs throughout his work, diminishing in intensity in his later years. In contrast to Emerson, Channing stressed persons as generic units who fulfill themselves by conforming to moral universals. In doing so, Channing asserted man's responsibility for his moral worth and hence man's likeness to God. He helped spearhead the liberal break from the Calvinist who, in spite of obsessive concern with self, sought to overcome, even to obliterate, selfhood, and to assert identity "through an act of submission to a transcendental absolute."[29] Emerson, carrying Channing's break further, argued that each person is free and unique and that his attribute of uniqueness is evidence that he is divine.

Emerson defended his thesis of individuation on psychological and theoretical grounds. The first has been voluminously documented. He told himself,

September, 1830, that "Every man has his own voice, manner, eloquence & just as much his own sort of love & grief & imagination & action. Let him scorn to imitate any being, let him scorn to be a secondary man, let him fully trust his own share of God's goodness, that correctly used it will lead him on to a perfection which has no type yet in the Universe save only in the Divine Mind" (III, 198-99). Such statements, of which there are many in his early journals and essays, are part of his attempt to justify to himself that a person who does his own thinking and follows his own path is not necessarily eccentric, and may very well be centered. He believed that he broke from the ministry to become a writer and a lecturer not out of quirkiness of character but from honest conviction that it was the best thing he could do for the welfare of his congregation and for the development of his unique talents. He left his church, unlike Jonathan Edwards, with dignity and graciousness.

Emerson's theoretic position on individuation has not been examined closely; it may be seen precisely when we once again play him off against Channing. Channing held that the "development of the divine attributes in ourselves is the realization not of what is peculiar to any individual, but what is common to all men."[30] However he sometimes appears to stress individuation of person:

> Were mind to perish there would be absolute, irretrievable destruction: for mind, from its nature, is something individual, an uncompounded essence, which cannot be broken into parts, and enter into union with other minds. I am myself, and can become no other being. My experience, my history, cannot become my neighbor's. My consciousness, my memory, my interest in my past life, my affections, cannot be transferred. . . . I can give away my property, my limbs; but that which makes myself, . . . my feelings, my hopes, these can never become parts of another mind.[31]

Channing is arguing that a mind is a simple, unmixed substance entirely separate and distinct from all other minds. He is not arguing for individuation of person. He seems to distinguish between a person as a generic unit ("something individual") and, after

75

Locke, as an individuated unit ("My memory"). That is to say, to clarify terms, let a person, i.e., a "mind," a center of (intelligent) consciousness, be represented by a white disk. A person's single generic identity consists in his separateness from all other white disks and his sharing with those disks the universal attribute of whiteness or consciousness.[32] Now let there appear on each disk a unique design. Uniqueness of person consists in the unique design of a mind which no other mind or person has or in part is. Implicit in the above passage of Channing are these distinctions. But there is no evidence that Channing placed much weight upon them, or indeed that he were aware of them at all.

Elizabeth Peabody reported that Channing, in 1825, said that "Perfection does not imply but excludes uniformity. If every one obeyed the will of God revealed to himself, no two would be alike . . . . The variety of the universe of matter is a faint symbol of heaven."[33] But this statement is an exception for Channing. However, I do not mean to insist that he would have denied the value of individuation. My point is that the trust of his thought and feeling is not toward it. If, in the twenties, he inspired Emerson to do "his thing," he, like Alcott, later dropped the theme. As the Transcendental movement developed, he concluded that its stress on uniqueness meant egotheism, rebelliousness, oddity, not God-given variety. Channing was a moralist who did not have a positive and abiding commitment to individuation of person. His dominant concern was to preserve the integrity of a person as a self-determining unit of spiritual substance that is responsible for embodying universal moral law. He was profoundly influenced by eighteenth-century ethical theory, particularly by that of Hutchinsonian and Edwardsean disinterested benevolence.[34] His early socialistic leanings while he was in Richmond, in contrast to Emerson's refusal to join Brook Farm, is symptomatic that he placed more importance on persons as generic than as individuated units. "Our nature is social," he said. "This is especially true in religion, the most social of all our sentiments"--a statement with which Emerson would not have agreed.[35] Whatever interest Channing had in individuation may have been in terms of continuity of idea as recorded evidence for determining moral worth.[36] But he was not concerned with individuation as a divine manifestation of the Absolute nor as an aesthetic enrichment of society. All persons, for Channing, should be predominantly the one color of Good.

From another point of view, Channing held to what Lovejoy calls "rationalistic individualism," the Enlightenment's "belief that--precisely because all individuals qua rational, are fundamental alike, and because this uniform element in them is the only important element--truth is to be attained by every individual for himself, by the exercise of his private judgment uninfluenced by tradition or external authority."[37] Channing, a Christian apologist, believed that society should be a corporation of generic units, each person being free in the sense that he is able to achieve independently uniform excellence. Thus Channing, who wanted to know if by "impersonality" Emerson meant that God expressed "moral impartiality," insisted that God is not only impartial in judgment but that he is not responsible for a person's character, that is, that a person is not predetermined to be depraved in the Calvinistic sense.[38] Persons for Channing are autonomous generic units whose "proper work" is the development of universal worth in themselves. (Emerson meant of course by calling God "impersonal" that God is not "a person;" he assumed that the Oversoul is impartial, and that a person is free.)

Emerson, on the other hand, argued for "romantic individualism" which is the belief that "the value of individuals [lies] chiefly, not in what is uniform but what is diverse or unique in them." Since for Emerson a person is an incarnation of the Oversoul, he shares with the Oversoul the category of one-of-a-kind; his uniqueness is proof of his divinity. A person is an end in himself who realizes his individuation through his unique "calling."

Explicitly, however, Emerson did not argue for "romantic individualism" in most of his writings. In "The American Scholar," for example, he accepts, with modification, specialization of calling but does not consider uniqueness of calling: more than one person can be "Man Thinking" or man working. Elsewhere he wrote that "the moment you describe

Milton's verse you use words implying, not creation but increased perception, second-sight, knowledge of what _is_, beyond the ken of others."[39] And in 1838 he stated that "every new mind ought to take the attitude of Columbus, - launch out from the ignorant gaping World, & sail west for a new world. Very, very few thoughts in an age" (V, 448). But neither of these statements is an argument for uniqueness of person. They are justifications for a person having a unique perception so that he can attain new and fuller knowledge of a universal. One must break habitual patterns to gain fresh insights that then can be had by everyone. Once the insight is achieved and communicated, its original uniqueness is worthless. But Emerson, in his stress on individuation, often implied that he wanted more than this, that he wanted a person to be absolutely unique, and end in himself.

A person must be either the Absolute or a unit whose uniqueness is necessary to the Whole, to be an end in himself. The first principle is ontological, the latter, aesthetic. Emerson implicitly assumed both positions. In the essay on Plato (1845), he spoke of the principle of Beauty, distinguishing it from that of logic: "art expresses the one or the same by the different. Thought seeks to know unity in unity; poetry to show it by variety." "The mind," he wrote, "returns from the one to that which is not one, but other or many; and affirms the necessary existence of variety; the self-existence of both, as each is involved in the other." In 1849 he noted that "I figure to myself the world as a hollow temple, & every individual mind as an exponent of some sacred part therein, as if each man were a jet of flame affixed to some capital, or node, or angle, or trigylph, or rosette, or spandyl, bringing out its beauty & symmetry to the eye by his shining" (XI, 161). Earlier in "Spiritual Laws," he had written: "Let the great soul incarnated in some woman's form, poor and sad and single, in some Dolly or Joan, go out to service and sweep chambers and scour floors, and its effulgent daybeams cannot be muffled or hid, but to sweep and scour will instantly appear supreme and beautiful actions, the top and radiance of human life." Dolly and Joan at once contribute to the welfare and beauty of society and, being "the great soul incarnated," are ends in themselves. Combining the above statements, and others like them, therefore, Emerson had an aesthetic -theological rationale for unique individuals who are ends in themselves contributing to the variety of the social whole. The Emersonian society, like a work of art, consists in a harmonious whole of individuated persons. If unity is lacking, an uneasy conglomeration of egotheists exists; if variety, a didactic commune in blank monotone. "We call the Beautiful the highest," Emerson said, "because it appears to us the golden mean, escaping the dowdiness of the good and the heartlessness of the true" ("The Transcendentalist").[40]

Emerson seldom used the aesthetic argument for individuation of person; he did so mainly after his early years when his thrust toward his own individuation was less personal and problematic. He could not have argued convincingly to the Boston congregation that he was resigning from the establishment to develop a personality that was its own excuse for being. But he could and did make the more practical and ethical claim that he thought that creeds were outworn and that he, by going his own way, was helping society by opening up fresh perspectives. A man must be a non-conformist to break habitual patterns. But again, this is not an argument, strictly speaking, for the inherent value of individuation of person.

V

Although Emerson stressed individuation of person, although he held from an absolute point of view that the Soul admits "no co-life," although he thought of friends as phenomenal, one may not logically conclude that his philosophy leads to "a state in which everything--theft, arson, murder--is permitted."[41] Throughout his work he guarded against egotheism of all sorts. Principles come before the ego. He ends "Self-Reliance" with the statement that "Nothing can bring you peace but yourself. Nothing can bring you peace but the triumph of principles." In Nature he wrote: "In my utter impotence to test the authenticity of the report of my senses . . . what difference does it make, whether Orion is up there in heaven, or some god paints the image in the firmament of the soul?

79

The relations of parts and the end of the whole remaining the same, what is the difference?" Ontology should not be confused with ethics. Where the drama is played, whether in the mind or "out there," is ethically inconsequential so long as the players abide by rules, so as as the relation of parts remain the same. Emerson diminished the "reality" of nature for religious not ethical purposes. He taught self-reliance in a world of absolute law. He never says "I am" at the expense of other people. The great man he speaks of in "Self-Reliance," like himself, "who in the midst of the crowd keeps with perfect sweetness the independence of solitude," is ethically superior to the Darwinian capitalist who thrives in a "real" world at the expense of "real" people. If Emerson denied, from a theoretic point of view, that persons are "real," he also thought it "strange that anybody who ever met another person's eyes, should doubt that all men have one soul" (V, 364).

Even so, he sought to explain on the level of the Understanding how Being can be at once One and Many; by doing so, he sought also an ethical theory. Particularly during the thirties and forties when he was clarifying his few major premises, he was interested in "Sympathy," in the ability of a person to identify with another person. He conceived the Over-Soul to be a kind of super-playwright who remains himself One while he is projecting himself imaginatively into the characters he is creating. Correspondingly, a person, he believed, by identifying himself with other persons repeats the cosmic paradigm on a microcosmic scale. "God is the substratum of all souls," he wrote in 1830. "Is not that the solution to the riddle of sympathy?" (II, 323). This riddle concerns how, in experiential terms, a person, a separate and distinct ego, can share himself with, in fact, at once remain himself and become, another person. Only mind can do this; a material thing cannot be one and many at the same time. Emerson tells us:

When I read a problem I would be a geometer; poetry, a poet; history, a historian; sermons, a preacher; when I see paintings, I would paint; sculpture, carve; and so with all things, the manifold soul in me vindicates its acquaintance with all these things. Similar delight we have in the admirable artist's, soldier's, or sailor's life. We individuate ourselves with him, and judge of his work. What is this but our first ride around our estate to take possession, promising ourselves with all, after a few visits more, to have an insight and give a personal direction to all the affairs that go on within our domain, which is the All? (II, 438; 1835).

A year later he observed: "I go to Shakespear, Goethe, Swift, even to Tennyson, submit myself to them, become merely an organ of hearing, and yield to the law of their being. I am paid for thus being nothing by an entire new mind, and thus, a Proteus, I enjoy the universe through the powers and organs of a hundred different men" (IV, 72). In 1846 Emerson promises that

We shall one day talk with the central man, and see again in the varying play of his features and the features which have characterized our darlings, and stamped themselves in fire on the heart: then, as the discourse rises out of the domestic and personal, and his countenance waxes grave and great, we shall fancy that we talk with Socrates, and behold his countenance: then the discourse changes, and the man, and we see the face and hear the tones of Shakespeare, --the body and the soul of Shakespeare living and speaking with us, only that Shakespeare seems below us. A change again, and the countenance of our companion is youthful and beardless, he talks of form and color and the riches of design; it is the face of the painter Raphael that confronts us with the visage of a girl, and the easy audacity of a creator. In a moment it was Michael Angelo; then Dante; afterwards it was the Saint Jesus, and the immensities of moral truth and power, embosomed us. And so it appears that these great secular personalities were only expressions of his face chasing each other like the rack of clouds. Then all will subside, and I find myself alone. I dreamed and did not know my dreams" (VII, 177-8).

Thus the problem of why Emerson was Emerson, "Why I was I," is solved as well as it can be for the

Understanding. Time and space are illusory. Alone as the Central Self, Emerson was also all other people.[42] "I, who suffer from excess of sympathy," he confesses, "proclaim always the merits of self-reliance" (V, 417).

Furthermore, "Sympathy" was a term for Emerson not only of ontology but of ethics. "The Deity in me and in them derides and cancels the thick walls of individual character, relation, age, sex, circumstance . . . and now makes many one" ("Friendship"). "Look at those who have less faculty," he urged in "Compensation," thinking of his feeble-minded brother, Bulkeley, "and one feels sad and knows not well what to make of it. He almost shuns their eye; he fears they will upbraid God. What should they do? It seems a great injustice. But see the facts nearly and these mountainous inequalities vanish. Love reduces them as the sun melts the iceberg in the sea. The heart and soul of all men being one, this bitterness of His and Mine ceases. His is mine. I am my brother and my brother is me." Although the principle of identity supercedes that of relation, self-reliance that of philanthropy, one should treat others as he would have them treat him because he is literally they. Through empathy, each of us, terrifyingly and wonderfully, is every one of us. Our ability to sympathize is evidence that we are not material in essence but divine spirit, that the universal is immanent in particulars.

VI

A person for Emerson consists in three terms: universality, generic identity, and uniqueness. In contrast to Channing who stressed the middle term (and to Jonathan Edwards who stressed the first), Emerson emphasized the first and last terms but by no means neglected the middle term in which the other two are fused. Yet he always gave God and the individual priority over society. He was primarily interested in self-culture, in "character," which are grounded on God; he was not fundamentally a "moral" writer.[43] He was a non-doctrinal evangelical who wanted to know God immediately and to have his unique character and hence his calling divinely sanctioned. Since his search for assured salvation was joined with his search for personal fulfillment, he did not resign from his church merely to seek another job. His daring embarkation for his true vocation was a divine mission on which he had to go alone. "The power which resides in him," he wrote in "Self-Reliance," "is new in nature, and none but he knows what that is which he can do, nor does he know until he has tried." His major essays are literally his autobiography. His literary art is the profession of his faith in the divinity of the unique individual.

In sum, Emerson left the ministry for the unstated reason that he sought assured salvation and did not find such salvation in the concept of a personal god, nor in persons, nor in following an occupation that did not allow him to fulfill his inherent talents. As early as 1827, two years before he officially became pastor of the Second Church, he wrote: "change that imperfect to perfect evidence & I too will be a Christian. . . . The nature of God may be different from what he is represented. I never behold him. I do not know that he exists" (III, 69). Emerson never conceptualized God; God for him was not a bounded form nor another person, another center of consciousness. God was more than a spark within and more than Supernatural Light without. God was closer to him than any covenant allowed: closer than a Father to a child, a mother to a fetus. The Over-Soul and he had no relationship whatsoever; it was that universal "unconscious" and "inaccessible region" of his Greater Self out of which his conscious ego kept emerging and nature kept being flung out before him.[44] This identity gave him ontological priority over nature, a central position in nature, and a holiness to his unique character and calling which was that of a religious artist.[45]

FOOTNOTES

1. Elizabeth Palmer Peabody, Reminiscences of Rev. Channing, D. D. (Boston, 1880), p. 379.

2. Emerson wrote: "Once Dr. Channing filled our sky. Now we become so conscious of his limits & of the difficulty attending any effort to show him our point of view, that we doubt if it be worth while. Best amputate." The Journals and Miscellaneous Notebooks of Ralph Waldo Emerson, ed. William H. Gilman et al (Cambridge, Mass: Harvard University Press, 1960-   ), V, 329. Hereafter references to this edition are included in the text with volume and page numbers.

3. Morton deCorcy Nachlas, A Study and Transcription of William Ellery Channing's Unfinished Treatise on Man, Dissertation (Chicago: The Meadville Theological School, June, 1942), p. 2.

4. Treatise on Man, pp. 31 and 35. Channing's thought on identity is derivative and vague. He concurs, for instance, with the Scottish School of philosophy. This group reacted particularly against Hume's scepticism about the self consisting in spiritual substance.

5. Dr. Channing's Note-book: Passages from the Unpublished Manuscripts of William Ellery Channing, ed. Grace Ellery Channing (New York, 1887), p. 12.

6. The Works of William Ellery Channing, D. D. (Boston, 1849), p. 4.

7. Peabody, p. 430.

8. Note-Book, p. 28.

9. Channing wrote in "The Moral Argument Against Calvinism:" "God is incomprehensible [but] not therefore unintelligible. . . . We do not pretend to know the whole nature and properties of God, but still we can form some clear ideas of him."

10. For an extended discussion of this point, see Robert Leet Paterson, The Philosophy of William Ellery Channing (New York: Bookman, 1952), p. 75 and passim.

11. I find no evidence that Channing considered seriously the problem about how God can be an "infinite" person when he defines "a person" as a unit distinct and separate from other persons. Later in the nineteenth century, Hermann Lotze argued that "true personality, an 'inner core' of selfhood 'previous to and out of' every relationship, is of its nature infinite and that our finite humanity informs us not of the necessary conditions of personal existence but only of the restraints which space and time impose on it." I quote Bernard M. G. Reardon who edited Religious Thought in the Nineteenth Century (London: Cambridge University Press, 1966), p. 126.

Frederick C. Copleston writes:

We are often told by theologians, that God is not 'a being', a member of a class with a plurality of members, an object among objects or thing among things. . . . At the same time it seems that unless we propose to use the word 'God' as a superfluous label for the world, we cannot refer to God or speak about him without distinguishing him from all finite things. In this case, however, how can we avoid speaking of him as 'a being'? We can of course describe God as infinite. But must not the infinite comprise all reality? If God is distinguished ontologically from finite things, does not the word 'infinite,' as applied to God, become an honorific title, signifying the greatest member of a class? In brief, the transcendent and infinite God cannot be a member of a class with a plurality of members. But it appears that we cannot think of him at all without implying that this is precisely what he is. Theistic talk thus seems to be incoherent. Matters are not indeed improved by embracing pantheism. For if finite things are said to be parts of God, what can this possible mean? (Religion and Philosophy, [New York: Harper, 1974], pp. 61-2).

This problem about how God can be an "infinite" person distinct and separate from men is referred to again in the next essay.

12. Works, p. 927.

13. Works, p. 965. In discussing Emerson's "relationship with his religious inheritance," David Robinson writes: "Emerson's sense of the moral life thus becomes like the vision of the ever-progressive heaven of his Unitarian predecessors" (Apostle of Culture [Philadelphia: University of Pennsylvania Press, 1982], p. 94). But at the same time one must remember that 1) Emerson was a mystic; the highest value he sought was non-relational. "Essence, or God, is not a relation or a part, but the whole" ("Compensation"). And 2) Emerson did not believe in personal immortality. In "Compensation," for example, his immense task was to prove that compensation for suffering exists in this life, not in another, as the orthodox preached. See the discussion of time and mysticism in Emerson in the following essay, "Commentary on Channing's Sermon, 'Father of Spirits'" (1823).

14. See Frederick I. Carpenter, "The Genteel Tradition: A Re-Interpretation," New England Quarterly, XV, 427-43.

15. March 5. In the "Address," delivered July 15, he wrote: "Historical Christianity . . . dwells with noxious exaggeration about the person of Jesus. The soul knows no persons." He does not, in the "Address," say much about God as God.

16. Freedom and Fate (1953; rpt. New York: Barnes, 1961), p. 23.

17. Christian Mysticism (New York: Meridian, 1956), p. 29.

18. Literary Transcendentalism (Ithaca: Cornell University Press, 1973), p. 15.

19. Quoted by Blakeney J. Richard, "Emerson and Berkeleian Idealism," ESQ, 58:93.

20. A. Robert Caponigri, "Bronson and Emerson: Nature and History," in American Transcendentalism, ed. Brian M. Barbour (Indiana: University of Notre Dame Press, 1973), p. 245. Frederick C. Copleston remarks that this was a problem for other Romantic philosophers, such as Fichte, Schelling, Hegel: "The problem which faced them was that of including, as it were, the finite within the life of the

infinite without depriving the former of its reality" (A History of Philosophy [New York: Doubleday, 1965], II, part I, p. 27).

21. The Journals of Ralph Waldo Emerson, ed. Edward Waldo Emerson and Waldo Emerson Forbes. 10 vols. Centenary Edition (Boston: Houghton Mifflin, 1909-1914), II, 101.

22. Alexander, Dod, and Hodge, Calvinistic Theologians, in their attack on Victor Cousin and Emerson, described the god of Transcendentalism as one "who returns to himself in the consciousness of man" (quoted in The Transcendentalists, ed. Perry Miller [Cambridge: Harvard University Press, 1950], p. 235).

23. The Magic Circle of Walden (New York: Holt, Rinehart, 1968), p. 114.

24. Emerson wrote: "The first quality we know in matter is centrality--we call it gravity--which holds the universe together, which remains pure and indestructible in each mote as in masses and planets. . . . To this material essence answers Truth, in the intellectual world--Truth whose centre is everywhere and its circumference nowhere. . . . And the first measure of a mind is its centrality, its capacity of truth, and its adhesion to it" ("Progress of Culture"). Poe also, we have seen, found immense philosophical significance in "Matter;" used Pascal's idea of a circle to express his philosophy; and conceived of each person as a deity. But Poe remained always at the level of the Understanding, believing in the reality of discrete persons in this world. For Poe this mortal stage of regression back to primal unity is a collection of heterogeneous gods without dominant immediacy of the existent universal to unify particulars. In other words, Poe had no sense of divine unity in experience. In contrast, Emerson reduced nature, including other persons, to phenomena, and left himself alone with God, as God, at ease with the variety of appearance.

25. Young Emerson Speaks, ed. Arthur Cushman McGiffert, J., (Boston: Houghton Mifflin, 1938), p. 258.

26. <u>Young</u> <u>Emerson</u> <u>Speaks</u>, pp. 207-209. Jacques Maritain, in this century, put Emerson's point succinctly: "The paradox of consciousness and personality is that each of us is situated precisely <u>at</u> <u>the</u> <u>centre</u> of this world. Each is at the centre <u>of</u> <u>infinity.</u> And this privileged subject, the thinking self, is itself not object but subject; in the midst of all the subjects which it knows only as objects, it alone is subject as subject" (quoted in <u>Four</u> <u>Existential</u> <u>Theologians</u>, ed. Will Herberg [New York: Doubleday, 1958], pp. 42-3).

27. See Quentin Anderson, <u>The</u> <u>Imperial</u> <u>Self</u> (New York, 1971).

28. Whicher, pp. 141-43.

29. Sacvan Bercovitch, <u>The</u> <u>Puritan</u> <u>Origin</u> <u>of</u> <u>the</u> <u>American</u> <u>Self</u> (New Haven: Yale University Press, 1975), p. 13.

30. Peabody, p. 365.

31. <u>Works</u>, p. 356.

32. See the second essay in this book.

33. <u>Reminiscences</u>, pp. 103-4.

34. What attracted Channing to "Hopkins was one aspect of Hopkin's system only, the concept of disinterested benevolence" (Conrad Wright, <u>The</u> <u>Liberal</u> <u>Christians</u> [Boston: Beacon Press, 1970], p. 28). See also David Robinson, "The Legacy of Channing: Culture as a Religious Category in New England Theology," <u>Harvard</u> <u>Theological</u> <u>Review</u>, 74:2 (1981), p. 225.

35. <u>Works</u>, p. 431.

36. Channing wrote:

The identity of self differs from all others. We call other things the same which retain the same general forms. We identify the tree today with that which occupied the same space--a hundred years ago, though it has not a particle which belonged to the latter, and has swelled to twice its size. The unbroken continuance of

the original organism is the only ground on
which we ascribe sameness to such different
substances. But the I which at this moment
remembers a past feeling or action is recognized as precisely the same being who so
acted and felt perhaps years ago. We detect in
it no fleeting particles. Memory recalls the
same self. So does the conscience, nor can we
still remorse by the suggestion that the old
agent has passed away, that we of this moment
are not the beings whose past errors we remember. Beneath the infinite crowd of our past
emotions and actions we meet continually the
same I, amidst all changes one and the same.
It is this permanence of the I which gives
unity to our shifting lives, which binds into
one our vast and various experience. On which
responsibility is founded. Which puts us in
possession of the past and future, which is the
condition of endless progress (Treatise on Man,
p. 34).

According to Channing, conscience and memory reveal
the "permanence of the I" "On which responsibility
is founded."

37. Arthur O. Lovejoy, Essays in the History of
Ideas (New York: Putnam, 1948), p. 82.

38. Peabody, p. 380.

39. Journals (1909-1914), II, 364.

40. Bercovitch comments: "Emerson's exhortation to greatness speaks directly to the paradox
of a literature devoted at once to the exaltation of
the individual and the search for a perfect community. Self-Reliance builds upon both these extremes. It is the consummate expression of a
culture which places an immense premium on independence while denouncing all forms of eccentricity
and elitism" (Puritan Origins, p. 176). From the
point of view of Reason, Emerson grounded himself on
God; was self-existent; had metaphysical priority
over society; and was the source of revolutionary or
creative energy. From the point of view of the
Understanding, he held that the perfect community is
a dynamic expression of unique individuals grounded
on the universal; each person seeks uniqueness not

for himself but for the purpose of contributing to the variety of the Whole.

Robinson writes that Emerson's intent in positing an impersonal deity "was not to worship a God who is a person, but to experience a God capable of taking his own personality, his limiting individuality away from him;" and that "self-culture ultimately becomes self-negation." But Emerson sought negation of the private ego because he wanted fulfillment of genius; and genius is the finite expression of the universal One, the temporal and spatial incarnation of the universal in a particular. This is why, as Robinson says, Emerson's "selfless denial of the ego . . . did not result in anything approaching a communitarian vision of society" (Apostle of Culture, pp. 130, 155).

41. B. L. Packer, Emerson's Fall (New York: Continuum, 1982), p. 175.

42. Lawrence Buell writes: "When it comes to presenting the self in its universal aspects, moreover, Whitman does not merely assert this claim in theory, but has the persona act it out, by imaginatively projecting into a series of identities or situations. In this way, the principles of spiritual metamorphosis which the Transcendentalists celebrate in the activity of nature is at last fully realized on the human level" (Literary Transcendentalism, p. 327).

43. Emerson wrote: "the necessity by which Deity rushes into distribution into variety and particles, is not less divine than the unity from which all begins" (Journals, [1909-1914], VI, 531). Emerson sought a balance between the extremes of the "All" and genius: "Unity or identity, and Variety; the poles of philosophy. . . . A too rapid unity or unification, and a too exclusive devotion to parts are the Scylla and Charybdis" (Journals [1909-1914], VII, 118).

T. S. Eliot, in "Tradition and the Individual Talent," raises the same problem that Emerson did about the relation of the universal and the particular. Eliot argues that the poet must extinguish his personality to achieve the "really new" in a great poem; that "the emotion of art is impersonal."

90

If by "personality" Eliot means private, then he and Emerson agree that great art cannot be private. And both would agree that a great poem must be "really new." By this phrase, I take Eliot to mean unique; a new great poem modifies the "ideal order" of already existing great poems because it is different from any one of those already existing unique great poems. Both Emerson and Eliot find a critical distinction between the unique-private (egotheism, an "immature" poem) and the unique-"really new" (genius, a great poem). Both men, in short, give us the same formula: an entity, whether a man or a work of art, realizes its unique particularity only when it is fused with a universal. For Eliot, a great poem is a unique expression of a universal aesthetic emotion; for Emerson, a genius is a unique incarnation of the Over-Soul. Both men distinguish between a unique particular in-and-for-itself, and a unique particular grounded on a universal. For both men, a goal of criticism is to distinguish between the private and the "really new"--in many cases, an extremely difficult task.

44. See, for a discussion of Emerson's position on the impersonality of God, Robinson, pp. 126-133. In general, I concur with his discussion but occasionally question his wording. For instance, he writes that Emerson held that the term "God" "is one name for an entity or phenomenon which can be known by other labels." But of course for Emerson "God" is not an "entity" nor a "phenomenon" nor a "person." Spirit is non-conceptualizable; the perceiver cannot be defined in bounded terms; only "matter" can be so defined.

45. Critics agree that Emerson's thought, during the late thirties and early forties, underwent a profound change from "optimism" to "pessimism." This transition was powered by the growing tension between the two worlds of Reason and Understanding, the latter demanding greater and greater attention. This struggle was manifested in Emerson's theology under various topics, as many critics have shown, each from his own perspective. To make a list: the tension was between the themes of the universal and the particular; the Me and the Not Me; the soul and nature; the deity within and the deity without; the unconscious and consciousness; impersonality and personality; the perceiver

and the perceived; the self as central and the self as one among many; vision and self-culture; eternity and temporality; mysticism and science; mysticism and history; mysticism and rational religion; spontaneity and discipline or self-denial; per-manence and growth; wildness and gardens; the individual and society; formal and free verse. Emerson broke from Unitarianism, we know, because he chose to stress content over form, the individual over the church, heaven over earth. That mortality pressed relentlessly as he aged, that the visionary gleam of his youth faded into the light of common day, as Wordswroth told him it would, is hardly surprising; it does for most of us who were lucky enough to have had a wonderful childhood. Even so, Emerson kept the faith in the central perspective; he remained haunted by the eternal mind.

"DIVINE IMPERSONALITY"

"In the midst of the personified impersonal, a personality stands here."

Ahab ("The Candles")

"To frame an adequate conception of deity, and set this forth in words, is not only above human capacity, but impossible in the nature of things."

Theodore Parker[1]

I

Of the charter members of the Transcendental Club, Alcott, Ripley, Emerson, Brownson, Clarke, Hedge, and of all the others who later joined or were associated with the group, only Emerson and Thoreau believed in an impersonal deity. "The 'thesis of personality'," Rusk writes, "was hardly more than Alcott's peculiar version of a religious opinion held by much of Concord and Massachusetts, including all the Emerson family, it seems, except Emerson himself."[2] Emerson, seeking assured salvation, found no empirical nor rational evidence for a personal god, and concluded that fundamental reality is impersonal. Indeed, the doctrine of "Divine Impersonality," as I have suggested, is the hallmark of the great Transcendentalists, Emerson and Thoreau (and probably Whitman). Later, post-Civil War Transcendentalists or "secondary transcendentalists," as Walt Whitman called them, Samuel Longfellow and particularly Samuel Johnson, leaned toward the doctrine but lacked Emerson's subtle and profound vision. This essay explores the definitions of God and man in terms of "personality" of Frederic Hedge, Bronson Alcott, Theodore Parker, and Samuel Johnson, so as to bring into sharper relief Emerson's point of view.

In general, early Unitarianism was part of the modern world's increasing tendency to image man with inherent worth who controls his own destiny. Transcendentalism, the rebellious child of orthodox Unitarianism, intensified this tendency, in fact, climaxed it, by arguing that God is immanent in man. The insistence that God is within man and the correlative insistence that intuition is the principal way of knowing God, characterizes Transcendentalism. For instance, Parker, in A Discourse of Matters Pertaining to Religion (Boston, 1842), argued against the Calvinistic god that was totally transcendent, against Norton's god that seemed merely an hypothesis based on probability and on the supposed empirical evidence of miracles; and argued for a god that was at once transcendent and immanent in man and nature, and that could be known by intuition. (And Channing clearly stands, on these issues, mid-way between Norton and Parker.)

Indeed, much of the theology of liberal Unitarianism in the last century consists in rationalistic attempts to define God and man based on the premise that God is in man, as well as being transcendent. These attempts range from Emerson's psychological pantheism to Hedge's theism in which the non-mediatorial "knowledge of God is . . . an intuition of the moral sense."[3] O. B. Frothingham in 1891 records that "the idea of God has passed through several phases. . . . The deity who was an individual has become a person; the attributes of personality, as commonly understood, have disappeared, so that pantheism has succeeded to a mechanical theism; God has become a name for our most exalted feelings, so that instead of saying 'God is Spirit,' some read 'Spirit is God'."[4] Thus Frothingham, at the end of the century, summed up the confused variety of conceptions of the transcendent and immanent deity that the early Unitarians began and that the Transcendentalists and Unitarian "scientific theists" accelerated. Certain features of the thought of Hedge, Alcott, and Parker illustrate Emerson's variance from the mainstream of Transcendental-Unitarianism, and reveal part of the quagmire of terminology among these independent thinkers.

Frederic Hedge, in his essay "Personality," stated that there are "three constituents of our humanity: 1. The unknown factor which constitutes the ground of our being. 2. The ego, or conscious

self. 3. The Person." In regard to the last, he
maintained that the "person" must be distinguished
from the "individual." "The person . . . is not the
individual proper, but the manifestation of the
individual to others, - the image he presents to the
world."⁵ Pointing out that the term "person"
derives from the Latin word "persona," Hedge held
that therefore "personality" is a "mask" or public
expression of the individual. In contrast, the
individual is the larger, unconscious, vague identity on which the person is grounded. Indeed, the
"individual," "the innermost nature of Man," of
which the personality is the mask, Hedge insisted,
cannot be known, either by another individual or by
that individual himself. Consciousness fades into
unconsciousness, and what is beyond consciousness
cannot be known. Thus consciousness defines the
individual only "laterally but not vertically;" it
distinguishes the self from other selves, but "it
does not reach to the root of our being."⁶

About this "root," Hedge continued, there are
two theories. The common notion is that "a separate
individual soul . . . [is] the ground and matrix of
the individual consciousness;" and the other theory
is that "all individual consciousnesses, all separate egos, have one universal Being for their common
ground." According to these distinctions, Hedge
would have held that Edwards and Channing, for
instance, represented the first theory, and Emerson,
the second. Surprisingly, Hedge himself said that
"I do not care to undertake the advocacy of either
of these views."⁷ In refusing to do so, he seems
to have disregarded the distinction between theism
and pantheism. The first theory assumes that
created individuals are metaphysically distinct and
separate from each other, and that the ground of
each individual, God, is distinct and separate from
each individual. And the second theory states that
all individuals and God are metaphysically one.
Evidently Hedge refused to commit himself to either
theory, at least in this essay, because he believed
that it is useless to speculate in conceptual terms
about that which is beyond consciousness, in this
case, the metaphysical nature of God and man.

Curiously, Hedge held that although we cannot know whether or not God is separate and distinct from us, that is, whether or not he is a person, we can and do know his personality. Defining personality as a "mask," he wrote: "All we can know of God is his personality: the manifestations of himself in action. Creation, providence, revelation, moral government,-- these constitute the personality of God. . . . Beyond these we cannot penetrate. We must not confuse the manifest God with the transcendental ground of the manifestation."[8] Again, whether this ground is an individual spirit or the "common ground" of all individual consciousness, he would not say.

Since Hedge could not conceptualize the transcendental ground of creation, he spoke of it in terms of analogy. And here again, his apparent lack of commitment to either theism or pantheism resulted in ambiguity. On the one hand, he argued that "However my philosophy may formulate its concepts of deity, the God whom I worship is a God who sees and hears, and thinks and loves, and pities and approves." On the other hand, he wrote: "I follow the analogy of the human microcosm. What the human soul is to the human individual, that I conceive God to be to the universe of things,-- its central soul, regent in all and present in all by diffused consciousness in every part of the human organism."[9] The first description of God, which is anthropomorphic, gives to God the attributes of an individual, i.e., thinking and loving; and the second, suggests pantheism. The problem for Hedge, as it was (and is) for other liberal theists seeking a humanism grounded on transcendence, was to understand how God can be at once separate and distinct from man and immanent in men. The theistic analogy, in conjunction with what he said elsewhere in "Personality," suggests that he believed that divine immanence in men is in terms of attributes (as it was for Channing). He stated that God is not a "bodily form" but the "moral image, the human attributes, the attributes of ideal humanity." In contrast, his pantheistic analogy implies that divine immanence is to be understood in terms of essence (as Emerson understood it). These two positions are not reconcilable. Wells writes that Leibnitz gave Hedge "a reconciliation between the extramundane God of pure theism and the cardinal principle of Spinozism, the immanence of Deity in creation."[10]   But the problem was too great for genuine reconciliation. Either God is an individual apart from men or he is not. Hedge's use of analogies or "symbolical" terms does not bridge the gap between these mutually exclusive positions. Analogies must be able to be interpreted literally to mean anything.[11]

Elsewhere Hedge wrote that "If I am to conceive of god at all as taking definite shape, it will be the human form. . . . But the mental concept does not necessarily imply a corresponding object. To suppose that God exists thus objectively concluded in a human form, is to suppose him spatially bounded, - an idea which reason refuses to entertain. Reason is satisfied with nothing less than the universe of being embodied in the Infinite Presence."[12]   But it is hard to correlate this statement with Hedge's belief in prayer: "I desire to enter into personal, conscious, mutual relations with the Power that rules. . . . The idea of a person in the Godhead answers this demand."[13] Men have relations with God; they can pray to him. But Hedge cannot logically hold this position and at the same time hold that his god is not "spatially bounded." Whatever else "spatially bounded" may mean, it must mean that God is other than men to whom men can pray. This is the same trouble Channing had when he said that God and men are distinct and separate and yet God is "infinite."

In other words, Hedge agreed with Emerson that "there is no way to God through the Understanding."[14]   God cannot be described, therefore, in terms of space and time that are modes of the Understanding. Yet God, according to Hedge, is an "individual" who is apart from man. But how can this apartness of God and man be understood in terms that are not spatial; that is, in terms that are not terms of the Understanding? To hold, as I have suggested, that the term "spatial" is a figurative expression which cannot be literally interpreted, leaves the relation of God and man either in obfuscation or in mystery, depending upon preference. Thus God for Hedge is an individual who is metaphysically apart from man, and whose apartness from man cannot be described in material or spatial terms.

Hedge's implicit purpose, of course, in giving ambiguous or contradictory descriptions of God was to attempt to describe the indescribable. He sought to solve the Transcendentalist's and the Radical's problem of how divinity can be conceived to be, in terms of the Understanding, at once immanent and transcendent. Emerson, on the other hand, seeking the experience, not the (impossible) conception, fused the human and divine in terms of perception: he was the center of the world. When he wrote that "the consciousness in each man is a sliding scale, which identifies him now with the First Cause, and now with the flesh of his body" ("Experience"), he meant this literally, not analogically. Although he and Hedge agreed that "there is no way to God through the Understanding," Emerson believed that the ego, perceiving the world through the eyes of Reason, is God perceiving the world in terms of the Understanding. It need hardly be said that Emerson climaxes the goal of the liberals, sought by Channing with his doctrine of man's likeness to God, to close the gap of mystery, in traditional religion, between God and man.

In the total context of his work Hedge was a Christian Transcendentalist whose thought was on the side of theism. He was an "enlightened Conservative" who distrusted Emerson's "intense reliance upon individual intuition," that is, upon personal experience at the expense of reason.[15] He was a Kantian for whom there was an unbridgable gap between the finite and the infinite. He therefore concentrated more on history which is the "personality" of God than on the transcendental ground behind phenomena. He believed that the attributes of God are known as they are manifested in "creation, providence, revelation, moral government;" that, as Kant held, "in and through ourselves . . . the eternal moral lives and works."[16] He was a supernaturalist insofar as he was a theist.

Emerson would have accepted Hedge's pantheistic "analogy of the human microcosm" but would not have accepted the notion that God thinks and loves as an individual apart from men, nor Hedge's "necessary anthropomorphisms" that imply separation between the essences of God and men. In a famous quotation, he wrote: "If, as Hedge thinks, I overlook great facts in stating the absolute laws of the soul; if as he seems to represent it the world is not a dualism, is not a bi-polar Unity, but is _two_, is Me and It, then there is the Alien, the Unknown, and all we have believed & chanted out of our deep instictive hope is a pretty dream."[17] In Emerson's sustained monistic continuum of God-ego-nature, a radical division of any kind between any of the three components of the sequence would destroy the sequence. One mind, according to Emerson, reaches vertically from the phenomenal world to the noumenal "root of our being" which is (the center of) God. "The soul is not twin-born but the only begotten . . . admitting no co-life" ("Experience"). He would have said that Hedge started "from without" not "from within." But Hedge would not accept Emerson's subjective idealism or psychological pantheism or "panpsychism" in which immanence excludes transcendence; or rather, in which immanence is transcendent.

Bronson Alcott, in 1868, stated bluntly that "I insist on Personal Theism."[18] However in the first year of his long friendship with Emerson, he seems to have been close to Emerson's theory of divine impersonalism. He recorded in 1838 that he and Dr. Channing "conversed mostly on the connexion of the Divine and Human Nature. I attempted to show the identity of the human soul, in its diviner action, with God. At this he expressed great dislike, even horror. He felt that doctrines of this character undermined the very foundations of virtue, confounded the nature of good and evil, destroyed human responsibility, and demolished free will."[19] Channing, we saw in the preceding essay, held above all that a person is a unit of spiritual substance, separate and distinct from all other units, a unit that is alone responsible for its essence which is moral and social. He criticized severely the Calvinist who submerged the creature's will in God's, and the Transcendentalist who held that the individual is absorbed, at death, in Deity. Consequently, he reacted in "horror" to Alcott's position in 1838 because Alcott was proposing such a pantheistic or monistic absorption.

But Alcott's views changed; in 1868 he wrote:
I can only ask you to distinguish finely that in yourself which differences you from

other persons essentially and that which unites and makes them one with yourself, also makes you one with them, indissolubly and forever. The unity is the Personality; the difference is the Individuality. . . . We must grow into and become one with the Person dwelling in every breast, and thus come to apprehend the saying "I and my Father are one," that is, perceive that all souls have a Personal identity with God and abide in Him.[20]

Odell Shepard believes that the idea in this quotation "is essentially the same idea with which Alcott had distressed Dr. Channing over thirty years before."[21] But Alcott is now arguing not for Emersonian impersonalism but for a theistic position similar to Channing's rather orthodox view of a divine society of separate and distinct persons, unified by the "Personality" or Spirit of God.

"Personality" and its related terms for Alcott referred obviously not to a "mask" of appearances of the individual, as it did for Hedge, but to a category of Being shared by all individuals. "The Person is the One in all the manifold phases of the Many, through which we transmigrate, and we find ourself [sic] perpetually, because we cannot lose ourself personally in the mazes of the many. Tis the one soul in manifold shapes."[22] With his doctrine of "Personalism," Alcott attempted to solve the problem of other Transcendentalists and Unitarian liberals about how to describe (and therefore to conceive clearly) the Deity as at once separate from men and immanent in men. He wrote that the "personality" is "the indivisible centre of the soul, or mind, which is a monad, so far forth as she is a person. Therefore Person is really that which exists,[23] inasmuch as it partakes of the divine unity." Alcott assumed that the "I" or soul or person is "a simple unity," "indivisible" (Channing's terms) that possesses universal attributes; that is, he assumed that a person is a single generic unit. When he claimed that "all souls have a Personal identity with God and abide in Him," he meant not that souls fuse with God, in the Emersonian fashion, but that they exist as separate entities[24] in love and harmony, filled with the Spirit of God.

101

As early as 1838 Alcott must have become aware of his tempermental and theoretical differences from Emerson. He commented that "Emerson's doctrines I like in the main . . . [but] I think his view of the social relations faulty. . . . Men are too purely ideas with him."[25] As Alcott became more familiar with Emerson's thought and exerted his own identity, he came to realize that for him the locus of "reality" was in relations among real people and not in solitary absorption in an impersonal One. He became, as it were, an "objective idealist" and a "personalist;" and Emerson remained loyal to subjective idealism and to divine impersonalism. Their disagreement is manifested particularly in their life-long debate about personal immortality. Alcott wrote in 1864 that he and Emerson "talked last night about the longevity of friendship, and . . . personal immortality. Certainly if immortality inhere in anything, we know it must be in persons; and to question the continuance of a connexion like the one I here intimate would be an impiety, if not an atheism, which I am the last of persons to espouse. If I have known life, I have known it not alone but in and through the reciprocation of it with a friend."[26] Emerson, on the contrary, held that we descend to meet, that friendship is only of this world of appearances. "I cannot deny it, O friend," he said, "that the vast shadow of the Phenomenal includes thee also . . . . Thou are not Being, as Truth is, as Justice is--thou art not my soul, but a picture and effigy of that."[27] Alcott, profoundly social, could not concur with Emerson that a person, a finite incarnation of the Oversoul, dissolves at death into universal mind, like a drop of water into the ocean; he desired other people, individual friends, in heaven.

Although Alcott believed that reality consists in relations among persons, he grew increasingly sensitive to the drawbacks of egocentricity. Shepard writes that "Alcott's theological doctrine of 'Personality' slowly modified his social and political thought. He came to condemn most radical measures of reform as 'Individualistic,' because he thought they dismembered society by ignoring that 'Personality' which all men hold in common."[28] Hence Shepard believes that "Alcott insisted more and more upon a personal rulership of the world so powerful that it would finally blot out all human differences. . . . Emerson could not accept this, whether because of some lingering Calvinism in him or because of his reluctance toward all intimate association."[29] Alcott did increasingly 1) deemphasize uniqueness of person and 2) emphasize moral or universal attributes of people; but he certainly did not, as Shepard implies, seek human dictatorship. Alcott, like Channing, found reality in relations among people as single generic units under the auspices of God; he increasingly placed social harmony above aesthetic variety, order above disorder, peace above revolution. Emerson, on the contrary, true to his profound sense of aloneness, true to his subjective idealism (that he, as ego, and God only existed) insisted upon uniqueness of person, upon the "necessary existence of variety" in the world of appearance.

Emerson, Shepard observes, liked the word "alone" and Alcott, the word "together." The term "alone" was used by Emerson to denote genius; and genius for him was the realization of uniqueness of person that is a temporal and spatial manifestation of the numerical oneness of the universal, of the divine solitude of the impersonal transcendental I. And the term "together" for Alcott referred not to fusion of individuals, here or hereafter, but to harmony among separate and distinct individuals. Alcott noted in 1878 that "the old topic of Personal immortality comes into our discussion, and I find my friend as persistent as formerly in his Individualism. . . . True to his convictions, he modestly rests in his Individualism, and is silent concerning what lies beyond."[30] Again, Emerson held to uniqueness of individuals in this world, and to dissolution of them at death; and Alcott, to immortal individuals, emphasizing single generic identity.

Believing in persons as fundamental reality, Alcott thought that "an impersonal God an absurdity," and spoke of "the Supreme Person," "the Unseen Personal Mind," "the Eternal I am." And Emerson wrote in his _Journal_ that Alcott "defended his thesis of personality last night, but it is not quite a satisfactory use of words. . . . I see profound need to distinguishing the First Cause as super-personal."[31] "I deny personality to God," he said elsewhere, "because it is too little, not too much. Life, personal life, is faint and cold to the energy of God."[32] A. C. Bartol wrote that "Pantheism is said to sink man and nature in God, Materialism to sink God and man in nature, and Transcendentalism to sink God and nature in man."[33] According to these definitions, Emerson was a Pantheist, not a Transcendentalist. In fact, one of his fundamental but little recognized disagreements with his radical friends was over the evaluation of man. He sought less to humanize God than to make man divine.

Theodore Parker, wishing to avoid the throes of argumentation over "personality," held: "God as being, not with the limitations of personality (that confounds him with man); but God with no limitations, infinite intellect; from the moral sense, infinite conscience; from the emotional, infinite affection; from the religious, infinite soul; from all truth, the whole Human nature names him Infinite Father."[34] In spite of his refusal to term God personal or impersonal, however, Parker was without doubt a theist, conceiving God in terms of an (intelligent) center of consciousness other than men. He "held that though God is different in kind from both matter and man, he must nonetheless be recognized as immanent in both. . . . There can be no distinction of supernatural or natural."[35] He stated that God is "the absolute object of reverence;" "the universal object of the human spirit."[36] "My definition," he wrote, "distinguishes God from all other beings." By this he meant, among other things, that God is a separate being from man.[37] Thus Parker, although he held that God is immanent in man, believed, like Channing and Hedge (and others) that this immanence consists in attributes only, not, like Emerson, in essence.

Like Alcott, Parker by temperment was more interested in relationships among people than in fusing with an Emersonian Alone. Within the amorphous Transcendental movement, he represents preeminently the opposite pole from Emerson. His god, like Channing's, although essentially indefinable, was a separate and distinct entity from (created) persons, the Father and Mother of mankind, with whom human beings should seek the highest social relationship. In distinction, Emerson found no assured

104

salvation in the human community. He speaks affirm-
atively in "The Method of Nature" of "that old
religion, . . . in the childhood of New England,
teaching privation, self-denial and sorrow;" teaching "not praise, not men's acceptance of our doing,
but the spirit's holy errand." "Every personal
consideration," he wrote in "Circles," "that we
allow costs us heavenly state." Although he thought
friendship one of the finest things he knew, he
found that "the best moments of life are these
delicious awakenings of the higher powers, and the
reverential withdrawing of nature before its God"
(<u>Nature</u>).

II

Emerson was criticized for his definition of
God as "Divine Impersonality" from different directions. Bartol (influenced in his theism by Alcott)
and Cabot concluded that Emerson's objection to
personality in God is "its likening him to man's
which is limited;"[38] it "seems to be nothing more
than limitation to an individual."[39] Parker
agreed with Channing, Ripley, and others, that
Emerson was too pantheistic and that his God was too
much of an idea."[40] In the "Divinity School
Address," Emerson spoke much about the soul and
about the "exaggeration of the personal" but little
about God, except to assure his audience that God
was not dead and can be known without a mediator.
Two months later, Henry Ware Jr., in his "Divinity
School Address," complained, "Take away the Father
of the universe, and . . . mankind becomes but a
company of children in an orphan asylum."[41] If
God is not a person, he continued, "an intelligent,
conscious agent; one who thinks, perceives, understands, wills, and acts," those who pray to him are
addressing only a meaningless abstraction. Bartol
noticed also that when Emerson "offered prayer . . .
it was impersonal, - to Infinite Wisdom and Goodness."[42]

Complaints like the above were numerous. Even
the Calvinistis attacked Emerson, claiming that he
had reduced God to "the substratum of all things"
and presents us, like Victor Cousin, with "a vague
personification of abstract principles."[43] Henry
Ware argued further that Emerson's position, as he

understood it, was not logical in that "veracity, justice, love . . . are qualities of being; and like all qualities have no actual existence of the substances in which they inhere."[44] Such qualities belong to persons, not to an impersonal It; to address qualities, abstractions, principles, merely in themselves, is rarified idolatry. Bartol asked Emerson, "You refuse Personality as a designation? Is there wisdom and no one wise, goodness and no one gracious, beauty and no one All-Fair?"[45] But again, Emerson, when questioned by Elizabeth Peabody if there were "not something in God corresponding to and justifying this human sensibility?" answered "No!"[46] Considering this sobering answer in conjunction with his statement that to represent God "as an individual is to shut him out of my consciousness," one must conclude that Emerson felt that immanent deity transcended the ways of man. Not sinking God in man, Emerson held that the essence of man is beyond humanity. This is the reason, incidentally, why it is simplistic to think that Emerson limited the incarnation of God in nature to the mere pastoral. He did so more than Thoreau; but neither man was adverse to including inhumanities of nature as projections of God in the unconscious. Nature, Emerson reminds us, "is no sentimentalist" ("Fate").[47]

III

Emerson's divine impersonalism surfaces after the Civil War in the later Transcendentalists, particularly in Samuel Longfellow and Samuel Johnson. The former stated that "we no longer think of Him as an individual being in any way apart from the universe. But as an all-pervading and all-including, and all-quckening Life; a really omnipresent Thought, and Love, and Will; not individual, yet personal, because Thought, and Love and Will are qualities of persons and not of things."[48] In Longfellow and Johnson we find the liberal reaction to the supernaturalism of Calvinism and rationalistic deism in extremely attenuated form. Deity is now immanent in creation, homogenized with the human. Yet Longfellow must ultimately be classified as a theist who held that God is in essence other than man. He wrote years later, in an attempt to counter a charge of subjectivism, that those "great ideas" in "the very structure of the human soul" are based on intuitions or perceptions of an object upon which they directly work," and on an "objective reality of divine things."[49] For Longfellow, God, known intuitively, had "objective reality," a proposition that Emerson would not have accepted.

Samuel Johnson is the closest of the post-Civil War Transcendentalists to Emerson. There are ideas and phrases in his work that are very similar to those of the older man. For example, he wrote, "One may so live in the divineness of principles that he no more seeks them in any outward appreciation than the eye looks out of itself to find the power of vision." "We know God by participation, not by observation:" "God is not an object, but an experience."[50] Implicit in this metaphor and in these statements is the psychological monism of Emerson. But Johnson really does not follow Emerson along these paths. How he varies is indicated in the following statement: "the worship of personages must give way to the worship of principles - the centrality of an Individual to the centrality of Ideas - the divinity or 'lordship' of a man to the Deity of the Infinitely Wise, and Good, and Fair."[51] The phrase "centrality of an individual" recalls Emerson's theme of centrality of self. But Johnson was not referring to Emerson's theme; he was speaking in a different context. He was opposing, as did Emerson, the exclusive embodiment of the universal in a particular person, such as Jesus. Deity is incarnated in all men: "Do we need a perfect personal incarnation? But this is impossible; only humanity itself can incarnate it. The Ideal hovers before us, unappropriated and free."[52] In this regard, Emerson perfectly agreed with Johnson. But Emerson, by the theme of centrality of self, had a far more profound, lyrical, and monistic perspective than Johnson. Johnson's view is that of the Understanding, not of Reason. His "Spiritual Pantheism" is not Emerson's psychological pantheism. Johnson, like Emerson, sought some kind of monism, but he did not begin from the center; he began "from without." Hence his vision lacks Emerson's genius; it lacks specific locality; the integrity of aesthetic concreteness is absent from it.

Rejecting Emerson's subjective idealism, standing outside the central perspective, Johnson in his vision could not fuse the universal and particular but spoke from an "objective" point of view. Assuming that he did not have ontological priority over other persons, he was far more interested than Emerson in social action, particularly Abolition. He was one among many in a democracy of persons; his god was separate in essence from individuals but immanent in them in terms of Principles and Ideals. Even so, he called himself a pantheist. He wrote: "It is an error to suppose that Spiritual Pantheism, because it absorbs all in God, is inconsistent with the belief in individual existences. It simply declares that their essential life is one in God, and that they must not be held to be outside and separate from this real being. Nor does it identify Deity with the mere sum of these distinct existences."[53]

For Johnson, then, God is a "real being" that is more than the sum of individual existences, "One Spirit that is over all."[54] This "real being" is manifested to individuals in terms of Principles or Ideals that are known by "imperishable intuitions." Under the influence of Lyell and Darwin, Johnson argued that the evolution of religion is of "ascending idealizations;" from the worship of natural things and forces, to that of the human form, to that of one man (Jesus), and finally to that of "Principles in themselves and in their own right; measured by no individual, nor age, nor form, nor institution. This is the highest Ideal, the one enduring recognition of God." Again, he writes: "to give the infinite over to visible form is to lose it. . . . We cannot see the eternal substance and life of the universe . . . not because deity is too far, but because it is too near. . . . God stands in all ideal thought."[55] A person, therefore, who follows his best thought realizes his potential divinity and acknowledges his affinity with the eternal Whole. In fact, Johnson said that he wanted "the largest and most liberal recognition of human nature."[56]

Drawn strongly on the one hand to Parker and on the other to Emerson, Johnson seems to have wavered between theism and pantheism. He rejected an other-worldly god, and sought a god beyond space and time and immanent in men. His god, like Parker's, is "Fatherly" and "Motherly," a real but not a supernatural being, separate from men, and known to them through intuition in terms of Principles. The direction of this difficult and vapid "Spiritual Pantheism" in which the essence of deity is neither supernature nor "within" (as in Emerson), is toward the humanization, even the socialization, of deity. In contrast, Emerson humanized God only in relation to Calvinism, and did not seek the "most liberal" human nature as highest reality. Emerson and the later Transcendentalists sought to bring God and man together in one Whole; but the former tended to make man divine, and the latter, to humanize the eternal.

Johnson argued for the worship of "Principles in themselves, and in their own right;"[57] that "Principles are real, not nominal."[58] He declared that "Unity is a universal principle, a loving spirit."[59] The Unitarian theists, however, were dissatisfied with these expressions. Bartol observed that "Nobody ever leaned, in his heart, on a law," and that "for sustenance there must be a response."[60] It seemed to the theists that if one posits absolute moral principles, he must posit also an absolute moral source that is therefore "personal." Furthermore, there was the underlying fear that mere principles by themselves would tend, by psychological osmosis, as it were, to become laws of "human nature;" and that "human nature," in turn, would be translated into individual people with relative value systems in pluralistic societies that at best had statistical morality and at worst were dominated by an "absolute" human source. When Johnson said that "Unity is a universal principle, a loving spirit," what did he mean? Did he mean that God is a loving spirit who is the creator and sustainer of universal moral principles? If so, then his god must be a person. Or did he mean that a human spirit who follows innate moral principles is divine? The ambiguity of the sentence exhibits the drift, for good or bad, of the liberal tradition from the belief in absolute a priori values to values empirically derived, and perhaps genetically coded. As Frothingham noted, "God has become a name for our most exalted feelings, so that instead of saying 'God is Spirit,' some read 'Spirit is God!'."

109

After the Civil War contention resumed between orthodox and liberal Unitarians. Many of the latter founded, in 1867, the Free Religious Association the constitution of which eventually read: "The objects of the Association are to encourage the scientific study of religion, to increase fellowship in the spirit, and to emphasize the supremacy of practical morality in all the relations of life."[61] Within this Association, two groups polarized: the Transcendentalists or intuitionists; and those who wished to establish religion on more rational and scientific grounds. Like Jonathan Edwards a hundred and fifty years earlier, the Transcendentalists found themselves passe in an age that was increasingly rationalistic, more of the head than of the heart.

Ghodes writes that "Transcendentalism . . . turned against itself when it showed itself friendly to the protests of science. Evolution, in so far as it was based upon materialism, denied its fundamental postulates of intuition and relegated it . . . to the realm of the discarded."[62] However the Transcendentalists, from their point of view, did not see themselves as enemies of science. Theodore Parker, for instance, sought rational and scientific verification of intuitive truths, and did not believe, Hutchinson writes, that "this kind of interest in scientific demonstration vitiated the whole intuitionist idea."[63] Samuel Longfellow, on safer grounds, believed that there was no need for religion and science to quarrel if science "does not claim to cover the whole ground and use the whole instrumentality of knowledge."[64] Samuel Johnson insisted that the "main postulates" of Transcendentalism were "essentially undisturbed by full acceptance of the results of science." Science needed the complement of idealism because "intelligence can be recognized behind and within laws of nature."[65] Although Parker's position inevitably aggravated the latent tension between reason and intuition, the position of Longfellow and Johnson did not. They, like Emerson (and Hedge), assumed that the worlds of Reason and the Understanding were mutually exclusive. On the other hand, Unitarian rationalists, represented for instance by F. E. Abbot, did hold that science claimed "the whole instrumentality of knowledge," and that the existence of Transcendental intuition could not be "proved scientifically." The predominant drift of free religion in the last half of the nineteenth century, therefore, was toward scientific rationalism and humanism, and away from non-cognitive knowledge. In terms of epistemology, certainly, Transcendentalism was an abberation in the rationalistic tradition of Unitarianism, earlier represented by Andrews Norton.

Within liberal Unitarianism, the empirical temper of the age worked against all theological assumptions. In fact, for both the "scientific theists" and the Transcendentalists, the idea of God became increasingly less prominent. The tendency of the former group, in spite of Abbot's stated belief that God is "an objective Person," was more humanistic than theistic; reason and evolution seemed to offer little or no evidence for a personal deity.[66] For the intuitionists, "Idealism" came to refer less to a philosophic system positing mind over matter than to human aspiration in itself. Ideals for Johnson were part of the evolution of human nature rather than immanent divinity. The dignity of mankind resided more in the fulfillment of innate ideals than, as Channing thought, in man's likeness to a supernatural god.

By the turn of the century, the scientific theists and the later Transcendentalists had blended, in the cruicible of free religion, to form a humanitarian philosophy of a priori values without an absolute personal source; an empirical, rational philosophy that held to innate knowledge of universal moral laws. In liberal Unitarian circles, a sense of divineness impregnated moral principles inherent in human nature. For example, Charles Fleischer, in 1911, wrote in honor of Theodore Parker: "What I want to assert is that enlightened and high-minded persons in general already pursue truth, beauty, goodness, justice, and whatever other ideals, for their own sake, because of the intrinsic worth and inherent attractiveness of these--not because God and the church command them. In other words, theology and ethics are separate though kindred human concerns, and the moral imperative is independent of the God-idea."[67] This statement argues that absolute moral principles are the essence of human nature, and all but ignores the possibility of the existence of a personal god. It expresses the ultimate humanization of Channing's supernatural personalism with its over-riding social emphasis; and the original rejection by Emerson of exclusive dogma and ritual, and the rejection of a personal god.[68]

V

The essence of the Unitarian tradition is the revolt against the Calvinistic condemnation of man; and the essence of Transcendentalism is the revolt against the Unitarian rationalistic tradition. These revolts were humanistic and epistemological. The early Transcendentalists, most of whom were Unitarian, broke from orthodox Unitarianism which held, in the words of Andrews Norton, that man is only "a creature of a day [who] cannot pretend to attain . . . any assurance concerning the unseen and the eternal;" that there is "no mode of establishing religious judgment, but by the exercise of reason . . . by forming probable judgment upon facts."[69] The Transcendentalists believed that they had greater assurance of God than mere probability allowed, and, in the words of Parker, that "we have direct access to Him, through reason, conscience, and the religious faculty;" that "if we are faithful, the great truths of morality and religion, the deep sentiment of love to man and love to God, are perceived intuitively."[70] The Transcendentalists were convinced that a person can know God directly through "intuition," and that this immediate knowledge is conceptualized in "the great truths of morality and religion" and realized through action. The movement was an enlightened manifestation of the reawakening of the evangelical spirit abroad in the country in the early part of the century.

Emerson, like other Transcendentalists, used the term "intuition" to describe immediate knowledge of absolutes: "We denote this primary wisdom as Intuition" ("Self-Reliance"). But he believed, in addition, that in revelation he knew the Over-Soul more intimately than the term "intuition" implies. When Parker said that "we have direct access" to God, he meant, presumably, that he knew immediately 1) spiritual attributes of God in himself and 2) God as a spiritual object, a separate center of consciousness, or at the least, God as a (mental)

112

"Otherness." Emerson agreed that he had immediate knowledge of divine attributes in himself but rejected the idea that God is a person. He found, once more, no rational or empirical evidence for an objective deity. He wrote in 1836: "As long as the soul seeks an external God, it never can have peace, it always must be uncertain what may be done & what may become of it. But when it sees the Great God far within its own nature, then it sees that always itself is a party to all that can be, that always it will be informed of that which will happen and therefore it is pervaded with a great peace."[71] Since the Great God is far within, Emerson held that he knew immediately divine attributes of himself and that he became aware, in moments of revelation, that he was one in essence or consciousness with god: "Man has access to the entire mind of the Creator, is himself the creator in the finite" (Nature).[72]

Revelation for Emerson was not a new dimension of consciousness known by an exclusive faculty, as it was for Edwards, Poe, and perhaps Parker, but a deepening of ordinary consciousness that gave numinosity to the multiplicity of the Not Me: "the soul in man is not an organ . . . is not a faculty, but a light . . . is the background of our being" ("Over-Soul"). In revelation, "all mean egotism vanishes; I become a transparent eyeball; I am nothing; I see all; the currents of the Universal Being circulate through me" (Nature). In revelation he as ego was nothing; and he saw all because he became God; because his ego fused with the mind of the Over-Soul. He was a "transparent eyeball" because the substantiality of the Not Me of the material eyeball faded away as the center of consciousness shifted from the particular ego to the universal I, as the ego became one in consciousness with its Greater Self.[73]

Although an epistemological dualist (Understanding and Reason), Emerson believed not in two separate worlds but in one world with two poles: the perceiver and the perceived; and that ultimate answers lie in the perceiver who cannot be defined in cognitive terms. Nature is not an alien entity but a projection of the perceiver, colored by the lens of the particular ego, reflecting the quality of perception of that ego. In a monism as complete as this, there are no other minds to know. Indeed,

Emerson, unlike Edwards, Channing, the Unitarian intuitionists and scientific theists, in short, unlike everyone else, had no epistemological problem about how to know nature and God.[74] His problem was about how to deepen and heighten the quality of consciousness so as to become increasingly aware that he was in essence God. He sought to view nature from the point of view of the Greater Self, not how to contact another (conscious) entity outside of himself.

From a strict point of view, Emerson's brand of Transcendentalism was a one man affair. Only he had the profound originality, the divine madness, if you will, to sustain the perspective of subjective idealism. Like Edwards, he looked with authority upon the world from the point of view of eternity. Frothingham calls Samuel Johnson "a true disciple of Emerson."[75] But Johnson, although an individualist and an idealist, bleached and half-personified the universal so that it seems a mere sentimental conflux of human hopes and dreams. His writings, including his nature descriptions, moreover, are morally high but imaginatively flat. Johnson had neither Emerson's stubborn subjective religious vision nor his ability to formulate in literary terms a viable Greater Self.

Emerson hid like a Purloin Letter his subjective idealism; its unseen presence is everywhere in his writings; it is the very structure of his vision. Even the liberal Unitarians, including Johnson, passed over, with commonsense incredulity, his position that other persons are phenomenal. George Ripley, at least, recognized the real Emerson when he remarked that Emerson "teaches that God and himself are the sole existences."[76] But the momentum of nineteenth-century liberalism was away from subjective, although enlightened, idealism and evangelicalism. The rationalism inherent in early Unitarianism blended with invigorated science after the Civil War, and left little room for an artist, like Emerson, whose self-reliance was God-reliance, not reliance on human community. Emerson led the attack on the concept of a personal god, but not for the purposes of replacing that concept with men in a pluralistic society. V. G. Allen observed in 1892 that "when we no longer localize Him as a physical essence in the infinite remoteness, it is easier to regard Him as ethical in His inmost being; righteousness becomes more readily the primary element [77] in our conception of His essential nature." But Emerson gave highest priority to values that did not correspond to human sensibility. Bartol was correct in arguing that absolute moral values logically necessitate an absolute personal source. But Emerson held that absolute values are not "human" and that therefore their source is not "personal."

In the history of religion, Emerson's ranking of priorities is not unusual. Like Edwards, Emerson sought "intense piety" and reacted against theologies that increasingly found reality exclusively among persons (of whom God is one) and neglected those ultimate and inevitable wastelands of human experience where other people are of no avail. "Souls," he said, "are not saved in bundles" ("Worship"). "When good is near you, when you have life in yourself, it is not by any known or accustomed way; you shall not discern the footprints of any other; you shall not see the face of man; you shall not hear any name;--the way, the thought, the good, shall be wholly strange and new. It shall exclude example and experience" ("Self-Reliance"). "If I recall the happiest hours of existence," he wrote late in life, "those which really make a man inmate of a better world, it is a lonely and undescribed joy, but it leads to joys ear hath not heard nor eye seen." [78] Putting eternity before (but not beyond) time, and regeneration before works, Emerson stands outside of (but not in opposition to) science and ethical societies. He sought salvation, and found other persons in emergencies no more helpful than dreams. The problem of evil is at the heart of his crisis philosophy; and his solution to this problem lay beyond the ego. To sensitive but existential souls who say that we have each other for solace and care, he would have said that this is not enough. He believed, Carpenter writes, that "moral living was good, but that divine grace was infinitely better." [79] Not worshipping the unknown god of Calvinism, he felt that he was "in the midst of a truth I do not comprehend, but which comprehends me." [80] This truth was the Impersonal Spectator or First Cause viewing, from great psychological depth, itself as the person, "Emerson," of Concord. Thus Emerson posited an absolute source of value and a transcendental audience for his ego, an audience that, even when he was alone, indeed, especially then, assured him that he was integrated into the very fabric of Being and Becoming.

FOOTNOTES

1. Views of Religion (Boston, 1906), p. 13.

2. Ralph L. Rusk, The Life of Ralph Waldo Emerson (New York: Columbia University Press, 1949), p. 424.

3. Frederic Henry Hedge, Reason in Religion (1967), p. 66.

4. Octavius Brooks Frothingham, Recollections and Impressions (1891), p. 296.

5. Frederic Henry Hedge, Martin Luther (1888), p. 285.

6. Hedge, Martin Luther, p. 283.

7. Hedge, Martin Luther, p. 284.

8. Hedge, Martin Luther, p. 289.

9. Hedge, Martin Luther, p. 294.

10. Ronald Vale Wells, Three Christian Transcendentalists (Columbia University Press, 1943), p. 119.

11. W. T. Stace writes concerning "psychological words" that "either they mean, when applied to God, the same things as they mean when applied to men; or, if they are metaphors, we must be able to say what the metaphors literally stand for; or they mean nothing at all" (Religion and the Modern Mind [Lippincott: N.Y., 1952], p. 16).

12. Hedge, Martin Luther, p. 312.

13. Hedge, Reason in Religion, p. 92.

14. Hedge, Reason in Religion, p. 36.

15. Joel Myerson, "Frederic Hedge and the Failure of Transcendentalism," Harvard Library Bulletin XXII, 409.

16. Hedge, Martin Luther, p. 29.

17. The Journals and Miscellaneous Notebooks of Ralph Waldo Emerson, ed. William H. Gilman et al. (Cambridge, Mass: Harvard University Press, 1960-), VII, 200. Hereafter references to this edition are included in the text with volume and page numbers.

18. The Journals of Bronson Alcott, ed. Odell Shepard (Boston: Little, Brown, 1938), p. 390.

19. Alcott, Journals, p. 85.

20. Quoted in Odell Shepard, Pedlar's Progress (Boston, Little, Brown, 1937), p. 494.

21. Shepard, p. 494.

22. Quoted by O. B. Frothingham in Transcendentalism in New England (New York, 1876) p. 254.

23. Bronson Alcott, Concord Days (Boston, 1872), p. 273. See also Gay Wilson Allen, Walt Whitman Handbook, [Chicago: Packard, 1946], pp. 190-1, 303, 306-7. Alcott was influenced by Whitman's use of the term "Personalism" and immediately adopted the term and "introduced it into American philosophy" (Walt Whitman Handbook, p. 303).

24. Journals, 306. Alcott wrote: "Personal identity is spiritual, not numerical, souls being one, bodies not" (Table Talk [Boston, 1877], p. 152). Compare this statement with the one by Emerson on page 69 in the previous essay. Both Alcott and Emerson, indeed, all the Transcendentalists, were of course philosophic idealists.

25. Journals, p. 98.

26. Journals, p. 362.

27. "Friendship."

28. Journals, p. 327, footnote by Shepard.

29. Pedlar's Progress, p. 495.

30. _Journals_, pp. 484-5. Shepard writes elsewhere that Emerson did not believe in personal immortality. "He thought that we go down like drops of water into the vast sea" (_Pedlar's Progress_, p. 510). On the whole, however, Shepard is admirably accurate in his discussion of the differences and similarities between Alcott and Emerson.

31. Quoted in Paul F. Boller, Jr., _American Transcendentalism_, (New York: Putnam, 1974), p. 28.

32. Quoted in James Elliot Cabot, A _Memoir_ of _Ralph_ _Waldo_ _Emerson_ (Boston, 1887), I, 341.

33. Cyrus Augustus Bartol, _Radical_ _Problems_ (Boston, 1872), p. 83. But Gay Wilson Allen writes that Emerson's statement, "Idealism sees the world in God," "proves that Emerson was not, as he was already being accused of being, a pantheist, who sees _God_ _in_ _the_ _world_" (_Waldo_ _Emerson_ [New York: Viking, 1981], p. 280). What one wishes to call Emerson depends on how one defines terms.

34. Quoted in _The_ _Transcendental_ _Revolt_ Against _Materialism_, ed. George F. Whicher (Boston: Heath, 1949), p. 80.

35. William R. Hutchinson, _The_ _Transcendental-_ ist _Ministers_ (New Haven: Yale University Press, 1959), pp. 105-6.

36. _Views_, pp. 25, 195.

37. _Theodore_ _Parker's_ _Experience_ as a _Minister_ (Boston, 1859), p. 80. William G. Heath writes: "Bartol's inability to embrace Parker's concept of 'absolute religion' . . . like the Oversoul, excluded the notion of a personal Creator" (A. C. Bartol, _On_ _Spirit_ and _Personality_, ed. William G. Heath, Jr. [John Colet Press: St. Paul, Minn., 1977], pp. xx-xxi). But Parker's thrust was social, like Alcott's. Given my minimal definition of "a person," a separate and distinct center of intelligent consciousness, Parker believed in a personal god.

38. _Radical_ _Problems_, p. 92.

39. Cabot, I, 340.

40. Quoted in John White Chadwick, _Theodore Parker_ (Boston: Houghton, Mifflin, 1901), p. 85.

41. Quoted in Kenneth Walter Cameron, "Henry Ware's 'Divinity School Address:' A Reply to Emerson'," _American Transcendental Quarterly_, XIII, 84-91.

42. In _The Genius and Character of Emerson_, ed. F. E. Sanborn (Boston, 1885), p. 113. About the time of the "Divinity School Address" Emerson gave up family prayers. See Ellen Tucker Emerson, _The Life of Lidian Jackson_, ed. Delores Bird Carpenter (Boston: Twayne, 1980), p. 79.

43. J. W. Alexander, Albert Dod, Charles Hodge, "Transcendentalism of the Germans and of Cousin and Its Influences on Opinion in this Country," in _The Transcendentalists_, ed. Perry Miller (Cambridge: Harvard University Press, 1950), p. 235.

44. Cameron, p. 86.

45. _On Spirit and Personality_, p. xxvii.

46. Sanborn, p. 169. David S. Reynolds writes: "The old question of why Transcendentalists avoided writing fiction may thus in part be answered by the fact that native religious fiction was moving progressively toward the earthly precisely when Transcendentalism wished to affirm the metaphysical" (_Faith in Fiction: the Emergence of Religious Literature in America_ [Cambridge: Harvard University Press, 1981], p. 121). Emerson and Thoreau, in their religious quests, sought divinity that, although immanent in man, was not "human" or "personal." Not surprisingly, therefore, they were not mainly interested in "fiction" and "persons," except, in the case of Emerson, insofar as the great man (One) represented the Many. Why "Transcendentalists" whose priorities were relational were not fiction writers, is another question. In any case, Reynold's valuable book supports, in its own way, the distinctions I make between Emerson and Channing; and provides, incidentally, a rich background to the subsequent essay on Hawthorne.

47. The Transcendentalists were not unaware of the lack of obligation nature shows man. Hedge spoke of its viciousness: "in the realm of Nature, of wild Nature, I find no proofs of moral life, no conscience . . . nor any pity for human woe" (Martin Luther, p. 321). Emerson would not have denied this, but both he and Hedge felt that "the Spirit will prevail." One difference between them is that Hedge, a theist, believed that God created the world in such a way that "Evil [presumably both moral and natural] is a necessary condition of development and moral growth"--a possibility that Hawthorne speculated about for a long time (Reason in Religion, p. 121). Emerson, on the other hand, recognizing the power of Being, believed that man, an incarnation of God, can by himself prevail over the absurd and meaningless. He might be called a Transcendental Existentialist.

48. The Radical, II, 522. This journal "was the chief organ of the heterodox of New England from September, 1865, to June, 1872" (See Clarence L. Gohdes, The Periodicals of American Transcendentalism [Durham: Duke University Press, 1931], p. 214).

49. Essays and Sermons, ed. Joseph May (New York: Houghton, Mifflin, 1894), p. 8.

50. Lectures, Essays, and Sermons, pp. 375, 370, 373.

51. The Worship of Jesus (Boston: Spencer, 1868), pp. 73-4. However, Johnson elsewhere refers to "the centre soul [which] . . . is all things, is ourselves" (Lectures, Essays, and Sermons, with a Memoir by Samuel Longfellow [Boston, 1883], p. 15).

52. The Worship of Jesus, p. 89.

53. The Radical, V. 490.

54. The Worship of Jesus, p. 87.

55. The Radical, VI, 276. Stowe Persons writes that Johnson clung to the "Emersonian concept of the Over-Soul. . . . Following the lead of the Concord seer, Johnson maintained that the evolution of higher forms out of lower in the natural sphere could only be explained on the assumption that the

process was a 'drawing out' of Mind" (Free Religion [New Haven: Yale University Press, 1947], p. 69).

56. The Radical, V, 487.

57. The Worship of Jesus, p. 17.

58. The Radical, V, 489.

59. The Radical, V, 19.

60. Heath, p. 124.

61. Quoted in Stowe Persons, Free Religion (New Haven: Yale University Press, 1947), p. 54.

62. Gohdes, pp. 253-4.

63. Hutchinson, p. 103. Elsewhere Hutchinson remarks: "Parker's apparent vacillation, often remarked upon, between a reliance upon intuition and a frenzied search for 'facts of demonstration,' is just one more sign of a dilemma that runs all through the thought and rhetorical enthusiasms of mid-century liberal and radical religion" (American Protestant Thought: The Liberal Area [New York: Harper and Row, 1968], p. 5).

64. Essays and Sermons, p. 2.

65. Lectures, Essays, and Sermons, pp. 419 and 356.

66. Persons, Free Religion, pp. 68 and 87; Sidney Ahlstrom, A Religious History of the American People (New Haven: Yale University Press, 1972), p. 607. To Abbot, Frothingham's statement applies: "pantheism has succeeded to a mechanical theism."

67. In Theodore Parker: Anniversaries of Birth and Death (Chicago: Unity Publishing Company, 1911), pp. 86-8.

68. By 1890, Persons writes, Unitarianism had come to hold to "a vague form of theism. . . . It saw the moral law inwrought in the nature of things" Free Religion, pp. 155-6. Insofar as "a vague form of theism" existed in Unitarian circles, my remarks are overstatements. But there were (and are)

Unitarians who believe in absolute values without believing in a personal god. For a short summary of the development of modern religious humanism, see Fred Gladstone Bratton, The Legacy of the Liberal Spirit (Boston: Beacon Press, 1943), pp. 228-34.

69. Quoted in The Transcendentalists, pp. 211-12.

70. Parker, Views, pp. 43, 300.

71. The Journals of Ralph Waldo Emerson, ed. by Edward Waldo Emerson and Waldo Emerson Forbes. 10 volumes. (Boston: Houghton Mifflin, 1909-1914), X, 453.

72. Elsewhere he wrote: "I grow in God. I am only a form of him. He is the soul of me. I can even with a mountainous aspiring, say, I am God" (quoted in Rusk, Life, p. 261).

73. Robinson gives a convincing interpretation of Emerson's use of the term "transparent," as in his "transparent eyeball." The term implies for Emerson "a state in which the self not only is unveiled and thus visible, but is really not a 'self' at all. Just as one sees through a transparent object to all around it, one sees 'through' a genuine man. . . . The transparent self is thus the negated self, if we think of self in the low and partial sense. But in terms of the 'whole' self, it is the self raised to the level of the universal" (David Robinson, Apostle of Culture [Philadelphia: University of Pennsylvania Press, 1982], p. 66).

74. Alexander, Dod, and Hodge shrewdly observed (and complained) that Emerson held to a god that he thought he could "thoroughly comprehend" (The Transcendentalists, p. 235). Neither Emerson nor Thoreau, however, thought that they could comprehend God in terms of the Understanding.

75. Recollections and Impressions, p. 209.

76. Fothingham, George Ripley (Boston, 1882), p. 271. I am increasingly impressed by how isolated Emerson was in his philosophy, even among his closest friends and immediate family. Lidian's

Christian fear of everlasting torment brings home
sharply the intellectual distance between her and
her husband (see Ellen Tucker Emerson, p. 205).
Only Thoreau, as I have said, embraced with Emerson
the doctrine of divine impersonalism; and no one,
not even Thoreau, practiced to the degree Emerson
did the perspective of subjective idealism. Alfred
Kazin speaks of Emerson's "extraordinary gift of
faith" and how "it left him superior to all his
trials. For all his outward mildness, he was an
exceptionally strong character. He knew his value,
he knew how to live with himself" (The New York
Review [January 21, 1982], p. 3). It is the purpose
of these essays on Emerson and Transcendentalism to
expose as clearly as I know how Emerson's
philosophic-psychological frame of reference in
which he achieved his remarkable ability "to live
with himself."

77. Quoted in Hutchinson, American Protestant
Thought, pp. 57-8.

78. Journals (1909-14), X, 453.

79. See "The Genteel Tradition: A
Re-Interpretation," New England Quarterly, XV
(1942), 427-43.

80. Quoted in Sanborn, p. 163.

COMMENTARY ON CHANNING'S SERMON, "FATHER OF SPIRITS" (1823)

"Theism is a half-way house between frank anthropomorphism of polytheism on the one hand and the idea of the all-inclusive Absolute on the other."

Frederick Copleston[1]

"Now it is by no means certain, that any thing which is dissolved by death is any way necessary to the living being in this its state of reflection, after ideas are gained. . . . It does not appear then, that the relation of this gross body to the reflecting being is, in any degree, necessary to thinking."

Joseph Butler[2]

I

William Ellery Channing and his wife, Ruth, sailed for England on May 27, 1822. On July 22, they interviewed Wordsworth whom Channing had early admired. He and the poet had a long talk, and near sunset they descended into Grasmere. "With the placid lake before me," Channing recorded, "and Wordsworth talking and reciting poetry with a poet's spirit by my side, I felt that the combination of circumstances was such as my highest hopes could never have anticipated."[3] The Channings subsequently traveled to France and Switzerland, then over the Alps to Rome where they spent the Winter. In the Spring they retraced their steps, arriving in London in early June, 1823. They visited Tintern Abbey and Coleridge, and late that summer, sailed for home.

Channing resumed preaching that October in the Federal Street Church in Boston, and one of the persons who heard him was Ralph Waldo Emerson, twenty years old, on the verge of a remarkable career. One Sunday in October, Emerson wrote in his Journal: "I heard Dr. Channing deliver a discourse upon Revelation as standing in comparison with Nature. . . . He considered God's word to be the only expounder of his works, and that Nature had always been found insufficient to teach men the great doctrines which Revelation inculcated. . . . Dr. Channing regarded Revelation as much a part of the order of things as any other event."[4] The sermon Emerson heard that Sunday in October is not extant, but the one printed here for the first time was delivered by Channing at the Federal Street Church in November, 1823; Emerson may have heard it. Since this sermon was written by Channing right after his return from meeting the English Romantics, one is not surprised to find that it contains suggestions of Transcendental themes. It therefore points to Channing's sermon, "Likeness to God," delivered five years later, which marked, Perry Miller wrote, the "commencement of themes that were to become standards among the more passionate of his [Channing's] adherents: namely, [we note with obvious reservation] that nature is the revelation of the divine rather than formal dogma, and that the approach to nature is properly to be made through insight and not through systematized and sterilized theology."[5]

Although the following sermon is entitled "Father of Spirits," its main theme is the greatness of the human mind. It exhibits what Henry Bellows considered to be Channing's two dominant ideas: reverence for human nature, and man's free will.[6] In his introductory remarks, Channing states that man consists in a glorious spirit and a frail body, and that the material world was made for the sake of the spiritual. As proof of this, he claims that whereas matter is static, dead, neither growing nor diminishing in quantity, the spiritual world is constantly enlarging and growing: with each new birth, a new member helps expand the great spiritual community. Of this community which extends from earth to heaven, God is the Father, and we humans are infants passing through a period of probation, destined for heaven.

Channing then concentrates on the human mind, and holds that it is both passive and active in regard to the physical and spiritual worlds. It receives impressions from nature; perceives order in nature; and actively modifies, through scientific

126

inventions and secondary qualities, the material world. However, he says, the mind finds the spiritual world of far more interest and relevance than the material world. In the spiritual world, the mind receives from other minds important information, secular and divine, and provides in turn those minds with its own knowledge and inspiration. In the spiritual world we will increasingly live, our actions guided by our "conscience" as we gain greater and greater harmony with God and our fellow spirits. Indeed, Channing writes, the soul naturally longs for the infinite where it will become "a recipient, a partaker" of the divine nature. We are spirits, he relates, who have "just begun to exist and improve;" we are in the "earliest stages of being," infant souls, essentially social, destined to ascend forever in the great family of souls. Or, as he says elsewhere, "this world's interest to [those in heaven] is as the birthplace of Immortal Minds, as the school where they are trained for Heaven."[7]

Channing concludes the sermon with the moral advice that "We belong to a social system, the great object of which is that intelligent beings should give themselves to one another." He warns his congregation against "spiritual suicide," of dissipating their minds "on a life of pleasure and amusement," and assures them once again that their minds are made to be temples of God. His rejection of the Calvinistic debasement of man is not mentioned but is assumed. Four years earlier, in "Unitarian Christianity" and in "The Moral Argument against Calvinism," he had attacked the doctrine of human depravity, and had grounded his attack on his faith in man's reason, virtue, and likeness to God. Even though he had referred to "our frail and fallible nature" in the former sermon, he had warned his audience in the latter that "we rate our faculties too meanly as well as too boastingly." The qualities of goodness and justice, he wrote in 1820, "are essentially the same in God and man, though differing in degree, in purity, and in extent of operation." "The ultimate reliance of a human being," he declared in answer to Calvinism, "is and must be on his own mind." In the Introduction to his <u>Works</u>, he stated that the soul "is an immortal germ, which may be said to contain now within itself what endless ages are to unfold. It is truly an image of the infinity of God."[8] "Father of Spirits," written a few years after the above sermons, and immediately following his visit with the great Romantics in England, continues the crescendo of his celebration of man that climaxed in "Likeness to God" which points, in turn, to Emerson's "Self-Reliance."

II

The rest of this essay consists in various notes comparing Channing and Emerson, so as to clarify their respective philosophies, and to delineate especially Emerson's thought.

Channing held that "strictly speaking, there is nothing below God sacred, save the human soul."[9] Yet he loved nature throughout his life. He wrote in 1798 (the year that Wordsworth and Coleridge published Lyrical Ballads): "there is a beach above a mile from town. . . . The towering and craggy rocks, the roar of the waves, the foam with which they dash on the shore. . . . I extend my arms towards them, I run to meet them, and wish myself buried beneath their waters. Sometimes my whole soul ascends to the God of nature, and in such a temple I cannot but be devout."[10] In 1822 he exclaimed, "The soul and nature are attuned together. Something within answers to all we witness without. . . . Nature breathes nothing unkind. It expands, or calms, or softens us. Let us open our souls to its influence."[11] And late in life Channing wrote in his sermon, "God Revealed in the Universe and in Humanity," that "Nature everywhere testifies to the infinity of its Author. . . . The Infinite is revealed in all things. I do not except the most common. The stone . . . the humblest flowers . . . this mighty living universe . . . each minutest particle speaks of the Infinite One. . . . Can you not discern the all-embracing, all pervading force that gives the primal impulse to the moving whole?" In 1839 Channing, in another passage reminiscent of Emerson's Nature, published three years earlier, stated that "To the man of the senses, nature is something substantial, the only reality. It subsists to him by its own power. As the senses lose their power over us, nature loses its rigid self-subsistence. The spirit within it, and of which it is the veil and shadow, shines out. We look on it as a phenomenon, and pierce beneath the surface to the deep, infinite power of which it is the mere sign and instrument."[12] And in "Likeness to God" (1828), Channing recorded that "the creation is a birth and shining forth of the Divine mind, a work through which his spirit breathes. In proportion as we receive this spirit we possess within ourselves the explanation of what we see. We discern more and more of God in everything, from the frail flower to the everlasting stars." When one comes upon such statements, he exclaims that here, certainly, is the source of Emerson.

But Channing does not celebrate nature above the Word in "Father of Spirits" nor evidently in the October sermon that Emerson heard. In fact, he never held nature in such high esteem as Emerson, and the examples quoted here of his stance toward nature do not jibe ultimately with the rest of his work. Even in "Likeness to God," his most Emersonian piece, Channing wrote that "It is possible that the brevity of these hints [in the last quotation] may expose to the charge of mysticism what seems to me the calmest and clearest truths," thus assuring the reader that he was not open to the charge of (turbulent, unclear) pantheism, that is, of believing that there is no separation between God, nature, and man. Channing occasionally expressed what appear to be Emersonian themes, but his consistent thrust was toward theism (and rationalism). His resolute and sustained stand for special miracles, for instance, is sufficient evidence that he did not believe in divine immanence in nature. In general, his treatment of nature is more like that of William Cullen Bryant, James Fenimore Cooper, Thomas Cole, than of Emerson and Thoreau.

Channing, an early Romantic, still found nature an artifact of the divine spirit rather than its incarnation, a "temple" in which he worshipped, "a work through which [God's] spirit breathes." But for Emerson nature was an extension of his own body through which his Greater Self breathed. And since God was within, nature, the projection of God in the unconscious, was "a great shadow pointing always to the sun behind us"--behind the "eye," not behind the

object (Nature).[13]   In turn, revelation, Emerson
believed, is a glimpse of Adam's vision, a moment
when the fallen ego is saved by fusion with the
Greater Self far within and nature is projected as a
perfect poem, a poem that is experienced immediately, beyond the analytical, rigidifying self-consciousness of the Understanding.   Emerson, not
Channing, of course, foreshadowed the twentieth-
century preoccupation with the Unconscious, for
life, religion, and art.

    The bracketed passage in "Father of Spirits"
that Channing omitted from public delivery indicates
more specifically his ontology of nature.   Like
other pre-Romantics, he reacted against the eighteenth-century version of the universe in which man
was a "puny, irrelevant spectator," a world which
had swept away

    the gloriously romantic universe of Dante and
    Milton, that set no bounds to the imagination
    of man as it played over space and time. . . .
    The world that people had thought themselves
    living in--a world rich with colour and sound,
    redolent with fragrance, filled with gladness,
    love and beauty, speaking everywhere of pur-
    posive harmony and creative ideals--was crowded
    into minute corners in the brains of scattered
    organic beings.   The really important world
    outside was a world hard, cold, colourless,
    silent, and dead, a world of quantity, a world
    of mathematically computable motions in me-
    chanical regularity.[14]

Opposing this view, Channing held that the "really
important world" consists in both primary and
secondary qualities, and that man provides the
latter.   God provides the framework of primary
qualities on which the human mind, as agent, imposes
the world of value.   He exclaimed that the active
soul "transmutes the colourless, silent, cheerless
earth into paradise."   "What charm is in nature is
spread over it by our own souls, and we create
through that intellectual power called association
the splendour and enchantment we enjoy."[15]   "I do
not say," he asserted, approaching his position from
another angle, "that the word exists in our thoughts
only.   But I do say that it derives its most interesting properties from the Mind which contemplates

it. For example, the forms of outward objects have doubtless actual existence; but they owe their Beauty--that mysterious charm--to thoughts and feelings which we blend with them, and of which they are but the reflected image."[16] The human mind for Channing is a "mighty enchantress" because it adds charm and beauty to the objective, quantitative factors of experience.[17] Thus Channing, in his philosophy of nature, was half-way between the view that primary and secondary qualities of nature exist independent of the human mind and Emerson's view that these qualities are projected through the ego. When Channing and Wordsworth, in July, 1822, descended into Grasmere near sunset, they were in agreement, as the poet said in "Tintern Abbey," that we "half-create" the world we experience.

Further (in regard to the bracketed passage) it is interesting to note, for the sake of the history of ideas, that Herman Melville wrote in Moby Dick, a quarter of a century later: "And when we consider that other theory of the natural philosophers, that all earthly hues--every stately or lovely emblazoning --the sweet tinges of sunset skies and woods, --yea, and the gilded velvets of butterflies, and the butterfly cheeks of young girls; all these are but subtile deceits, not actually inherent in substances, but only laid on from without; so that all deified nature absolutely paints like the harlot, whose allurements cover nothing but the charnel-house within" ("The Whiteness of the Whale"). Channing, at the beginning of the American Romantic movement, utilized Lockean epistemology to escape the passive Lockean understanding, the Newtonian mechanism of nature, and the depraved soul of Calvinism: man's mind, he said, was active and cooperative with God in creating experience the reality of which consisted in both primary and secondary qualities. And Melville, at the end of that movement, used the same epistemology to cry in anguish at mankind for its impotence, guillibility, and blindness. Melville, filled with scepticism, acutely sensitive to evil, feared that mankind was pitifully white-washing submerged and malicious forces of existence. But Channing, with faith in a good deity behind appearances, praised man as co-creator of the grand universe.

Channing believed in extended material space filled, as he said in "Father of Spirits," with stars that are lamps "for the awe, and guidance of the soul." He observed repeatedly, as did the age, that "the human mind loves the infinite, loves it in the vast heavens, the countless stars, and in boundless prospects of the earth and ocean"-- because infinite space correlates with infinite Spirit. Unafraid, Channing was drawn out of his finitude by sidereal space; his soul, yearning for the other world, his true home, followed the guiding stars upward through friendly space toward the Father. Emerson, on the contrary, not having faith in an external god, found no solace in the apparent material immensity of the heavens. In "Life and Letters" (1867), he isolated what he thought was one of the most important causes of the growth of the new religion:

> I think the paramount source of the religious revolution was Modern Science; beginning with Copernicus, who destroyed the pagan fictions of the Church, by showing mankind that the earth on which we live was not the centre of the Universe . . . but a little scrap of a planet rushing round the sun in our system, which in turn was too minute to be seen at the distance of many stars which we behold. Astronomy taught us our insignificance in Nature.

But, he continued, "we presently saw also that the religious nature in man was not affected by these errors in his understanding. The religious sentiment made nothing of bulk or size, or far or near; triumphed over time as well as space." Emerson countered the idea of his insignificance in nature with keener appreciation for philosophic idealism. Many years earlier, in 1832, he wrote: "Do you believe that there is boundless space? Just dwell on that gigantic thought. Does not idealism seem more probable than space upon whose area what is, the family of being, is a mere dot, & the thought of men or angels can never fathom more than its verge? All is lost in the bosom of its great night."[18] In "The American Scholar," Emerson alluded to the same subject: Modern science shows us "system on system shooting like rays, upward, downward, without centre, without circumference." The trouble was, he believed, that "we know nothing rightly, for want of perspective" ("Nature," 1844). In the right per- spective, although "a man is a little thing in the midst of the objects of nature, yet, by the moral quality radiating from his countenance he may abolish all considerations of magnitude" ("Manners"). This "moral quality" or "religious sentiment," this subjective power of Virtue, of Being, radiated from Emerson, abolishing magnitude, making nothing of bulk or size, far or near, because he was in truth the center and ground of nature. He quotes the "materialist" Condillac: "we never go out of ourselves; it is always our own thought that we perceive;" and adds, "what more could an idealist say?"[19] Empty space was nothing beyond Emerson; it was a flatness in his mind, merely a sensation of vastness-at-the-center-of-which-he-was.

This is not to say, however, that Emerson, in regard to his idealism in general, sought to eliminate nature (of which space is a part) in principle. The subject and object, the One and the Many, are interdependent. Creation, he held in distinction to Calvinism, is necessary. It is true that Emerson wrote that in revelation, nature withdraws before its god. But this is simply the process of getting priorities straight. When the ego, with the eyes of Reason, reads the divine text of nature correctly, that is, reads those "essences unchanged by man," the ego's "instinctive belief in the absolute existence of nature" is marred, and nature is seen to be amenable (as words are for a poet) to the saint's remodelling of matter into paradise. We must destroy the old world of fallen nature, which is the result of our distorted vision, to be able to create a new world. Emerson entitled <u>Nature</u>, <u>Nature</u>, because he wished to celebrate nature as <u>divine</u> art, the sacred text that for him replaced the Bible as an "objective" reference. He desired also to distinguish his position from that of supernaturalism which looks away from divine immanence. Of any other supposed reality beyond this world, he had only scorn: "Other world! There is no other world. God is one and omnipresent: here or nowhere is the whole fact."[20] In short, Emerson held that the object, although dependent on the subject, is necessary in his bi-polar monism of mind, and that harmony between the two exists, if at all, only here and now.

David Robinson argues that out of the "doctrines of the God within, Channing was able to

133

fashion a definition of religion as progressive moral activity of 'growing likeness to the Supreme Being'," but that this doctrine and this definition were fundamentally at odds: the doctrine of divine immanence implies perfection now, and the definition of religion as progressive implies perfection in the future. Furthermore, Robinson believes that this contradiction appears also in Emerson's thought, that in fact it "turned out to be Emerson's major dilemma--the Relation between progress and perfection," between the active will and the mystical experience.[21] As time went by, Robinson continues, Channing placed increasing emphasis on "energy, expansion, and growth," and Emerson, on the mystical Now.

There is no doubt that Channing loved the Infinite in time (and space) and that Emerson sought immediate salvation. In so far as they both spoke of spiritual progress, they meant (as Channing's seed-image suggests) the unfolding of potential spiritual attributes of the soul. But in fact Channing (rather inconsistently) conceived of this spiritual progress less in terms of the organic metaphor than in terms of linear or historic time. He was more interested in growing increasingly like the Father than in savoring his immanent divinity. His basic image of human nature, in spite of his seed image, is therefore not in organic terms but in familial and linear terms. He envisioned mankind to be a bundle of infant souls growing, according to the model of Jesus, in spiritual education, through historic time, in this world and in heaven, toward their parent and antitype, God. In contrast, Emerson conceived of "progress" to be manifested in terms of the self-contained teleology of the organic metaphor, as a bud flowering, as a circle widening from a center. "The soul's advances," he wrote in "The Over-Soul," "are not made by gradation, such as can be represented by motion in a straight line, but rather by ascension of state, such as can be represented by metamorphosis --from the egg to the worm, from the worm to the fly." Historic time, in which Jesus was embedded and the future abstract, was of secondary interest; all of God is Now. Emerson speaks to the individual of immediate salvation; Channing, to a community of souls about the perfect life to be.[22]

Furthermore, it is quite true, as I have pointed out and as Robinson states, that Emerson recognized that "the experience of mystical timelessness could not be summoned at will . . . which implied that the experience was the product of a will separate from his own, and therefore beyond his control." But that this recognition by Emerson marks a loss of "self-reliance" and shows a clear affinity with the [Calvinistic] doctrines of elect but irresistible grace," as Robinson believes, is not as evident. Channing, in his rationalistic supernaturalism, placed emphasis on the free-will of the individual ego. Emerson, by positing the Over-Soul as the universal "Unconscious," by blending the individual consciousness and will with God, placed the center of action and of reality beyond the individual ego. Indeed, Emerson based the existence of all creation on the immediate action of the divine. In a passage reminiscent of Edwards, he wrote that God is "One without whom no man or beast or nature subsists; one who is the life of things, & from whose creative will our life and the life of all creatures flows every moment, wave after wave, like the successive beams that every moment issue from the Sun. Such is God, or he is nothing. What is God but the Soul at the centre by which all things are what they are, & so our existence is proof of his?"[23] Even though Channing might not have denied this statement, he stressed the independence of the ego-will from the will of God. Emerson, by fusing God and man, retained the Calvinistic sense of divine immediacy that he felt Unitarianism, in its rationalism, had lost; and eliminated the ultimate ethical arbitrariness of the Calvinistic god, on which the doctrine of election was based. On the other hand, Emerson argued (although the openness of his universe narrowed as he aged) that man, the finite incarnation of the Over-Soul, controls to some degree, on the level of the Understanding, the world in which he lives. As ego, however, man can only prepare himself psychologically, read nature, and wait passively for the revelatory voices of the Greater Self, the Universal unconscious. These voices ultimately confirm self-reliance.

In his philosophy of persons, Channing sought "the reciprocation of the human and divine, preserving the unity of substance without confounding

135

the distinction of personality."[24] God is immanent in each individual person in terms of universal attributes. Yet Channing, although standing in theory and in character against all forms of pantheism, made himself a few statements that border on religious monism. He wrote: "We are known more interiorily by Him, than we are known to ourselves. Moment by moment, the Loving God sustains us."[25] "I am persuaded by his agency . . . . Through Him am I this instant thinking, feeling, and speaking."[26] Perhaps these statements express more Channing's lingering feeling for the old sovereignty of God than his dangerous attraction to the new pantheism of Emerson. Or perhaps he, like many deeply religious people, felt, at one time or another, so close to what he believed to be the divine presence, that he seemed to lose his identity. Whatever the reason, the above statements, like his few passages of apparent nature-mysticism, are not characteristic of his thought. We are told that he used the term "Father" to refer to God, instead of the terms "Unity" or "Trinity," to make the universal less abstract.[27] In doing so, he chose a personalistic term that reenforced his belief in the distinction between God and man. In spite of his gestures toward pantheism, in spite of his mystically inclined nature passages, Channing, once again, "was nothing, if not ethical."[28] "Goodness cannot be given" anymore than can depravity.[29] He insisted above all on the integrity of the human will; personal identity consisted in the character or moral quality of a person determined by the independent will of that person. "Our own will," he said, "seems to work out our welfare."[30] Each human being is a discrete unit: "the thinking, feeling, willing Principle within remains One, underived and indivisible Essence."[31] A person is "a recipient, a partaker" of the nature of God, as a child is of the nature of his parents. But the "indivisible" essence of a person is not identical, as it was for Emerson, with the divine essence.

Finally, Emerson used Channing's phrases, "Father of Spirits" and "Father of all Spirits" only, so far as I have been able to determine, in his sermon, "Consolation for the Mourner." This sermon was delivered February 20, 1831, twelve days after Ellen Tucker died. In it the heart-stricken man assumed personal immortality, a position he later abandoned, if he were not already doing so. Apparently Emerson reverted, during this time of intense loss of his first love, to Channing's serene faith in persons and in everlasting life. Indeed, this speculation is all but proved true when one returns to Emerson's letters and discovers that on the day Ellen died, he wrote Aunt Mary Moody: "I do not know but it is true that I have never known a person in the world in whose separate existence as a soul I could so readily & fully believe."[32] This statement read another way suggests that Emerson had already commenced, when Ellen died, to question the substantial reality of persons and the outer world; that he was already beginning to set up defenses against the threat to his personal uniqueness; that even she whom he nearly idolized was, finally, only phenomenal; that in fact "the soul knows no persons."[33] Perhaps he was able to recuperate from her death, from the deaths of his brothers, from that of Waldo, from his own haunting illnesses, because he learned how to diminish nature of first-class reality. His subjective idealism was at once a defense mechanism, a tool to build with, a weapon for self-reliance. He used it to weaken the world so that he could conquer death and re-build the world. Tactics are all.[34]

FOOTNOTES

[1] _A History of Philosophy_, VII, part 1, p. 41.

[2] _Analogy of Religion_ (1736; rpt. New York: Ungar, 1961), p. 23.

[3] _Memoir of William Ellery Channing_ (Boston, 1851), II, 218.

[4] _The Journals of Ralph Waldo Emerson_, ed. Edward Waldo Emerson and Waldo Emerson Forbes, 10 vols. Centenary Edition (Boston: Houghton Mifflin, 1910-1914), I, 290-1.

[5] _The Transcendentalists_ (Cambridge: Harvard University Press, 1950), p. 22.

[6] Henry Whitney Bellows, _William Ellery Channing_ (New York, 1880), p. 10.

[7] _The Perfect Life_ (London, 1888), p. 172.

[8] _The Works of William E. Channing, D. D._ (Boston, 1886), p. I.

[9] Elizabeth Palmer Peabody, _Rev. Wm. Ellery Channing, D. D._ (Boston, 1880), pp. 198-99.

[10] _Memoir_, I, 77.

[11] _Memoir_, II, 203.

[12] _Memoir_, II, 430.

[13] In discussing the relative priorities Emerson gives to mind and matter (based on fundamental assumptions of his religious stance), B.L. Packer writes that Emerson "seems to suggest that natural phenomena are somehow being extruded through us like tooth-paste--or, as Burke prefers to put it, like offal" (_Emerson's Fall_ [New York: Continuum, 1982], p. 58; and Burke, "I, Eye, Ay--Emerson's Early Essay 'Nature:' Thoughts on the Machinery of Transcendence," in _Transcendentalism and Its Legacy_, ed. by Myron Simon and Thornton H. Parson [Ann Arbor: University of Michigan Press, 1969], p. 20). But Packer and Burke know very well that their

metaphors destroy the spirit of the poem; that they are not even good translations. Although Emerson was Victorian in his attitude toward sex (almost unforgivably so in respect to Whitman), he embraced the common, the familiar, the low, all those essences of nature unchanged by man as the living art of the creative Over-Soul. Suggestions, however brilliant, that Emerson was neurotic in his philosophic priorities are merely potshots in the endless scuffle between naturalists and idealists.

[14] A. E. Burtt, The Metaphysical Foundations of Modern Science (New York: Doubleday, 1954), pp. 234-39.

[15] William Ellery Channing, "Treatise on Man:" A Study and Transcript of William Ellery Channing's Unfinished Treatise on Man. Dissertation. Meadville Theological School. By Morton de-Corcy Nachlas, Chicago, 1942. Page 9.

[16] The Perfect Life, p. 101.

[17] This bracketed passage is echoed in a much later sermon, "The True End of Life;" and the phrase at the end of this passage, the "Mighty enchanter," i.e., the human mind, is echoed specifically in The Treatise on Man: "Nature by impulses on the organs of sense invites the mind to pour forth her boundless treasures, and obedient to the summons the mighty enchantress sheds over the moist heaven and earth, spring, and autumn, cloud and ocean, a profusion of beauty which she cannot herself comprehend" (p. 9). Since signs of this bracketed passage, and in fact of the entire sermon, are found in later writings of Channing, and since the sermon was written right after his visit with Wordsworth, one concludes again that this visit helped Channing to crystalize his philosophy.

[18] The Journals and Miscellaneous Notebooks of Ralph Waldo Emerson, ed. William H. Gilman et al (Cambridge, Massachusetts: Harvard University Press, 1960-), IV, 26.

[19] "The Transcendentalist."

[20] "The Sovereignty of Ethics."

[21] "The Legacy of Channing: Culture as a Religious Category in New England Thought," _Harvard Theological Review_, 74:2 (1981), 221-239.

[22] Tension seems to exist between the ideas of the organic metaphor and true creativity. If evolution, history, and biography, are simply the unfolding realizations of what is already potential in the seed, how can mankind be truly creative? How can the self-enclosed teleology of the organic metaphor be anything but closed? Does Emerson hold that the organic process is open-ended, with all that that implies?

[23] _Journal_ (1960), IV, 33.

[24] Peabody, p. 309.

[25] The _Perfect Life_, p. 53.

[26] The _Perfect Life_, p. 54.

[27] Peabody, pp. 69-70.

[28] John White Chadwick, _Old and New Unitarian Belief_ (Boston, 1894), p. 59.

[29] The _Perfect Life_, p. 80.

[30] The _Perfect Life_, p. 80.

[31] The _Perfect Life_, p. 63.

[32] The _Letters of Ralph Waldo Emerson_, ed. Ralph L. Rusk (New York: Columbia University Press, 1939), I, 318.

[33] "Divinity School Address."

[34] Herbert W. Schneider, in his revision of his early evaluation of Emerson, writes that Emerson's

> conception of the ego, though central, is not transcendental. It is the empirical focus of the world of intentions and final causes. His seeing of all things in personal perspective is not a mental structure that is imposed on an alien world; it is a thoroughly practical philosophy, the ideology of Emerson's self-

reliance. His building of his own world in poetic imagination is at the same time his practical appropriation of the real world. He is not interested in the formal essence of objects; he is intent on the world's meaning for him. . . . The whole effort of such an analysis of the world aims at making the individual at home in the world, well-disciplined for both thought and action, or rather for a type of reflection that integrates existential and mental relations" ("American Transcendentalism's Escape from Phenomenology," in Transcendentalism and Its Legacy, p. 218). This passage highlights Emerson's existential Transcendentalism in relation to Channing's rationalistic supernaturalism.

FATHER OF SPIRITS (1823)

by William Ellery Channing, Sr.

God is manifested in his works. His perfections become visible by their operation and
effects. We know him by the beings he has created,
by the purposes for which he made them, and by his
methods of accomplishing his ends. On this account
the knowledge of creation, especially of the highest, noblest spirits, is important, for in these as
in a mirror, we see the image, expression, reflected
glory of their author.

The creation may be divided into two great
provinces or regions, the spiritual and the material, both closely connected with, yet immeasurably
different from, each other. They both surpass our
comprehension, existing in extent, in vastness,
although in this respect as in every other, we have
reason to suppose that the spiritual far exceeds the
material, for the former is constantly enlarging
itself and receiving additions, whilst the latter
seems to preserve its original dimensions. Our
earth, for example, we have reason to suppose,
retains always the same portion of matter without
increases or diminutions, and the heavenly bodies,
though exhibiting some inexplicable changes, are
essentially the same as in all ages--whilst we know
that the great spiritual family is constantly
receiving new members, that the birth of every child
is the addition of a new and immortal intelligence
to the spiritual world. We know, that through the
principle of improvement, - that glorious distinction of mind from matter, - this universe of
mind in general is constantly enlarging itself, and
will spread and ascend and grow in splendor and
happiness through eternity.

It is the great glory of God that he is the
Father of Spirits, and in this light I wish to
discourse of him. To show this glory, I propose to
consider the greatness of the only Spirit with which
we are acquainted, I mean the human mind, perhaps
the lowest intelligent being in the creation, yet
fitted to give us magnificent conceptions of the

spiritual world. My object in this is not only to set forth the glory of the great spiritual father, but to impress on you and myself the important truth, that each of us, in possessing a soul, possesses an infinite treasure, has an infinite trust and duty of enquiry into its condition and prospects, the growth and salvation of our spiritual nature.

Many men and perhaps the majority are so far creatures of sense that they are more struck with the content and glory of the material than the spiritual system, more impressed with matter than mind, and think that more of God's greatness may be seen in the former, that the outward universe is only a habitation [or] palace of art. It is indeed a splendid palace, but splendor is lavished on it only for the sake of its illustrious inhabitants. The stars, lighted up in infinite space, are but lamps for the awe, and guidance of the soul. Mind is the great end of God, his true offspring and representative, to which all nature is a minister, for whom suns shine, seasons revolve, and the Heavens are spread out in a volume, and which is to endure though the earth be shaken, and the heavens grow old and pass away.

At present however we know only our own spirits, and these are in their infancy, imprisoned in frail bodies with which they constantly sympathize. And still more, they are passing through a solemn probation, engaged in a fearful conflict with flesh and the world, in which the glory and power of their spiritual nature are often mournfully obscured. Yet to a reflecting man, the human spirit, even in its present state, is a wonderful work, far superior to every thing around, a bright manifestation of God; and to this our attention will now be confined.

To perceive the greatness of the human mind, we must consider its connection with the material and spiritual worlds, must consider how vast, I might say, how immeasurable its capacities are of receiving from both [worlds] knowledge, goodness, and happiness, and of giving, communicating to both in return. First, its comprehension and energy in regard to the outward creation indicates a noble nature. The vast universe it regards as its inheritance. It ranges from the immeasurably distant stars to the unorganized dust at our feet. Through every province of nature, through the earth, air, sea, the mineral, vegetable, animal kingdoms, not satisfying itself with superficial glances, but analyzing, comparing, bringing together scattered appearances, tracing likeness in seeming different operations, discriminating those which are most similar, and by these processes it has ascended from causes to effects, from particular facts to general principles, until it has gradually gathered the great outlines of the universe. Nature, you know, is not a place book, but [is] full of mysteries and apparent irregularities, its most important elements and operations being concealed. The first impressions which it makes [are] so often confused and erroneous that an unreflecting man quite mistakes the world in which he lives. But the mind, quickened by difficulty to patient watching and laborious experiment, has penetrated beneath the veil into the processes, purposes, and general laws of the creation, so as to discern every where a beautiful harmony, order, connection, and mutual influence, and subservience to the general weal. Not satisfied with enquiring into the parts of nature which minister to the comforts of life, it employs itself in measuring the orbits of the heavenly bodies, and in tracing the subtle invisible elements out of which all things are made, and not content with judging the present order of nature, it travels back to the beginning of the world, pierces the crust of the earth, scales its mountains, to gather the [secrets] of its formation and revolutions. The past acquisitions of the mind in natural knowledge, when joined with its unattainable thirst for new and wider views, with its impatience of any bounds of discovery which can be prescribed to it, plainly bespeaks a capacity which nothing created can fill, which is intended to spread itself forever through the immeasurable universe. It is truly astonishing that in one mind, and one which began to think but a few years ago, such vast and distant regions of the creation as the earth and heavens should be comprehended. The activity too with which the mind traverses this extent, sending its thoughts with a speed which mocks the lightning, from land to land, from age to age, from world to world, is another fact which would amaze us were it less common. The strong grasp too which it takes of these objects, by which it identifies them with itself, and can recall them at pleasure for improvement or qualification, is another indication of greatness. It acquires a property in what it has seen and thought upon, incomparably higher and purer than men have in any worldly possession. It carries the universe, as it were, within itself. A spirit like Newton's, though immured in a dungeon, would still range through, inherit, and enjoy by the power of thought, the regions of the creation which it had before explored. Milton, blind and in darkness, still created with delight the scenes where nature's beauty had touched and melted, and its grandeur awed and swelled his soul; and in describing paradise, he saw a more glorious creation under a richer light than had ever been offered to the bodily eye. If great possessions constituted greatness, what are we to think of the mind, which becomes proprietor of whatever it meets and contemplates in its excursions through all the kingdoms of nature?

But as yet we have not considered the most interesting relation of the mind to the outward world. It is placed here not only to contemplate, to be a quiet learner, but to be an agent. It not only receives the idea or image of nature into itself but impresses itself on nature, turning its knowledge into action, and exerts wide and increasing influence on what surrounds it. It not only explores, but even combines, directs the laws of the creation, and armed with these energies, changes the face of the earth, and makes innumerable products of nature minister to human comfort and enjoyment. The body seems to have been made weak, that the power of mind might be made more conspicuous. It is surprising what empire the mind has gained over the material world, how by fire it subdues and moulds the metals into instruments of labour, and by these subdues the earth, and gives new and most various forms to its production, until in the progress of arts, vast regions become fruitful fields, and populous cities are erected, and the mud hut, which first offered scarcely a shelter from the elements, rises into a magnificent structure, and the ocean is made a path, and the [wind] becomes minister to our speed, and the stars of heaven our guides, and the most distant countries are linked together, and the harvests are brought to our very door. This power of mind over nature, being enlarged by every dis-

145

covery, cannot be limited. It has been multiplied indefinitely by the application of steam alone, and future ages will accomplish what once it would have been deemed insanity to suggest as lying within the reach of human agency. When I see the mind subjecting the elements, leaving traces of itself on so many regions, bending shapeless matter to so many ends, moulding it into so many useful forms, spreading enchantment and beauty with a few coarse materials over the blank canvas, and extracting forms of transcendent loveliness and grandeur from the stubborn rock, I am struck with its persevering, triumphant, inexhaustible energy; I can prescribe it no boundary; I am sure it is destined to accomplish great purposes in the creation.

[There is another view of the power of the mind over the material world, perhaps too refined to be understood by those not accustomed to reflect on such subjects, but which is true and very interesting. The glory, beauty, grandeur, which we admire in the material world, do not belong primarily to that world, but are the results of ideas connected with it by the mind, or rather are qualities of mind associated with it and suggested by it, so that what charm is in nature is spread over it by our own souls, and we create through that intellectual power called association the splendor and enchantment we enjoy. I may not be understood by all, and perhaps those accustomed to this train of thinking are not aware how much the mind furnishes from its own resources, and glorifies with its own excellencies the creation in which it dwells. (The mighty enchanter working unconsciously.)][1]

I have now spoken of the capacities of the soul in relation to the material universe, but in speaking of this, I have hardly touched on its true greatness, for in perceiving and acting on material nature it is employed on what is inferior to itself, converses with a lower kind of existence, meets nothing worthy to be its associate, and if confined to this, never develops its highest principle. Let us then proceed to our second great division, which is the relation of the mind to the spiritual universe. The proper object of mind is mind. The power of the soul in which its true dignity dwells is the power of knowing and acting on itself and

146

other souls, of discerning, pursuing, loving and enjoying spiritual excellencies, of ascending above all created mind to the first, supreme, all glorious mind, and of identifying itself, if I may so speak, by esteem, love, and self-consecration, with God and his spiritual family. The foundation of this high knowledge, action and happiness, is laid in the faculty of conscience, with which every man is gifted, which discerns and enjoins the right and the good, which commands and forbids as a sovereign, and sits as a judge and representative of God in the human breast, which can vent guilt with pangs of remorse which are faintly shadowed forth by the gnawing worm and devouring fire, or encourage sanity and virtue, by gentle, peace-instilling whispers, sweeter and more thrilling than the music of the spheres. Through this power, when enlightened by revelation, strengthened by obedience, and God's spirit, the mind attains, not merely to virtues which prevent [evil] demands, but to a refinement and exaltation of moral and religious sense, to a thirsting and striving for unspotted purity and self-sacrificing love, and inflexible rectitude and entire devotion to God, which however resisted and occasionally overbourne by sense and sin, shed a divine lustre round our nature, and indicate a being formed for perpetual moral progression. Such a mind may be said without exaggeration to become the proprietor and heir of the whole spiritual creation, still more than of the material, for it identifies itself by esteem, love, and sympathy with all good and improved beings. So numerous are these ties in the spiritual world, and so vigorous the circulation and diffusive tendency of virtue, that it is reasonable to believe that every being, who becomes capable by purity of receiving holy influences, will share in and be enriched by, and advanced by the improvements of every other purified spirit in the universe. This, I say, is not exaggeration. The truth is that all our conceptions on this subject are poor and mean. We never rise to the height of this great argument. We cannot indeed comprehend now the powers to be developed, the treasures to be gained by an immortal mind. To assist us, however, we have examples in our present imperfect state, of humans deeply smitten with the love of goodness and greatness. There have been those which have pressed toward perfection with an intenseness of desire, which danger, pain and death, could not relax; and

147

there are still those which glow with an unquench-
able ardor of admiration and love, as they read or
hear of tried and triumphant piety and virtue, or
anticipate a meeting with apostles and prophets, and
the just made perfect in Heaven. This I say takes
place in the human mind now, in its infancy, amidst
great imperfections, under the pressure and burdens
of this tempted and mortal life. Is there danger of
speaking of such a nature too thoroughly?

But the highest view of the mind, I have as yet
but suggested, and I approach it with a deep feeling
of my inability to do it justice. I refer to its
power of ascending above the world of matter and
spirit, to the first and infinite spirit. If there
be greatness in conceiving of great objects, if the
mind becomes sublime by the perception of and
feeling of sublimity, then how great is this human
soul, for it conceives and feels the infinite God.
It is capable of hearing and does hear the voices
with which nature through its vastness proclaims its
author, and understands the witness which the powers
and virtues of intelligent beings bear to their
spiritual source. That vast conception, infinity,
is a noble indication of human capacity, and design
of our nature. Amidst all man's degeneracy, follies
and crimes, we see that he was made for something
infinite, and that nothing below this can meet the
whole wants of his soul. In his very vices, we see
the insatiableness and craving of a soul, which this
world's possessions and pleasures cannot fill. We
see him striving to cheat himself [of] the idea of
something exhaustless and unlimited in the inferior
goods to which he gives his heart. The human mind
loves the infinite, loves it in the vast heaven, the
countless stars, and in boundless prospects of the
earth and ocean. It shows this love in its curiosity which, forsaking the old and familiar, presses
toward to the unknown, in its desperation to feign
character and joys of a purity and duration unknown
in this world, and in its admiration of men whose
affections are wide and overflowing, or whose genius
expatiates in untrodden and interminable fields of
thought. This is a view of the soul, inexpressibly
ennobling, that it tends towards the infinite, and
shows that it was made for him to whom only this
sublime attribute belongs.

I know not indeed what more can be said of any mind in any world than that it is capable of a living, profound, affectionate sentiment or conviction of God, - for this sentiment has in it the principles of everlasting spiritual growth. It is the germ of an infinite thought, for it gains strength and brightness and extension from every new disclosure of nature and providence, there being through the whole extent the manifestation of the divinity. Besides this sentiment, this thought of God when it lives and grows in us has always a transforming, assimilating power, so that the mind in perceiving him, becomes a recipient, a partaker of his nature, imbibing his disposition, and moral perfections, and adopting as its own his vast and beneficent purposes, and thus returning itself to him by the strong bonds of likeness, affinity, and sympathy. The splendour, vastness, happiness, to which such a mind must attain in an existence of constant progress, and perpetual approximation to its infinite source, we can only express by saying that it passeth understanding.

I have spoken of the power which the mind has of perceiving, understanding the spiritual world; but I ought to add here as under the first head, it is made not only to perceive other minds and to be acted upon, but to act and make large communication in return. The power of soul over soul is vastly greater and nobler than over the material creation. We belong to a social system, the great object of which is that intelligent beings should give themselves to one another. The mind has the power of bringing forth and imparting all its possessions, and the agency of a single mind is often vast and astonishing. A man of highly gifted intellect, confined to his closet, sends forth thoughts which electrify both continents, and influences the capacity to improve the human race. Nor is this all, - many a great mind which lived ages ago has through writing and history acted on all future ages, and whilst empires have fallen, its domain has continued and enlarged, so that we now derive spiritual life, light, heat from the flames that burnt in a soul which existed thousands of years before our birth. The light of intellect beams over the tracts of ages and flashes across oceans, and never grows dim. Who does not know the power which mind may exercise over mind[?] Who of us has not

149

been absorbed by the writings or discourses of such a gifted intellect, and been conscious of new powers of thought and feeling under its quickening agency[?] Let us not forget that this intellect is not a prodigy, but a spirit which has just begun to exist and improve and made such small advances that we shall all of us one day look down upon its acquisitions and eloquence which now astonish, as on the imperfect conceptions and lispings of infancy. If such then be the influence of mind on mind in its earliest stages of being, what must it be in that state where spiritual bonds and connections are infinitely more multiplied and stronger than on earth. How literally may Christ's words be fulfilled, that a righteous soul shall shine as the sun in the kingdom of God.

My Friends, I have been obliged to omit many interesting views, for want of time, - but enough has been said, I trust, to give some conception of the greatness of the human spirit. The instructions to be derived from these views are various and important. We learn from them the glory of God, the Father of all spirits. We learn the reason or ground of the expansive and wonderful method he has employed for the redemption of the human soul, for we see that the soul is great enough for the interpretation of the love of God. But these topics I must defer. I will only say, learn my friends to think reverently of your minds. Feel that no ruin throughout the universe is so mournful and awful as the ruin of the soul. Beware of spiritual suicide. Do not quench the light of heaven in you by intemperance or any excess. Do not dissipate and waste your minds on a life of pleasure or amusement. Do not bury them in low, worldly cares. Do not sever them from God, the true life. Feel that they were made to be his temples, and by prayer and watching and labour for purity and virtue, invite him to enter and make them his everlasting abodes.

Federal Street, Nov. 1823

FOOTNOTES

[1] In the margin, Channing wrote: "This paragraph omitted as too refined."

HAWTHORNE: CALVINISTIC HUMANISM

"We belong to a social system, the great object
of which is that intelligent beings should give
themselves to one another."
                              "Father of Spirits"

"There is a wisdom that is woe; but there is
woe that is madness."
                              Ishmael ("The Try-Works")

I

In spite of his dark temperment, Nathaniel
Hawthorne did not believe in human depravity, at
least as it was defined by Jonathan Edwards: "the
prevailing effectual tendency" of all mankind to do
evil, "a propensity in all to sin immediately . . .
continually and progressively."[1] Nor strictly
speaking did he believe in inherited guilt. He
would not have agreed with Edwards that "there is no
reason can be brought, why one man's sin can't be
justly reckoned to another's account, who was not
then in being."[2] Hawthorne did not condemn
anyone, especially a newborn child, even though a
Pyncheon, to eternal punishment. However he did not
deny that a person inherits the consequences of good
and bad choices of preceding generations. The theme
of The House of the Seven Gables is that a bad act
of one generation, like a seed, darkly blossoms in
following generations, a sound sociological conclusion. Hawthorne meant by inherited guilt no more
than what Emerson meant by "sin" in "Heroism:"

Life is a festival only to the wise. Seen from
the nook and chimney-side of prudence, it wears
a ragged and dangerous front. The violations
of the laws of nature by our predecessors and
our contemporaries are punished in us also.
The disease and deformity around us certify the
infractions of natural, intellectual and moral
laws, and often violation on violation to breed
such compound misery. A lockjaw that bends a
man's head back to his heels; hydrophobia that
makes him bark at his wife and babes; insanity
that makes him eat grass; war, plague, cholera,

famine, indicate a certain ferocity in nature, which, as it had its inlet by human crime, must have its outlet by human suffering. Unhappily no man exists who was not in his own person become to some amount a stockholder in the sin, and so made himself liable to share in the expiration.

Roderick in "Egotism" says that his snake is a "family pecularity" but adds that "I have no faith in this idea of the snake's being a heirloom. He is my own snake, and no man's else's." Neither Emerson nor Hawthorne believed that we today deserve eternal damnation because our ancestors were limited human beings, like ourselves. They agreed, however, that we inherit psychological and environmental conditions that incline us to evil.

In "The Custom-House" Hawthorne half-facetiously stated that he, the representative of his Puritan ancestors, "hereby take shame upon myself for their sakes, and pray that any curse incurred by them --as I have heard, and as the dreary and unprosperous condition of the race, for many a long year back, would argue to exist--may be now and henceforth removed." Hawthorne transfers his ancestor's guilt for their crimes onto himself, and hopes that, by this act, the curse will be removed. But he does not ask God to forgive his ancestors; the curse is sociological, given by narrow-minded men, to be forgiven, if at all, by enlightened descendents, like Hawthorne, who realize how fallible and wrong-headed mankind can be.

After seeing the wretched condition of the children in the London slums, Hawthorne concluded that "the whole question of eternity is staked here. If a single one of those helpless little ones be lost, the world is lost!"[3] In fact, one of these children reminded him that he himself was, in some sense, responsible for "all the sufferings and misdemeanors of the world," and that that child was "the offspring of a brother's iniquity being his own blood-relation, and guilt, likewise, a burden on him, unless he expiated it by better deeds" (VII, 353). These statements are not Calvinistic; they are protests over social conditions and exclamations of hope that compensation for suffering somehow exists. Hawthorne felt that people are too dominated by circumstances to be held as responsible for evil as the Calvinists believed. He meant by these statements, on the one hand, that no man is an island; that responsibility of all for the miserable condition of some is so heavy that it may be likened to Calvinistic guilt; that people commit a sin of omission when they do not vicariously identity with the downtrodden, have pity, mercy, forgiveness. He meant, on the other hand, that even were the world to become paradise today, the suffering of those who lived yesterday and who cannot share this paradise, must be accounted for or absolute Justice does not exist, and eternity is lost. These statements belong to a world that is pathetic but without metaphysical guilt; they express hope for eventual compensation, and presume mankind essentially innocent and capable of good works.

Indeed, Hawthorne, further manifesting the ethical liberalism of the time, and in sharp contrast to Edwards, believed that probably people are neither good nor bad in essence, that perhaps they retain, although buried under layers of sorrow and illusion, an original Adamic essence.[4] "It is the credit of human nature," he wrote in The Scarlet Letter, "that, except where its selfishness is brought into play, it loves more readily than it hates" ("Another View of Hester"). Dimmesdale's "guilty sorrow, hidden from the world" would have been "pitied and forgiven" by the world's "great heart" ("The Interior of a Heart"). Even in the London slums he saw "the bright, intelligent merry face of a child whose dark eyes gleamed with vivacious expression through the dirt that incrusted is skin, like sunshine struggling through a very dusty window pane" (VII, 339). "The earthliest human soul," he wrote, "has an infinite spiritual capacity and may contain the better world within its depths" ("The Old Manse"). "If we would know what heaven is before we come thither," he stated, "let us retire into the depths of our own spirits, and we shall find it there among holy thoughts and feelings" (IX, 244-45). Hawthorne's affirmations, often faint, were as much a part of who he was, and what his art is, as were his exclamations of gloom.

His artistic sensitivity to the complexities and ambiguities of secret sin were underlaid by ordinary humaneness and tinted by cosmic, if not worldly, optimism. His faith in human affection, his hope for universal justice, his denial of absolute evil, complement and balance his dark temperment and scepticism of the possibility of metaphysical knowledge.

In his notebook in 1842, Hawthorne jotted down the following metaphor:

> The human heart to be allegorized as a cavern; at the entrance there is sunshine, and flowers growing about it. You step within, but a short distance, and begin to find yourself surrounded with a terrible gloom, and monsters of diverse kinds; it seems like Hell itself. You are bewildered, and wander long without hope. At last a light strikes upon you. You peep towards it, and find yourself in a region that seems, in some sort, to reproduce the flowers and sunny beauty of the entrance, but all perfect. These are the depths of the heart, or of human nature, bright and peaceful; the gloom and terror may lie deep; but deeper still is the eternal beauty.[5]

But two years later Hawthorne published "Earth's Holocaust" in which the narrator sees the human heart as a "foul cavern" "wherein existed the original wrong of which the crime and misery of this outward world were merely types." On the surface these statements seem to conflict; but not sur- prisingly the narrator of the "Holocuast" modifies his statement about "the evil principle" in the Heart with the phrase, "If true it were." He then proceeds to tell us that since the Head is not capable of purifying the Heart, the Heart must purify itself. He does not ask God for help; he is too humanistic and sceptical of the relevance of whatever deity there may be. He means that mankind cannot save itself by reason, only by human af- fection. But whether or not mankind will save itself, he does not say. He denied that the Heart is evil in essence but was non-committal about the destiny of mankind.

Moreover Hawthorne, like many of his liberal religious friends, believed that men do not deserve absolute punishment for the simple reason that, although free, their capacity for wisdom is extremely limited. Jonathan Edwards argued that "moral inability is as absolute as natural inability;" and Dr. Channing, that "to suppose that He punishes us for . . . an inability seated in the will, is just as absurd as to suppose him to punish us for a weakness of sight or of limb."[6] Hawthorne felt mankind too controlled by causes beyond the conscious will to be responsible completely for its actions; and thus, incidentally, he was more interested in the consequences than the motivations of wrong-doing. In other words, he preferred to see mankind within a liberal, humanistic context than a Calvinistic one.

Emerson wrote in "Experience" that "the intellect names it [sin] shade, absence of light, and no essence. The conscience must feel its essence, essential evil. This it is not; it has objective existence but not subjective." Hawthorne, not a philosophic idealist like Emerson but a "moral" writer more in the tradition of the Scotch Common Sense School of Philosophy, would have reversed this statement to read that evil has subjective but no objective existence. But both men agreed that evil is not metaphysical.

In high Edwardsean style, Hawthorne intoned in "The Haunted Mind" of "the guilty hour," "this nightmare of the soul, this heavy, heavy sinking of the spirits; this wintry gloom about the heart; this distinct horror of the mind blending itself with the darkness." But again, Hawthorne, although not agreeing with Emerson that the unconscious depth of the mind is surely haunted by deity, was not a Calvinist. He observed in 1840 that "Lights and shadows are continually flitting across my inward sky. . . . It is dangerous to look too minutely into such phenomena. It is apt to create a substance where at first there was a mere shadow" (IX, 219). He believed that the Puritans, Reverend Hooper, Catherine in "The Gentle Boy," Miriam in The Marble Faun, all his victims of blackness, like Ahab in Moby Dick, looked "too long in the face of the fire," turned their backs "to the compass" of the human Heart, and created in themselves a substance

156

where there is only shadow.[7] When he wrote "sin,"
he meant a problem of the human Heart or psyche, not
a mystery of God.

Deliberate ambiguity about the origin and
nature of moral evil occurs throughout Hawthorne's
works because of his orthodox terminology. He used
terms like "sin," "imperfection," "guilt," to
intensify his fiction. Associated with the agon-
izing theology of the Puritans, these terms intensify his fiction and suggest that the limitations
of mortality are due to an ancient generic crime by
mankind against God; they imply that what we human
beings are is somehow cosmically wrong. Hawthorne
obviously weighed with great seriousness this
possibility. But again, he did not claim that this
theory is true or even probable. The doctrine of
Original Sin is, after all, an hypothesis, not a
fact, and he sought the existential truth of human
nature. For another reason, the doctrine unjustly
blames mankind who, as John Locke said, could not be
blamed for what it cannot remember, if in fact there
is anything to remember that could explain the moral
condition of mankind. Hawthorne speculated about
different proposed answers to the cause of mankind's
limitations--why he dies, why he is subject to pain
and sorrow, why he commits crime--but he had no
definitive answer.

If Herman Melville, in his famous review of
Hawthorne's _Mosses_ _from_ _an_ _Old_ _Manse_, meant by the
phrase, "Something, somehow like Original Sin," that
Hawthorne believed in absolute human depravity, he
was wrong. If he meant that Hawthorne held that we
inherit physical and psychological conditions that
incline, not determine, us to commit acts of evil,
he was of course correct. Hawthorne might even have
agreed that a person may respond to situations from
some modifiable genetic base. He wrote in _The_
Scarlet _Letter_ that "the whole system of society is
to be torn down, and built up anew. Then, the very
nature of the opposite sex, or its long hereditary
habit, which has become like nature, is to be
essentially modified, before women can be allowed to
assume what seems a fair and suitable position"
("Another View of Hester").

Now the above distinctions about human nature
are not without differences. They are distinctions

157

between a philosophy like Calvinism and philosophies that admit the darkness of mankind but believe that this darkness is not the essence of mankind and that it can be in theory worked out by mankind. Worlds apart are the medieval belief that all men are depraved because one man long ago disobeyed God, and that God sustains this depravity; and the liberal belief that men, in essence either good or morally neutral, are in practice morally imperfect because they unavoidably have only limited wisdom.

II

Although Hawthorne did not believe in the doctrine of Original Sin, he felt that a true appreciation of human nature includes a recognition of its dark propensities. In fact, he held that one cannot live a normal life unless he makes this acknowledgement. For example, Young Goodman Brown, in a desperate effort to save himself and his young wife, Faith, from being initiated into the knowledge of human nature, cries out, "Faith! Faith! . . . look up to heaven and resist the wicked one." He did precisely the wrong thing (whether or not his experience was a dream). He should have joined the fraternity of sinners, and accepted the fact that he, like them, sought the forest at night. He would have been able, then, in the daylight of common-sense, to have understood his neighbors, to have sympathized with, pitied, and even forgiven them. Ironically he falls because he refuses to accept his fall; he remains young because he never morally matures. There are two kinds of faith in the tale: Brown's faith in "heaven" which is his private belief in his own ethical superiority that damns his townsmen; and Brown's wife who stands for a faith in humanity that is deep and strong because it is based in part on the full recognition that all people, including herself, are fallible. This is the kind of faith, Hawthorne tells us, that can lead one to whatever salvation there is on earth. Since Brown does not understand this, he distrusts everyone, the creation in general, and dies an unhappy man.

Likewise, Aylmer in "The Birthmark" cannot accept the truth of human nature. The tragedy of this tale is not Georgianna's "liability to sin, sorrow, decay and death" but Aylmer's "sombre imagination" (the underside of his fanatic idealism) that renders the birthmark a "frightful object." He blackens in hateful entity characteristics of mortality not necessarily evil in themselves. Aylmer denies the very definition of mankind, and imposes upon his wife private plans or "ideals" inappropriate to humanity. Her birthmark is a sign of imperfection only from his own un-realistic ideal point of view. The "swains," on the other hand, adore it as a beauty-mark of her humanness and sexuality. The weight of the theme of this tale is not on human depravity as such; it is on Aylmer's failure to accept the integrity of our very nature, and on his fanatical efforts to "improve" it at the cost of another human being.

This is not to say that Hawthorne discarded idealism or the refusal to accept human nature as it is now. Georgianna, although gullible to some degree to Aylmer's aspiration, praises him for it. The "actual" must be tempered by the ideal, the earth by intuitions of "heaven." But it must be tempered within the boundaries of given human nature. Aylmer, a man of the Head, not of the Heart, is like Catherine in "The Gentle Boy" who "violated the duties of the present life and the future, by fixing her attention wholly on the latter." He should have looked "beyond the shadowy scope of time, and living once for all in eternity, [found] the perfect future in the present." Thus true human affection (reality) consists in the right mixture of heaven and earth; it is not paradisiacal but composed of mature sorrow and joy. Although Aylmer and Georgianna fail in their love, Edgar and Edith in "The Maypole of Merrymount" from the moment they had "truly loved subjected themselves to earth's doom of care and sorrow, and troubled joy." The trick in improving this twilight world is to do so without violating the sanctity of the human heart, without compounding darknesses, without treating people as objects. Reformers must learn, Hawthorne discovered at Brook Farm, that principles are not to be placed above people. For Hawthorne, people are more important that "God."[8]

III

The Marble Faun, the last of Hawthorne's major
novels, is his definitive statement, as ethical
connoisseur, of his aesthetic appreciation of the
subtle interplay of light and shadow, of good and
evil, in human life. Like Kenyon who climbs the
Faun's tower high above the variegated landscape and
tries to grasp "without the aid of words" the
meaning of the panorama, Hawthorne, in the novel,
toured the history of man in the Italian context,
and produced a sophisticated but enigmatic picture
in which an absolute meaning of good and evil is
beyond the understanding of words.

In the Faun Hawthorne debates with himself
about two ways of looking at the role of evil in
human affairs, playing off against each other what
may be termed the Neoplatonic and the Augustinian
views of evil. He accepts totally neither view.
The former view, represented by Hilda, is that Good
is a priori; that evil is the absence of Good; and
that knowledge of evil is not necessary for moral
growth.⁹ In contrast to the simple, animal-like
Donatello from whom "we should expect no sacrifice
nor effort for an abstract cause," Hilda is divine
Goodness, principled Virtue. She exists in what
Milton (whose bust is in Kenyon's studio) called a
"state of rectitude," with a disposition to do what
is right "as being naturally good and holy."¹⁰
She believes that "precepts of Heaven are written
deepest within us," and her heart is "all purity and
rectitude." For her the (hypothetical) Fall of Man
was not fortunate.

Miriam, on the other hand, represents the
Augustinian view of evil. She believes that evil is
necessary for moral growth; that higher good arises
from a synthesis of evil and lower good. She also
concurs with Milton who also said that "it was
called the tree of knowledge of good and evil from
the event; for since Adam tasted it, we not only
know evil, but we know good only by means of evil.
For it is by evil that virtue is chiefly exercised,
and shines with greater brightness."¹¹ Miriam
argues that "the crime--in which he [Donatello] and
I were wedded--was . . . a blessing . . . a means of
education, bringing a simple and imperfect nature to

160

a point of feeling and intelligence which it could have reached under no other discipline." For Miriam, the Fall was fortunate.[12] Thus Hilda, representing an absolute view, argues that evil is not necessary; and Miriam, representing the relative view that may be grounded on an absolute view (Hawthorne was not sure), argues that evil is necessary for moral growth.

Since Hilda represents absolute Good not relative to evil, she expresses the corollary that when pure virtue acts in the world it is not polluted by the world. She asks, must "care for the spotlessness of our own garments keep us from pressing the guilty ones close to our hearts, wherein for the very reason that we are innocent, lies their securest refuge from further ill?" Her implicit answer is expressed by Plotinus who held that "There is no absolute depravity of the human will. . . . The descent of the soul into this world is no mere fall, because it is in harmony with the general cosmic design of the Creator. It is rather a mission entrusted to the soul." Following Plotinus, the Florentine Circle believed that "It is the privilege of the soul that in order to contemplate higher being it need not break violently away from lower being; and that, owing to the same primal impulse of love, it looks upward with faith and downward with care." "Here is shattered one of the fundamental presuppositions of Augustinian dogma, the doctrine of the incurable corruption of the will, which by the fall has been diverted and cut off from its source for all time."[13] In the Plotinian view, which Hilda represents, mankind need not know, nor be polluted by, evil to be Good.

These Neoplatonic views are woven into the variegated tapestry of Hawthorne's (Victorian and Transcendental) ethical imagination. In "Egotism," Rosina bends over Roderick "with the shadow of his anguish reflected in her countenance, yet so mingled with hope and unselfish love that all anguish seemed but an earthly shadow and a dream." Ilbrahim, in "The Gentle Boy," has "instinctive rectitude" and is a "gentle spirit [who] came down from heaven to teach his parent a true religion." Hilda, disagreeing with Miriam, holds that "there is no chasm, nor any hideous emptiness under our feet, except what the evil within us digs. If there be such a chasm,

161

let us bridge it over with good thoughts and deeds, and we shall tread safely to the other side. . . . As the evil of Rome was far more than its good, the whole commonwealth finally sank into it, indeed, but of no original necessity." For Hilda, only Good is real and has "original necessity." She, by Goodness alone, can "purify the objects of her regard by the mere act of turning such spotless eyes upon them."

Near the end of the novel, Kenyon states that "sin has educated Donatello, and elevated him;" and asks Hilda, "Is Sin, then . . . like sorrow, merely an element of human education, through which we struggle to a higher and purer state than we could otherwise have attained?" Hilda corrects Kenyon who has been confused by Miriam, and says definitely No. If Donatello had been educated by sin, then moral growth condones crime. And surely Hawthorne himself did not mean that; he denied in part through Hilda that such growth necessitates additional agony of mankind. He meant perhaps that the murder of the capuchin was the occasion, but not a necessary occasion, of the Faun's maturity and the growth of true affection between him and Miriam. His position seems to be that, given the way the world is, knowledge (not an act) of evil is necessary for moral growth and full participation in the human race--a commonsense conclusion. But he was not willing to say that there is a metaphysical fiat that the way the world is now is the way the world must be.

Most critics side with Miriam against Hilda and believe that Hawthorne in his heart did also. I agree. Miriam, with her explosive warmth and sophisticated sensitivity to "the reality of evil," is certainly the kind of person the twentieth century admires. Hawthorne's tales, as I have said, support the view that human beings are morally profound only by knowing of evil. He concurred with Milton who, although he wrote in Comus about a lady of rectitude, stated in Areopagitica that he could not "praise a fugitive and cloistered virtue." Yet Hawthorne firmly believed, as we have seen, that there is real danger in over-emphasizing the limitations or "imperfections" of human nature, of reading into these limitations metaphysical significance for which there is no evidence. Thus, in spite of his admiration for Miriam, he would not commit himself to the proposition that there must be a dialectic of good and evil. He weighs Miriam's affirmative qualities against her sordid ones, the obscure origin of which seems to be incestuous and cultural centricity. She has, like Satan in _Paradise Lost_, secret fits of madness; she is an accomplice to murder; a "self-painter" who doubts that "God sees and cares for us."[14] Her Hebraic temperment paralyzes her genuine creativity and ultimately exiles her from her lover and friends. Like Satan again, she suffers gradual decay, so that at the end of the novel she kneels under the "heathenish" eye of the Pantheon, "glides" away "without a greeting," and is exiled in "obscurity." In sum, Miriam, although the most human of the characters in the novel, nevertheless has a depth of blackness that Hawthorne, seeking a balance between extremes, could not accept. She is the actual flesh and warm humanity he was drawn to, the blackness and lack of faith in the ideal that he felt sick about. Kenyon not without reason admires her only from a distance.

But Hawthorne could not embrace Hilda either. Enlightened, sceptical, physically vigorous, he accepted as dogma neither the Neoplatonic nor the Augustinian view of evil. Hyatt Waggoner believes that Hilda is "Hawthorne's tribute to Sophia."[15] If so, it is a tribute with severe qualifications. Hilda is a "stainless maiden" who "is utterly sufficient to herself" and has "no need of love." She carries a "sharp steel sword" of justice, is "a terribly severe judge" who rejects Miriam with "involuntary repellent gestures." Too much a Realist in the old sense, she sacrifices people for principles; her nurtured innocence of evil is physically emasculating. We are told but are not convinced that she is eventually, by means of sorrow, "softened out of the chilliness of her virgin pride." Such statements are backhanded slaps at "maidens" and "angels" about whom, and about "holy love," Hawthorne had strong reservations. The above traits Hawthorne, with critical self-awareness, deliberately gave to Hilda.

Hawthorne, living in the actual, longing for the ideal, was suspended in tension between the two views of evil that Hilda and Miriam represent. On

the one hand, he would have agreed, for example,
with Frederic Hedge, his contemporary and a Transcendentalist, who believed that evil is "a necessary
condition of development and growth;" that evil is
"a necessary accompaniment of finite being; a
condition inherent in the act of creation; a con-
sequence resulting from the very limitations which
bound individual existence."[16]   On the other hand,
he would not discard the Hilda-Alcott hypothesis
that there may be some people who know Good without
knowing evil; and that these people evidence the
reality of a moral universe in which evil is not
necessary.[17]   In a passage in the Faun that seems
to sum up Hawthorne's dilemma, if not confusion,
about the mystery of good and evil, Kenyon says:
"Every life, if it ascends to truth or delves down
to reality, must undergo a similar change [to
Donatello's]; but sometimes, perhaps, the in-
struction comes without the sorrow, and often the
sorrow teaches no lesson that abides with us."   If
there is sense to this passage, it is that human
beings, if they mature morally, become aware of good
and evil (and choose good).   Some, like Donatello,
Miriam, Hester, Robin, become conscious of them
through sin and sorrow; others, like Hilda,
Ilbrahim, (Billy Budd), know them intuitively, or at
least do not need to know evil to know good; and
some, like Goodman Brown and Aylmer, learn nothing
at all from sin and sorrow.   In other words, the
philosophic answer to the question, Why does evil
exist? can be grasped, if at all, Hawthorne thought,
only "without the aid of words."

Kenyon's choice of Hilda over Miriam expresses
of course Hawthorne's belief in Absolute Good in
spite of the dark forests of the world that beckon
the human psyche.[18]   Kenyon meditates on "the
sepulchral darkness of the catacomb" from which he
found "no path emerging" and on his own finitude
among the crumbling "landmarks of time:"   "You
behold the obelisks, with their unintelligible
inscriptions, hinting at a past infinitely more
remote than history can define.   Your own life is as
nothing, when compared with that immeasurable
distance; but still you demand, none the less
earnestly, a gleam of sunshine, instead of a speck
of shadow, on the step or two that will bring you to
your quiet rest."   If Kenyon, by choosing "a gleam
of sunshine" over a warm-blooded shadow, fails to

become "a consummate artist," it is because Hawthorne believed that Kenyon with Hilda will more likely find "something dearer to him than his art . . . the greater strength of human affection."

The problem with Kenyon's choice is that the reader feels it to be more of the Head than of the Heart. The novel, however, is not a literary failure; it is an expression of a philosophic dilemma. It expresses perfectly the religious predicament that Hawthorne and much of his culture were in. He was torn between his faith in fading Absolutes and his sceptical humanism intensified by religious liberalism. Kenyon's choice of Hilda over Miriam is not simplistic nor sentimental. A careful reading of the novel, I have tried to show, reveals the genuine tensions in that considered choice. Although we today might be, Kenyon could not have been contented with the sensuous Miriam haunted by a dark past. Hawthorne needed, as his love letters to Spohia show, a domestic deity to counterbalance his profound tendency toward isolation and religious scepticism.[19]

IV

It is ironic that Hawthorne prepared his Mosses in the chamber of the Old Manse where Emerson had written Nature, a radical metaphysic that proclaims above all that a person can find reality by himself, apart from others. For Hawthorne, compassionate people, not God, are the salvation of mankind; love is more fulfilling than art. In "The Hall of Fantasy," for example, there are no lovers, only artists. The Hall, which will be "likely to endure longer than the most substantial structure that ever cumbered the earth," is a monument to the laudable awareness of the possibility of something higher than this world. But the Hall is not "eternal" nor alive; only people are who are in loving reciprocity. Love for Hawthorne is the living embodiment of the ideal and the actual, hints of heaven and tender understanding of the "fallen creature." Owen, the artist of the Beautiful, truly loves Annie but does not have his love reciprocated. Nevertheless his mechanized ideal, although shattered, is a spiritual achievement. Owen, like

165

Aylmer, is praised for his idealism; but both men would have been far happier if their love had been fulfilled. Had Owen "found Annie what he fancied, his lot would have been so rich in beauty that out of its mere redundancy he might have wrought the beautiful into many a worthier type than he had toiled for." An art object for Hawthorne is not a living fusion of the ideal and the actual, not a living Romance. It is, as Annie intuited of the butterfly, "spiritualized machinery," a symbolic arrow only. Only love is for its own sake, not art.[20]

But there are few fulfilled lovers in Hawthorne's tales. The many ways people fail to communicate and to love and the consequences of these failures is the dark theme of his work. Yet the pathetic rarity of affection did not negate for him the belief that it is the only viable ideal, the absolute standard, by which failures are judged. His tales are jeremiads in fiction in which tension is generated by pitting off the actual and the ideal, what people are against the implications of what they could be. His belief that people can be loving creatures stands in judgment behind his intricate examinations of the dusky layers of personality that surround the bright center of the human heart. Unfortunately, it is dubious, in spite of his praise of human affection, and in spite of his apparently successful marriage, that Hawthorne himself ever adequately realized the reality of that affection. The "magnetic chain of humanity" seems to have eluded him. Emerson, after attending Hawthorne's funeral, spoke of "the painful solitude of the man, which, I suppose, could no longer be endured, and he died of it."[21] It is ironic again that Emerson who preached solitude and supreme self-reliance lived a life far less lonely than Hawthorne who dreamed of human affection. As Emily Dickinson, an admirer of Emerson, said, "Success is counted sweetest/By those who ne'er succeed."

V

Henry James wrote that for Hawthorne, as for the Puritans, "the consciousness of _sin_ was the most

important fact of life."[22]   But it was not "sin"
that absorbed him; it was the secrecy and loneliness
of people.   Emerson once said to him, "We must get
rid of Christ;" and Hawthorne replied, "No, Mr.
Emerson, we cannot do without Christ," that is,
without understanding and forgiveness that are
essential for the endurance of the human race.[23]
Commenting on Michael Angelo's statue of Jesus,
Hawthorne thought it too hard, and asked "for at
least a little pity, some few regrets, and not such
a stern denunciatory spirit on the part of Him who
had thought us worth dying for."[24]   If Hawthorne
believed in a god, it was certainly not the puritan
god, nor the rational, educated Unitarian god.   It
was a catholic god of faith without Catholicism; it
was a god who asks for social openness, who sym-
pathizes, forgives, and offers hope to the hidden
and downcast, not for an earthly millenium but for
compensatory happiness somewhere beyond this world.
Hawthorne, like the liberal Unitarians, rejected
orthodox dogma, but he was sadly convinced that
human nature is pitiful, not necessarily perfectible
as Dr. Channing thought; in this sense, he was not a
humanist.

    "In the common use of the world," one critic
wrote, "Hawthorne was not a religious man; for he
rarely attended church, and he had no interest in
ecclesiastical formalities.   No man who has written
in this country, however, was more deeply influenced
than he by those spiritual ideas and traditions
which may be properly called Unitarian."[25]   In
some disagreement, F. O. Matthiessen stated that
Hawthorne "was like the Unitarians only in that he
shared Theodore Parker's concern to distinguish
between the transient and permanent in Christianity."[26]   In what sense was Hawthorne religious?
Certainly he was not religious in "the common sense
of the word."   In what sense was he Unitarian?   He
would not have accepted Parker's Absolute Religion
which was a Christian theism of deep social concern
and belief in the necessity of prayer.

    But without doubt the liberal religious views
of the day influenced Hawthorne's theological
thought and his philosophy of ethics.   The liberal
views permeated his intellectual and household
atmosphere.   To state the obvious: he knew personally Bronson Alcott, Emerson, Thoreau (his

best friend when he lived in Concord), James Freeman
Clarke (who officiated at his marriage and at his
funeral), George Ripley (at Brook Farm), Theodore
Parker (who doubted that Hawthorne "understood his
own genius or comprehended his philosophic meaning
of many of the circumstances or characters found in
his books"),[27] Margaret Fuller, Dr. Channing,
Reverend William Henry Channing (particularly when
Hawthorne was in England), Ellery Channing, and many
more of the radicals and liberals. His wife was an
active Christian Unitarian; her sister, Elizabeth
Peabody, was Dr. Channing's amanuensis, and
Hawthorne's long-time friend whom he may have at one
time courted.[28] It would be surprising indeed if
Hawthorne had not been influenced by the Trans-
cedental-Unitarian debates over the definitions of
God and man, over the existence of divine immanency,
over the role of ethics in religion, over the nature
of good and evil, over the emphasis to be placed on
this world and the next, and so on. The massive
Hawthornian criticism by scholars of this century
who have scorned the liberal tradition has tended to
cover-up Hawthorne's intimate and prolonged exposure
to religious liberalism. At the very least,
Hawthorne agreed with the liberals about negatives.
With them, he opposed Calvinistic theology and
ethics; and he agreed with Emerson and Thoreau in
denying the validity of religious formulations,
dogmas, and static symbolism. If Hawthorne did not
agree with the liberals about the nature of man (and
the degree of his disagreement, I have tried to
suggest, is open for discussion), he joined them in
holding that man, not God, is the center of attention; that all men are essentially equal in terms
of absolute moral standards; and that mankind does
not deserve eternal punishment.

"Despite occasional pious references to a
creator . . . there is little indication that
Hawthorne . . . has any concern with traditional
concepts of a god that is a personal, conscious
deity."[29] One goes too far, however, in calling
him an agnostic. Hawthorne wrote: "But God would
not have made the close so dark and wretched, if
there were nothing beyond; for then it would have
been a fiend that created us, and measured out our
existence, and not God. . . . So out of the very
bitterness of death, I gather the sweet assurance of
a better state of being."[30] Statements like this

are not, it seems to me, merely paying lip-service to the notion of an ultimately meaningful creation--if lip-service is defined to mean that Hawthorne thought one thing and said another. Without doubt, he did pay lip-service sometimes to conventional Christian beliefs. The critic must judge Hawthorne's religious stance, however, on the basis of all his work, not on just chosen statements. It is not easy for anyone to determine what he does and does not sub-consciously believe; and one is not sure whether or not Hawthorne himself knew exactly what he believed. Yet there is no convincing evidence that he had faith in an active deity; the concept of a personal god plays no positive role in any of his fiction or in his other writings. But his constant awareness of the strangeness of experience; his habit of positing a hypothetical state of higher existence, a state more than, and other than, an earthly millenium, implies that he assumed that mankind is not entirely of this world. He speculated, "our next state of existence, we may hope, will be more real,--that is to say, it may be only one remove from reality. But, as yet, we dwell in the shadow cast by time, which is itself the shadow cast by eternity."[31] Austin Warren writes that "While seriously concerned with human mysteries, Hawthorne found himself persistently attracted to the strictly supernatural as well."[32] "I find that my respect for clerical people, as such," Hawthorne wrote, "and my faith in the utility of their office, decreases daily. We certainly do need a new revelation--a new system--for there seems to be no life in the old one."[33] Hawthorne, like Emerson, Thoreau, and the radical Unitarians, objected to outmoded religious forms rather than to essential religious content.

Although he said that he wished that he could write more realistically, Hawthorne was by no means a Naturalist in temperment.[34] He was a Romancer whose imaginative life resided in a neutral territory between the actual and the ideal. This territory, although neutral, was not agnostic because Hawthorne, residing there, had made some kind of committment to something other than mortality and Naturalism. As Warren says, "By 'romance' . . . he means . . . the freedom to see men in the light of Eternity, to see the Supernatural surrounding the natural."[35]

Furthermore, even characters like Hilda, representing absolute value, cannot be psychoanalyzed away completely without doing irreparable damage to the tension in his fiction. They may beg Freudian analysis for critics today, but what they stand for in part cannot be cancelled unless the question of religion in Hawthorne in general is cancelled.[36]

Conservative in his evaluation of man, Hawthorne was, in relation to Calvinism, liberal in ethics because he sympathized with, pitied, and to a large extent forgave, mankind for its moral ills. Like the Unitarian liberals who held to a vague concept of deity, he believed in absolute moral values known intuitively: mankind has the "simple perception of what is right" ("The Old Manse"). He would have agreed, again, with Frederic Hedge who wrote: "I think we have abundant evidence of an original sense of moral obligation, a feeling of the difference between right and wrong . . . very imperfect, indeed, very crude . . . but not wholly dormant, not utterly inactive."[37] Moreover, he would have concurred with Hedge's philosophy of evil: "God has implanted no propensity in man which is evil in itself. . . . Every property with which he has endowed us is good in itself, and only by perversion and excess, in the absence of a moral and controlling power, productive of evil."[38] Hawthorne felt guilty about the children in the London slums because, although he would probably never see them again, he believed that he and they belonged to a moral whole. As Hilda said to Miriam, "While there is a single guilty person in the universe, each innocent one must feel his innocence tortured by that guilt." This may be a sentimental point of view, but it is precisely the position, as we have seen in a preceeding essay, of many liberal Unitarians during the nineteenth century. In no way was Hawthorne an ethical pluralist; he would not have held to a morality based on statistics.[39] He lived still within the framework of a faint monotheistic universe.

VI

In sum, Hawthorne appreciated the Calvinistic temperment toward evil but had too much sympathy and pity for mankind to structure his dark sensitivity with Calvinistic theology. His genius lay not in Italy but in Salem and Concord, among the ruins of Calvinistic abstractions that were still efficacious as artistic symbols. He shrank the Calvinistic hell to human psychology, and shifted the focus of the love of God to the love of human beings, believing that this love is the highest truth we can know. Thus unlike Emerson, he held that other persons are first-class reality; and like Channing that "we belong to a social system, the great object of which is that intelligent beings should give themselves to one another."[40] However Hawthorne had much less faith than Channing in a personal god, and consequently relationships among human beings for him took priority over any relationship with any god or with any absolute standard of value that excluded human beings from being of primary importance. In fact, he held that moral worth, on which "salvation" rests, is determined by a person's relation not to a god or to some inhuman ideal but to his fellow man. And these relations, Hawthorne felt, are man's responsibility; only we are responsible for our destiny: "Our welfare depends on ourselves" (IX, 124). "At the last day . . . man's only inexorable judge will be himself, and the punishment of his sins will be the perception of them" (X, 205).

Hawthorne believed that a person consists in two worlds, a soul and a body, and that he fulfills his nature by accepting his longing for a better and higher world and the limitations of mortality. On the one hand, a true human being does not forsake the faith that there is absolute moral value independent of evil; and on the other, he understands that "fallen" mankind knows good only by knowing evil. He acknowledges that he, like other fallen creatures, is liable to sin, sorrow, decay, and death. By making this acknowledgement, he is able to comprehend with the Heart the pathetic fallibility of all men and the moral necessity for compassion and mercy toward others. Hence he grows morally and is deserving of heaven by partaking in "fallen" or imperfection human nature. He is purified of evil thoughts and deeds through the virtues of compassion and mercy, and so can enter heaven with a truly "unspotted life."[41] For Hawthorne, then, not glorification of a sovereign god, not fanatical adherence to an "ideal" absolute that sacrifices human happiness, but compassion and mercy are the saving virtues. He was convinced that "what is wrong can be righted by nothing unless by love."[42]   His model was the human Christ, not the inhuman Jehovah, nor, for that matter, the impersonal Over-Soul.

Hawthorne complained in 1856 that Melville, "as he always does," reasoned "of Providence and futurity, and of everything else that lies beyond human ken."[43]   He wrote in "The Old Manse" that he admired Emerson as "a poet of deep beauty and austere tenderness, but sought nothing from him as a philosopher." He might have added that he sought nothing from anyone as a philosopher. Yet he owed much to the liberal tradition. It justified his rejection of religious ritual and dogma, and helped him, with its stress on humane ethics, to humanize his Calvinistic sensibility.[44]

FOOTNOTES

[1] *Original Sin*, ed. Clyde A. Holbrook (New Haven: Yale University Press, 1970), pp. 120 and 134.

[2] *Original Sin*, p. 410.

[3] *The Complete Works of Nathaniel Hawthorne*, ed. G. P. Lathrope (Boston, 1882-83), VII, 332. Hereafter references to the *Works* are incorporated into the text.

[4] Hawthorne defined "reality" in terms of value, and held on the one hand that harmonious relations among people is reality; that this reality, if anything does, foreshadows eternity; and on the other, that a lack of harmony among persons is experienced in terms of non-reality or illusion. He noted in 1840 that "Indeed, we are but shadows; we are not endowed with real life, and all that seems most real about us is but the thinnest substance of a dream,--till the heart be touched. That touch creates us,--then we begin to be,--thereby we are beings of reality and inheritors of eternity" (IX, 223). In 1842, the year of his marriage, he concluded that "all gloom is but a dream and a shadow, and that cheerfulness is the real truth" (IX, 315). As one approaches the top of the scale of value, through human affection, positive sympathy, "the magnetic chain of humanity," things become increasingly less illusory and more real. But as one descends through hate, pride, all sorts of mental abstractions, such as idealisms, that cut one off from people, things become increasingly distorted and shadowy.

In tale after tale, Hawthorne associated evil with illusion. The serpent in Roderick's breast "was but a dark fantasy, and what it typified was as shadowy as itself." Elizabeth considers how to withdraw Reverend Hooper from "so dark a fantasy, which, if it had no other meaning was perhaps a symptom of mental disease." Young Goodman Brown had a dream about going into the woods at night. In The Scarlet Letter, Hawthorne tells us that "it is the unspeakable misery of a life so false as his [Dimmesdale's] that it steals the pith and substance

out of whatever realities there are around us, and
which were meant by Heaven to be the spirit's joy
and nutriment. To the untrue man, the whole universe is false,--it is impalpable,--it shrinks to
nothing within his grasp. And he himself, in so far
as he shows himself in a false light, becomes a
shadow, or, indeed, ceases to exist" ("The Interior
of a Heart"). Hawthorne used terms like "illusion"
to give an accurate rendering of the texture of the
experience of evil, and to counteract a false
metaphysics of evil.

In other words, Hawthorne did not believed in
the devil, nor in active evil outside of mankind,
nor in evil in man sustained by the will of God from
generation to generation. For example, we are not
to ask on one level if Goodman Brown's experience in
the woods was "an actual Satanic experience or a
dream" (Q. D. Leavis, "Hawthorne as Poet," in
Hawthorne: A Collection of Critical Essays, ed. A.
N. Kaul [New Jersey: Prentice-Hall, 1966], p. 37).
No matter what the metaphysical status of his
experience, it severely affects him. But the
narrator himself raises the question about the
reality-status of that experience, and does so in a
way that does not call into question either the plot
or the texture of that experience. That is to say,
the question is not relevant to the plot or to the
character development in the story. It is a question asked by the narrator about the ontology of
Brown's experience. The evil Brown encounters, on
Hawthorne's scale of reality, is "actual" from the
low perspective and nothing from the absolute
perspective--just as for Emerson, in the section
"Idealism" in Nature, nature is "real" from the
practical standpoint but illusory from the spiritual
standpoint; and just as for Edwards, evil is real
from the sinner's view but "an approach to Nothing"
from the divine view (in Jonathan Edwards, Selections, ed. Clarence H. Faust and Thomas H. Johnson
[New York: Hill and Wang, 1962; rev. from 1935], p.
33, "Notes on the Mind"). Hawthorne would have
agreed with Emerson who wrote in "Swedenborg" that
"pure malignity can exist is the extreme proposition
of unbelief . . . it is atheism." Hawthorne's
constant use of terms like "illusion" in respect to
"sin," "guilt," "evil," are reminders that for him
there is something more real than evil in this
twilight world. He was always careful not to

174

subvert his refusal to affirm that evil has metaphysical reality.

[5] The American Notebooks, ed. Randall Stewart
(New Haven: Yale University Press, 1932), p. 98.

[6] See William Ellery Channing: Unitarian
Christianity and Other Essays, ed. Irving H.
Bartlett (New York: Bobbs-Merrill, 1957), p. 41-2;
p. 41, footnote.

[7] "The Try-Works."

[8] Hawthorne himself was shrewder than many of
his critics believe, and was not in danger of
naively sacrificing the actual to the ideal. He
wrote Sophia, October, 1840: "When we shall be
endowed with spiritual bodies, I think they will be
so constituted that we may send thoughts and feelings any distance, in no time at all, and transfuse
them warm and fresh into the consciousness of those
we love" (Julian Hawthorne, Nathaniel Hawthorne and
His Wife [Boston, 1885], I, 223). He placed this
Victorian passage also into his notebook at that
time, but added: "after all, perhaps it is not wise
to intermix fanatastic ideas with the reality of
affection. Let us content ourselves to be earthly
creatures, and hold communion of spirit in such
modes as are ordained to us" (IX, 224). "Such modes
as are ordained to us," for Hawthorne, help define
human beings: spirits possessing physical bodies,
inclined (not determined) toward moral darkness, who
seek happiness, who sorrow, decay, and die. This is
what we are, and to try to deny this fact, to try to
be an "angel," leads to perversion, isolation, and
unhappiness. There may be a better world to come,
but in the meantime we should content ourselves,
thinking of heaven, with human finitude and the
given modes of communication.

[9] Bronson Alcott wrote: "Greater is he, who
is above temptation, than he, who, being tempted,
overcomes. The latter but regains the state from
which the former has not fallen. He who is tempted
has sinned; temptation is impossible to the holy"
(quoted in The Transcendentalists, ed. Perry Miller
[Cambridge: Harvard University Press, 1950], p.
306). Emerson stated: "our moral nature is vitiated by any interference of our will. People

represent virtue as a struggle, and take to themselves great airs upon their attainments, and the
question is everywhere vexed when a noble nature is
commended, whether the man is not better who strives
with temptation. But there is no merit in the
matter. Either God is there or he is not there. We
love characters in proportion as they are impulsive
and spontaneous" ("Spiritual Laws"). I argue that
Hawthorne genuinely struggled in his Heart between
the Platonic view and the orthodox view that knowledge of evil is necessary for moral status. The
twentieth century finds Alcott's and Emerson's
position manifestly untrue.

[10] Milton, Christian Doctrine, chapter 10.

[11] Milton, Christian Doctrine, chapter 10.

[12] Critics differ about whether or not
Hawthorne argues in the Faun for the doctrine of the
Fortunate Fall. For instance, Roy Male believes
that "almost every page of the book indicates that
without sin and suffering moral growth rarely, if
ever, results" (Hawthorne's Tragic Vision [New York:
Norton, 1957], p. 175). Hyatt Waggoner feels that
"The plot gives no clear answer to the largest
question explicitly posed by the novel" (Kaul,
p. 168).

[13] Ernst Cassierer, Platonic Renaissance in
England (New York: Gordian Press, 1970), pp. 101,
103.

[14] Book IV, lines 128-30.

[15] The Recognition of Nathaniel Hawthorne (Ann
Arbor: University of Michigan Press, 1969), p. 253.
Matthiessen writes: "In his treatment of [Kenyon
and Hilda's] relationship Hawthorne has obviously
interwoven many strands of his own relationship with
his wife; but the unintended impression of
self-righteousness and priggishness that exudes from
these characters brings to the fore some extreme
limitations to the standards Hawthorne took for
granted" (American Rennaissance, [New York: Oxford
University Press, 1941] p. 356). But Sophia wrote:
"Mr. Hawthorne had no idea of portraying me in
Hilda. Whatever resemblance one sees is accidental"
(quoted in James R. Mellows, Nathaniel

Hawthorne in His Times [Boston: Houghton Mifflin, 1980], p. 518). However, Sophia's sister, Elizabeth Peabody, saw a resemblance between Hilda and Sophia: "There was one kind of thing she could not bear, and that was, moral evil. Every cloud brought over her horizon by the hand of God [natural evil] had for her a silvery lining; but human unkindness, dishonor, falsehood, agonized and stunned her,--as, in The Marble Faun, the crime of Miriam and Donatello stunned and agonized Hilda. And it was this very characteristic of hers that was her supreme charm to Hawthorne's imagination. He reverenced it" (Julian Hawthorne, I, 248).

[16] Reason in Religion (Boston, 1867), p. 121.

[17] Ellen Tucker Emerson wrote of her mother: "Her principles were that she ought to forgive. Every injustice, every slight, every wrong to her that anyone was guilty of lived before her mind and caused her permanently the same resentment that she felt at the first moment. . . . She ought to treat these false friends well, but it wasn't true to do so. She ought to forgive. How could she forgive, for they considered wrong right, and wrong that hurt her so terribly?" (The Life of Lidian Jackson Emerson, ed. Dolores Bird Carpenter [Boston: Twayne, 1980], p. 128). Lidian and Sophia aggressively found much of their Victorian identity in believing that they were super-sensitive antenae to fading absolutes in an increasingly pluralistic world.

[18] Waggoner writes: "One of the things Hawthorne must have meant when he declared himself 'saved' by his marriage was that he had found Sophia's buoyant faith a needed counter-balance to his own dark questionings. So Kenyon might be wiser in the ways of the world but Hilda, as we are often reminded, was wiser in religious truth. Kenyon might well ask her to guide him home, in Hawthorne's view of the matter" (Kaul, pp. 167-8).

[19] See for a discussion of "The Domestication of Theology," Amanda Porterfield's Feminine Spirituality in America (Philadelphia: Temple University Press, 1980).

[20] See R. K. Gupta, "Hawthorne's Treatment of the Artist," New England Quarterly, XLV, 65-80, for

a discussion of the role of art in Hawthorne. I question Gupta's statement that for Hawthorne "faith in art is the one eternal thing in a world of ephemeral, changing form." Matthiessen writes: "We remember that at the time of his one great emotional experience, giving himself in love to Sophia Peabody, he was already in his middle thirties, and therefore felt with exceptional acuteness the release from the prison of himself. That was what caused him to declare, with a fervency so rare for him, 'We are not endowed with real life . . . till the heart is touched. That touch creates us,--then we begin to be.' The experience was no mere interlude of romantic passion" (<u>American Renaissance</u>, p. 345).

[21] <u>Journals of Ralph Waldo Emerson</u>, ed. Edwards Waldo Emerson and Waldo Emerson Forbes (New York: Houghton Mifflin, 1909-1914), X, 40.

[22] <u>Hawthorne</u> (1879; rpt. New York: Collier-Macmillan, 1966), p. 22.

[23] Moncure Conway, <u>Emerson at Home and Abroad</u> (Boston, 1882), p. 185.

[24] Moncure Conway, <u>Life of Nathaniel Hawthorne</u> (1890; rpt. New York: Haskell House, 1968), p. 176.

[25] George Willis Cooke, <u>Unitarianism in America</u> (Boston, 1902), p. 430.

[26] <u>American Renaissance</u>, p. 232.

[27] Quoted by Austin Warren, in <u>The Recognition of Nathaniel Hawthorne</u>, ed. B. Bernard Cohen (Ann Arbor, University of Michigan Press, 1969), p. 183.

[28] See Mellows, p. 6.

[29] Jac Tharpe, <u>Nathaniel Hawthorne</u> (Carbondale: Southern Illinois University Press, 1967), p. 13.

[30] Mellows, p. 298.

[31] Julian Hawthorne I, 325.

[32] Warren, p. 181.

[33] Matthiessen, p. 361.

[34] That is, Hawthorne was not a materialist. A small example illustrates his position: Robert Danforth asks Owen Warland if he is trying to discover perpetual motion, and Owen answers: "It can never be discovered. It is a dream that may delude men whose brains are mystified with matter."

[35] Warren, p. 184. Hawthorne would have approved of Ishmael's statement in Moby Dick: "Doubts of all things earthly, and intuitions of some things heavenly; this combination makes neither believer nor infidel, but makes a man who regards them both with equal eye" (Chapter 85).

[36] For example, see Frederick Crews, The Sins of the Fathers (New York: Oxford University Press, 1966), for a fascinating psychoanalytical study of Hawthorne.

[37] Martin Luther and Other Essays (Boston, 1888), p. 235.

[38] Reason in Religion, p. 138.

[39] Hawthorne would not have agreed with W. T. Stace, for instance, who argues that "morality has a secular base," that "moral rules simply are rules of human happiness. And if so, they will be universal and not relative . . . in exactly the same way . . . as rules of safety and health are so" (Religion and the Modern Mind [New York: Lippincott, 1960], pp. 294, 305.

[40] "Father of Spirits."

[41] In "Fancy's Show Box" Hawthorne argued that evil thoughts in themselves are not evil or sinful, and that only when such thoughts are actualized is sin committed and guilt felt. Indeed, he said that "in truth, there is no such thing in man's nature as a settled and full resolve, either for good or evil, except at the very moment of execution." "It is not until the crime is accomplished that guilt clinches its grip upon the guilty heart." And yet, Hawthorne continued, thoughts and acts are closely related, and no one should "disclaim his brotherhood, even with the guiltiest, though his hand be clean,"

179

because "his heart has surely been polluted by the flitting phantoms of iniquity." Furthermore, he believed that when a person knocks "at the gate of heaven, no semblance of an unspotted life can entitle him to entrance there." In short, all men are acquainted with sin; and only those men who are penitent for their thoughts and/or deeds, and are merciful towards others for their thoughts and/or deeds, will enter heaven. As Hawthorne put it: "Penitence must kneel, and Mercy come from the footstool of the throne, or that golden gate will never open." If we are to change this world to (or exchange it for) a world free of even the thought of evil, we must have compassion and forgiveness. Thus knowledge of evil for Hawthorne is necessary for a profound moral knowledge of this world, but it may not be necessary for knowledge of the Absolute. Emerson, since he had stronger faith than Hawthorne in the Absolute, gave knowledge of the Over-Soul priority over knowledge of the relationships among men.

[42] Said by Newton Arvin in American Pantheon, ed. Daniel Aaron and Sylvan Schendler (New York: Delacourte Press, 1966), p. 96.

[43] Quoted by Randall Stewart in American Literature & Christian Doctrine (Baton Rouge: Louisiana State University Press, 1958), p. 78. Also (VIII, 374-5).

[44] Hawthorne, in 1855, was invited to the Unitarian Church in Liverpool, England, of which W. H. Channing was the minister. He declined the invitation because of "a long contemplated and unavoidable absence from town," but wrote to the church that he was delighted "to find here the descendants [in England] of that revered brotherhood a part of whose mission it was to plant the seeds of liberal Christianity in American. . . . And it seems to me a noble and beautiful testimony to the truth of our religious convictions that . . . the liberal churches of England and American should . . . have arrived at the same results; that an American . . . still finds himself in brotherly relations with the posterity of those free-minded men who exchanged a parting pressure of the hand with his forefathers . . . and that we can all unite in one tone of re-ligious sentiment" (Julian Hawthorne, II, 61).

Julian Hawthorne wrote elsewhere that "On Sundays Mrs. Hawthorne, with the two elder children, would go to the Unitarian chapel in Renshaw Street . . . but Hawthorne himself never attended church, that I remember" (Julian Hawthorne, II, 22).

THOREAU'S "DIAMOND BODY"

"March 7 [1852] . . . Going through the
high field beyond the lone graveyard, I
see the track of a boy's sled before me,
and his footsteps shining like silver
between me and the moon."

Thoreau

I

During the early eighteen-fifties Henry David
Thoreau was working on three major projects, the
extensive interior remodeling of Walden, the writing
of the Journal, and of the Indian Notebooks. The
"discrepancy" between the first two of these projects, according to Sherman Paul, is that "while the
bulk of his later Journals records a terrible
struggle, the published work of the same period
affirms his faith."[1] A symptom of this discrepancy is that Walden is crowded with sun images, and
the Journal, particularly during the summers of
these years, contain passages about moonlight of
which there is almost no mention in Walden. These
passages are part of the record of how Thoreau
retreated into his "real" or universal self to
maintain his identity and to regain sanity.

The years following Thoreau's stay at the pond,
critics have noted, were the most difficult of his
life. He was failing as a publishing writer and a
popular lecturer; his friendships were
dissatisfying; his youth was vanishing. He bewailed
his shameful and "pitiful conduct," awakened "to an
infinite regret" to find himself "not the thorough-
fare of glorious and world-stirring inspiration, but
a scuttle full of dirt." Overriding all problems
was the necessity to be who he was, a necessity that
at once haunted him and sustained his confidence.
He stated in the Journal, December, 1851, with
immense but abbreviated honesty, that "My dif-
ficulties with my friends are such as no frankness
will settle. . . . My nature, it may [be] is secret.
Others can confess and explain; I cannot. It is not
that I am too proud, but that is not what is wanted.

182

. . . I am under an awful necessity to be what I am. If the truth were known, which I do not know, I have no concern with those friends whom I misunderstand or who misunderstand me."[2] Yet, in spite of this negative content, the _Journal_ does not contradict but complements _Walden_. It gives us the difficult ground of mood and thought out of which the golden persona of _Walden_ grew, and therefore must be consulted to understand in depth the rebirth pattern which culminated in the book.

Thoreau added to _Walden_ after 1849 a great deal of new material concerning experiences following his pond adventure, but he omitted his moon journeys. He made this omission, we may speculate, because he was unaware that these journeys represented in part his sub-conscious battle against guilt and depression. That he was not aware of their significance is exemplified by his inability to handle them convincingly in a formal context. For example, his essay, "Night and Moonlight," constructed out of many of these passages and delivered as a lecture, October, 1854, borders on the sentimental. He apologized for his night wanderings, made a pun on "moonshine," and ended the essay with unearned dancing sunbeams. He recognized his failure, if not its significance, when he admitted that "I have not put darkness, duskiness, enough into my night and moonlight walks" (IV, 147). Thoreau spoke with authority in the relatively spontaneous moon passages embedded in the miry context of actual subsistence in the _Journal_; but he could not consciously handle them by themselves in a formal essay. They symbolized areas of mental unrest of which he was probably never fully aware.

The first three versions of _Walden_ were not satisfactory to Thoreau. "Time had to pass," Shanley[3] writes, "before he could achieve the right focus." Thoreau began to gain this focus after 1849: version IV shows tremendous growth; and V "more adequately represented the moral and spiritual problems he had sought to settle by his way of life."[4] Since most of the material Thoreau worked with while writing _Walden_ was extremely personal, he labored to release and to distance himself as critic from that material. He observed right after the death of his brother in 1842 that "I have lived ill for the most part because too near myself. I have tripped myself up, so that there is no progress for my own narrowness. I cannot walk contentedly and pleasantly but when I hold myself far off in the horizon" (I, 322). Thoreau's retreats into Nature, away from the irritation of civilized egos, were searches for the lucid "bone-set" of identity. In the early forties he narrowed at the death of his brother and saved himself by distancing himself at the pond and by creating a book about himself and John. In the early fifties he hardened more inexorably; this time he lost himself in moonlight walks, and found momentary salvation in the dynamism of impersonal interiority and by completing, in terms of myth, the reality of his personal affirmation.

Thoreau's principal battle was with the spectral inertia of privateness. Perry Miller has charged him with mouthing "the more extravagant solipsism of his master," and other critics have commented on his preoccupation with the point of view of the self as central.[5] We have seen, in the fourth essay, Emerson's treatment of this perspective of centrality of self, and how it evidenced his conviction of his divinity. In theory, Thoreau agreed with Emerson about the significance of centrality. But in practice his task, during these difficult years, a task which he never completed, was to distinguish between the loneliness of ego-centricity and the aloneness of the soul or "real self." His conclusion in 1842 after the death of John, for instance, that "I am my destiny. . . . The soul which does shape the world is within and central," may be interpreted as less an expression of ego-centricity than as an early indication of his orientation, in times of stress, toward the solace of the Emersonian doctrine. Nine years later, July, 1851, he pondered the reality-status of other persons, especially the phenomenal paradox that although the empirical ego is central there are in fact other selves: "I am always struck by the centrality of the observer's position. He always stands fronting the middle of the arch, and does not suspect at first that a thousand observers on a thousand hills behold the sunset sky from equally favorable positions" (II, 296). Like Emerson, he countered the solipsistic implications of centrality with a statement that each person is, paradoxically, the center of the universe. In the Spring of 1852, he stated firmly, as though conclusively answering an insistent personal question, that "Man is but the place where I stand, and the prospect hence is infinite. It is not a chamber of mirrors which reflect me. When I reflect, I find that there is other than me" (III, 382). In this year also, he added to Walden the ebullient statement: "wherever I sat, there I might live, and the landscape radiated from me accordingly."

However, although in theory and in practice Theoreau combatted solipsism, he could only slow his "long descent into loneliness, which lasted from 1851 to 1857."[6] At the same time he was philosophically accepting the existence of other selves, he was faced with the lack of friendship. He endured and, for moments, even thrived and created, by moving beyond ego-centricity and introspective privateness with their insoluable problems, not into society, but into Nature and ultimately into God. He sought the universal ground of all selves, the substantial "other than me," the centralizing interiority of the "real self."

Between 1849 and 1855 Thoreau's interest heightened in Eastern philosophy.[7] Shanley feels that although we cannot characterize exactly the kind of material Thoreau added to Walden after 1849, we know that he added, during the years 1850-51, "all or most of the quotations from Chinese and Hindu writings."[8] Thoreau's most famous statement about the doctrine of the "real self," which is associated with Eastern thought, is found in the chapter, "Solitude," in Walden. He lifted this statement out of (and slightly altered it from) a paragraph he had entered in the Journals for August, 1852 - once again during the time of his discouraging struggles and his most intense moonlight walks. He was, he said, "conscious of the presence and criticism of a part of me, which, as it were, is not a part of me, but spectator, sharing no experience, but taking note of it, and that is no more I than it is you. When the play, it may be the tragedy, of life is over, the spectator goes his way. It was a kind of fiction, a work of the imagination only, so far as he was concerned." In this passage Thoreau referred significantly to life as possibly tragic, passed beyond the perspective of space-time centrality of self, and resided as a detached observer of the world.

The Indian scriptures, V. K. Chari claims, were "undeniably" the source of Thoreau's "idea of the self as the ground of all experience, and the spectator of the scene of the world, and the further conception that this self is the common self of all; . . . that man's surface mentality does not constitute his real self [which] is the fundamental thesis of Vedanta."[9] In the Journal the paragraph preceding the spectator passage refers to thoughts similar to the above philosophy; and in Walden the spectator paragraph includes a reference to "Indra." In a letter to Harrison Blake, February, 1853, Thoreau wrote: "You words make me think of a man of my acquaintance whom I occasionally meet, whom you, too, appear to have met, one Myself, as he is called. Yet why not call him yourself? If you have met with him and know him, it is all I have done; and surely where there is a mutual acquaintance, the My and Thy make a distinction without a difference."[10] Thoreau was convinced that impersonal interiority was the ground of empirical selves, a doctrine he doubtless heard originally from Emerson and found supported in Emerson's oriental library. Furthermore, since he believed that "The unconsciousness of man is the consciousness of God," he assumed that his personal unconscious blended with the infinite mind (I, 119).[11]

In addition, Thoreau held, speculating along lines confirmed for him by Eastern thought, that neither personal nor impersonal interiority was empty but alive with non-empirical realities known to the sub-conscious mind in terms of archetypal dream imagery. During the early fifties he remarked on experiencing the unconscious in several ways. May, 1851, after taking ether to have his teeth removed, he said that "You are told that it will make you unconscious, but no one can imagine what it is to be unconscious. . . . The value of the experiment is that it does give you experience of an interval between one life and another" (II, 194). This passage lies between one on "the Yogin absorbed in contemplation" and one about himself lying in moonlight on the outskirts of town.

186

March, 1852, Thoreau recorded his transmigration.

> I am conscious of having, in my sleep, transcended the limits of the individual, and made observations and carried on conversations which in my waking hours I can neither recall nor appreciate. As if in sleep our individual fell into the infinite mind, and at the moment of waking we found ourselves on the confines of the latter. On awakening we resume our enterprise, take up our bodies and become limited mind again. We meet and converse with those bodies which we have previously animated. There is a moment in the dawn, when the darkness of the night is dissipated and before the exhalations of the day commence to rise, when we see things more truly than at any other time (III, 354).

Five years after having his teeth pulled, he is still reflecting on his remarkable experience with ether, and writes in serious fun that "When I took the ether my consciousness amounted to this: I put my finger on myself in order to keep the place, otherwise I should never have returned to this world" (VIII, 142; 1856). In 1841 he commented that "The nearest approach to discovering what we are is in dreams" (I, 253). And almost twenty years later he observed: "I am surprised that my affirmations or utterances come to me ready-made,--not forethought,--so that I occasionally awake in the night simply to let fall ripe a statement which I had never consciously considered before. . . . As if we only thought by sympathy with the universal mind, which thought while we were asleep" (XIII, 238). Thoreau believed, moreover, that the instinctual powers "are to a certain extent a sort of independent nobility, of equal date with the mind, or crown,--ancient dukes and princes of the regal blood. They are perhaps the mind of our ancestors subsided in us, the experience of the race" (I, 487). "I demand," he wrote in "Walking" and foreshadowing Jungian thought, "something which no Augustan nor Elizabethan age, which no culture, in short, can give. Mythology comes nearer to it than anything." Thoreau would not have insisted on specific content of the interior world, but he believed, beyond doubt, in such a reality. His escape from privateness and debilitating depression, during the early fifties, lay in the increased realization, dramatized by moonlight walks, that the unconscious is universal, rejuvenating, and creative.

Eastern thought not only confirmed for Theoreau the doctrine of the real self and the importance of interiority but substantiated his use of the moon as symbol for contemplative detachment. "The Hindoos," he wrote in 1850, "are more serenely and thoughtfully religious than the Hebrews. They have perhaps a purer, more independent and impersonal knowledge of God. . . . It is only by forgetting yourself that you draw near to him" (II, 3). "What extracts from the Vedas I have read," he observed, associating Hindu thought with moonlight, "fall on me like the light of a higher and purer luminary, which describes a loftier course through a purer stratum-- from particulars, simple, universal. It arises on me like the full moon after the stars have come out, wading through some far summer stratum of the sky" (II, 4). In the Bhagavadgita, Thoreau's favorite book of the East which is filled with the doctrine of the real self, Krishna says that "That radiance which proceedeth from the moon, sheddeth soft beams over the earth . . . all this splendor is of Me." In his essay on the moon, Thoreau asked of that light, "Why not study this Sanskrit?" and observed: "The Hindoos compare the moon to a saintly being who has reached the last stage of bodily existence."[12]

Thus Thoreau's moonlight journeys, taken during the early fifties, the time of his greatest distress and of his writing of the last versions of Walden, were dramatizations of his contemplative withdrawals into interiority which was, he believed, the ground of all finite selves and filled with archetypal imagery. This "religious" retreat into impersonal reality helped to distance him critically from himself, to give him the right perspective on the private content he was struggling to mold into the lyrical Walden. Elsewhere in the spectator passage in Walden, he wrote that "With thinking we may be beside ourselves in a sane sense. By a conscious effort of the mind we can stand aloof from actions and their consequences; and all things, good and bad, go by us like a torrent." This is precisely

what he had to do to be able to sift out "superfluous and irrelevant material," to bring to light
other material that had been buried, to deepen and
to shape important content.

We may theorize that Thoreau even approximated
at times, in his own way, what Carl Jung calls the
"superior personality . . . the holy fruit, the
diamond body . . . which is out of reach of intense
emotional involvement and therefore from the world
[that] sets in after the middle of life and is
actually a natural preparation for death." This
"diamond body," Jung holds, is gained "If the
unconscious can be recognized as a co-determining
quantity along with the conscious;" "the center of
gravity of the total personality shifts its position. It ceases to be in the ego which is merely
the center of consciousness, and instead is located
in a hypothetical point between the conscious and
the unconscious which might be called the self."[13]
Thoreau's experience under ether, his dreams, his
moonlight walks, during the early fifties, were
psychic journeys of submergence into creative
interiority; these journeys were symptomatic of the
shift of his total personality that allowed him to
endure as a person and to complete his book. He
wrote in 1856: "Both a conscious and unconscious
life are good. Neither is good exclusively, for
both have the same source" (IX, 37).

II

Following are many of Thoreau's descriptions of
his moonlight walks, and commentaries on them. The
analytical tool for these commentaries is Jung's
thought. Both he and Thoreau, we have seen, held
that consciousness is grounded on, or shades into,
the impersonal, universal "unconscious."[14] They
believed that for mental health we must recognize
the content of the unconscious, and accord it equal
status with that of the conscious mind. Furthermore, they were convinced that modern man stresses
abstract thought and public morality to such a
degree that he represses his instinctual needs for
the sake of his public image or persona; we try
desperately to conform to the demands of our

189

intensely conscious society. But the repressed needs of our animal life, which Jung calls our "shadow," are part of our total psyche; they demand recognition; they provide "wild" energy and indeed primordial wisdom for our survival and creative life. A person is a complete individual, therefore, when he harmonizes his primitive shadow with his social presence. Conversely, a person who seeks psychic wholeness must contact the repressed content of his unconscious, and in some way recognize its integrity.

Jung came to believe that the mind, like the body, contains the history of its evolution. Behind our ego lies our personal unconscious; and behind that is the collective unconscious or our universal memory. This memory contains, according to Jung, the impressions of all the experiences of our race, our species, indeed, of our entire psychic evolution. If we had exact recall, we could remember back through aeons to the very beginning of life. But we cannot remember the content of our collective unconscious in all its multiplicity. However, we can recall, according to Jung, when we are free of the grip of our conscious egos, that content in terms of "archetypes." Archetypes are latent memory norms of ancient patterns and techniques of behavior which evolving mankind has found efficacious in understanding and satisfying its typical needs. When we are in psychic health, therefore, our instinctual needs are satisfied by conforming to the primitive rituals of these universal behavior patterns. When we do not have wholeness of personality, we instinctively seek the "magical" wisdom of archetypes to correct our deviation. Archetypal symbols are the language of these ancient patterns.

These symbols, furthermore, have "numinosity," a psychic aura that seems not of this world. When we relax our willful egos and become open and sensitive to the dim language of the collective unconscious, our concrete experience seems to float in an aura of memories of ancient creatures who have had the same type of experience.

Thoreau, in his moonlight walks, relaxed the power of his conscious mind, and opened himself to the contents of the supra-personal unconscious. In many ways, therefore, the territory he sauntered through may be seen as archetypal. With an instinctive urge, he was seeking psychic health, self-containment, detachment, and incubation of new creative energy.

The chief symbol for the yearning for psychic wholeness, Jung has shown, is the mandala or circle; and clearly the moon was a mandala for Thoreau. After the imposed clarity of daylight or ego-consciousness had faded, he wandered, as in a dream or transcendental meditation, through a half-emerged obscurely-lit landscape of archetypes. The disk of the moon floated above him, symbolizing his search for wholeness, his yearning to recognize, for the sake of sanity, the vaster interior world and to synthesize the needs of that world with his conscious world in a transcendent reality of a more individuated self.

On May 16, 1851, Thoreau wrote: "A splendid full moon tonight. Lay on the rock near a meadow ....In the moonlight what intervals are created! The rising moon is related to the near pine tree which rises above the forest, and we get a just notion of distance . . . myself, a pine tree, and the moon, nearly equidistant." Thoreau sought a balanced state of mind, the peace of adequate perspective, elimination of ego-trivia, the determination of who he really was. On June 11, he recalled:

> Last night a beautiful summer night, not too warm, moon not quite full....I feared at first that there would be too much white light, like the pale remains of daylight, and not a yellow, gloomy, dreamier light . . . but when I got away from the town and deeper into the night, it was better. I saw it was necessary to see objects by moonlight as well as sunlight, to get a complete notion of them. . . . When I rose out of the Deep Cut into the old pigeon-place field, I rose into a warmer stratum of air. . . . I seem to be nearer to the origin of things. There is something creative and primal in the cool mist . . . fertility, the origin of things. An atmosphere which has forgotten the sun, where the ancient principle of moisture prevails . . . in a moonlight night . . . your

feet meet no obstacles. It is as if it were not a path, but an open winding passage through the bushes, which your feet find. . . . [In moonlight] our spiritual side takes a more distinct form, like our shadow which we see accompanying us. . . . The wind blows, the river flows, without resting. There lies Fair Haven Lake, undistinguishable from fallen sky. The pines seem forever foreign. . . . My shadow has the distinctness of a second person, a certain black companion bordering on the imp.

In moonlight Thoreau moved among "the archaic language of the unconscious."[15] His identification with primal forces is extraordinary. He is in a land forgotten by sun, a place warm, moist, womb-like. Things are uncanny; the wind of fertility blows; his shadow seems a bewitched native of the place, a small trickster. He himself is detached, drifting through the bushes like a disembodied spirit. Two days later, June 13, 1851, he records:

Walked to Walden last night (moon not quite full) . . . how valuable was some water by moonlight, like the river and Fair Haven Pond, though far away, reflecting the light with a faint glimmering sheen, as in the spring of the year. The water shines with an inward light like a heaven on earth. The silent depth and serenity and majesty of water! I saw a distant river by moonlight, making no noise, yet flowing, as by day, still to the sea, like melted silver reflecting the moonlight. Far away it lay encircling the earth. . . . I saw the moon suddenly reflected full from a pool. A puddle from which you may see the moon reflected, and the earth dissolved under your feet. The magical moon with attendant stars suddenly looking up with mild lustre from a window in the dark earth. . . . I observed also the same night a halo about my shadow in the moonlight. . . . The light of the moon, - in what age of the world does that fall upon the earth? The moonlight was as the earliest and dewy morning light, and the daylight tinge reminded me much more of the night. There were the old and new dynasties opposed, contrasted, and an interval between, which time could not span. Then is night, when the daylight yields to the nightlight. It suggested an interval, a distance not recognized in history. . . . The white stems of the pines, which reflected the weak light, standing thick and close together while their lower branches were gone, reminded me that the pines are only larger grasses which rise to a chaffy head, and we the insects that crawl beneath them. . . . By moonlight we see not distinctly even the surface of the earth. . . . As I approach the pond down Hubbard's Path, after coming out of the woods into warmer air, I saw the shimmering of the moon on its surface, and, in the near, now flooded cove, the water-bugs, darting, circling about, made streaks or curves of light. The moon's inverted pyramid of shimmering light commenced about twenty rods off, like so much micaceous sand. But I was startled to see midway in the dark water a bright flame-like, more than phosphorescent light crowning the crests of the wavelets, which at first I mistook for fireflies . . . and I saw that even this was so many broken reflections of the moon's disk . . . so many lustrous burnished coins poured from a bag with inexhaustible lavishness . . . and I saw how farther and farther off they gradually merged in the general sheen, which, in fact, was made up of a myriad little mirrors reflecting the disk of the moon. . . . And on the bottom I saw the moving reflections of the shining waves, faint streaks of light revealing the shadows of the waves or the opaqueness of the water. . . . As I climbed the hill again toward my old bean-field, I listened to the ancient, familiar, immortal dear cricket sound under all others . . . the general earth-song.

Surely Thoreau, in his moonlight journeys, was touching the content of the deep unconscious.[16] The vague terrain, totally different from the world of surfaces of direct sunlight, lay before him, half-emerged from the liquid ground of darkness. The silver river flowed under the reflected moon, like the silent substratum of time, like Being and Becoming. Thoreau himself floated over the earth, free of gravitational pull, in the soft wind that pervaded the world like a divine spirit. The magical water shone, and shone within itself; the total scene quivered with the light of the mandala moon. Names of present real places, like "Hubbard's Path" and "my old beanfield," seemed to fuse with archetypal familiarity and shine with numinosity. Thoreau was at once humble and divine: he was a small young thing hiding among the white hairs of pine trees; his shadow had a halo around it, a sign perhaps of developing hero identity. The cricket, like a "bush soul" or protecting companion of the great earth, comforted him with its familiar archaic sound. Indeed, Thoreau himself, the cricket, the moon-disk above, and the silent waters below, seemed a symbol of a balanced wholeness of interior life. On June 14, he wrote:

> Full moon last night. . . . A serene evening.
> . . . All nature is abandoned to me. You feel
> yourself - your body, your legs, - more at
> night, for there is less beside to be distinct-
> ly known . . . I see indistinctly oxen asleep
> in the fields, silent in majestic slumber, like
> the sphinx, - statuesque, Egyptian, reclining.
> . . . When a man is asleep and day forgotten,
> then is the beauty of moonlight seen over
> lonely pastures where cattle are silently
> feeding.

> June 15. . . . After walking by night
> several times I now walk by day, but I am not
> aware of any crowning advantage in it. I see
> small objects better, but it does not enlighten
> me any. The day is more trivial.

> June 22. . . . To be calm, to be serene! .
> . . Sometimes we are clarified and calmed
> healthily . . . by some unconscious obedience
> to the all-just laws, so that we become like a
> still lake of purest crystal and without an
> effort our depths are revealed to ourselves.

> July 6. . . . I walked by night last moon,
> and saw its disk reflected in Walden Pond, the
> broken disk, now here, now there, a pure and
> memorable flame unearthly bright, like a
> cucullo of a water-bug. . . . What an immeasur-
> able interval there is between the first tinge
> of moonlight which we detect, lighting with

mysterious, silvery, poetic light the western
slopes, like a paler grass, and the last wave
of daylight on the eastern slopes! It is
wonderful how our senses ever span so vast an
interval, how from being aware of the one we
become aware of the other. And now the night
winds blows, - from where? What gave it birth?
It suggests an interval equal to that between
the most distant periods recorded in history. .
. . I turn and see the silent, spiritual,
contemplative moonlight shedding the softest
imaginable light on the western slopes of the
hills, as if, after a thousand years of polishing, their surfaces were just beginning to be
bright, - a pale whitish lustre. Already the
crickets chirp to the moon a different strain,
and the night wind rustles the leaves of the
wood. A different dynasty has commenced. Yet
moonlight, like daylight, is more valuable for
what it suggests than for what it actually is.
It is a long past season of which I dream . . .
a more sacred and glorious season. . . . Ah,
there is the mysterious light which for some
hours has illustrated Asia and the scene of
Alexander's victories, now at length, after two
or three hours spent in surmounting the billows
of the Atlantic, comes to shine on America.
There, on that illustrated sand-bank, was
revealed an antiquity beside which Nineveh is
young. Such a light as sufficed for the
earliest ages. . . . What if there are some
spirits which walk in its light alone still?
who separate the moonlight from the sunlight,
and are shined on by the former only? I passed
from dynasty to dynasty, from one age of the
world to another age of the world, from Jove
perchance back to Saturn. What river of Lethe
was there to run between? I bade farewell to
that light setting in the west and turned to
salute the new light rising in the east.

There is some advantage in being the
humblest, cheapest, least dignified man in the
village, so that the very stable boys shall
damn you. . . . I am not above being used, aye
abused, sometimes.

July 7. The intimations of the night are
divine, me-thinks. . . . I have been to-night

with Anthony Wright to look through Perez
Blood's telescope. . . . I am still contented
to see the stars with my naked eye. . . . Only
thought which is expressed by the mind in
repose - as it were, lying on its back and
contemplating the heavens - is adequately and
fully expressed. . . . The sound of crickets
. . . is a mark of serenity and health of mind.

    July 10. . . . I am always struck by the
centrality of the observer's position.

Thoreau carefully edited and rewrote his Journal;
and in these passages he was concerned to give us,
as accurately as possible, the record of his therapeutic experiences in darkness and moonlight. He
perceived oxen, in the generic night, sphinx-like,
perhaps an archetype of "the dragon of the abyss,
representing the might of the Earth Mother."[17] He
senses the ancient ceremonial of feeding, of gaining
sustenance -- and one recalls Sherwood Anderson's
"Death in the Woods," a story of moonlight and
feeding. When he is unconsciously obedient to
universal laws, Thoreau says that he perceived his
interior world. On a later night, he speaks about
moonlight polishing the hills, possibly a stone
mandala symbolizing the gradual and arduous emergence of his self-contained individuation. He
rationalizes his lack of identity in daylight
consciousness; counters this with a reminder of the
soul's central position; and synthesizes the two
with a reference to his "guardian spirit," the
cricket, whose voice "is a mark of serenity and
health of mind." He rejects the telescope, as he
did the established church, as a medium to knowledge
of reality. Experience, undistorted by the human
will, is the true expression of his interior world
which is the real world. He continues:

    July 11. . . . With W. E. C. go forth to
see the moon, the glimpses of the moon. . . .
Some woods are black as clouds; if we knew not
they were green by day, they would appear
blacker still. . . . Now we are getting into
moonlight. We see it reflected from particular
stumps in the depths of the darkest woods, and
from the stems of trees. . . . How remarkable a
lesser light can be when a greater has de-

parted. How simply and naturally the moon presides! 'Tis true she was eclipsed by the sun, but now she acquires an almost equal respect and worship by reflecting and representing him, with some new quality, perchance, added to his light, showing how original the disciple may be who still in midday is seen, though pale and cloud-like, beside his master. Such is a worthy disciple.

The leaves are shining and lowing. We wade through the luxuriant vegetation, seeing no bottom. . . . The frogs are eructating, like the falling of huge drops.

In Baker's orchard the thick grass looks like a sea of mowing in this weird moonlight, a bottomless sea of grass. Our feet . . . must know the earth in imagination only. . . . The clouds are peculiarly wispy tonight . . . The rails of the fences shine like silver. We know not whether we are sitting on the ruins of a wall, or the materials which are to compose a new one. I see, half a mile off, a phosphorescent arc on the hillsides, where Bartlett's Cliff reflects the moonlight. Going by the shanty, I smell the excrements of its inhabitants.

July 12. . . . Now at least the moon is full, and I walk alone, which is best by night. . . . I go forth to be reminded of a previous state of existence. . . . I see a skunk on Bear Garden Hill stealing noiselessly away from me, while the moon shines over the pitch pines, which send long shadows down the hill. Now, looking back, I see it shining on the south side of farmhouses and barns with a weird light. I smell the huckleberry bushes. I hear a human voice . . . it is far away. . . . There is more serenity and more light. . . . Looking down from the cliffs . . . the whole world below is covered as with a gossamer blanket of moonlight . . . this simple and magnificent stillness, brooding like genius.

July 16. . . . Me thinks my present experience is nothing; my past experience is all in all. . . . My life was ecstasy. In youth, before I lost any of my senses, I can remember that I was all alive, and inhabited my body with inexpressible satisfaction. . . . The morning and the evening were sweet to me, and I led a life aloof from society of men. I wonder if a mortal had ever known what I knew. . . . Let me forever go in search of myself. . . . May I be to myself as one is to me whom I love, a dear and cherished object.

July 19. Here I am thirty-four years old, and yet my life is almost wholly unexpanded. . . . There is such an interval between my ideal and the actual in many instances that I may say I am unborn. . . . I am contented. . . . The society which I was made for is not here.

July 21. . . . Now I yearn for one of those old, meandering, dry, uninhabited roads, which lead away from towns, . . . on which you can go off half-cock and wave adieu to the village; along which you may travel like a pilgrim, going nowhither. . . . There I can walk, and recover the lost child that I am.

July 23. . . . My genius makes distinctions which my understanding cannot, and which my senses do not report.

Aug. 7. . . . Moon half full. . . . The wind now rising from over Bear Garden Hill falls gently on my ear. . . . I distinguish the modest moonlight on my paper. As the twilight deepens and the moonlight is more and more bright, I begin to distinguish myself, who I am and where. . . . I recover some sanity, my thoughts are more distinct, moderated, and tempered. . . . The intense light of the sun unfits me for meditation. . . . I am sobered by the moonlight. I bethink myself. . . . I see Fair Haven Pond from the Cliffs, as it were through a slight mist. It is the wildest scenery imaginable. . . . You all alone, the moon all alone, over-coming with incessant victory whole squadrons of clouds.

Aug. 8. . . . On Conantum I sit awhile in the shade of the woods and look out on the moonlit fields. . . . I could lie out here on this pinnacle rock all night without cold. To lie here on your back with nothing between your eyes and the stars, - nothing but space.

Aug. 12. . . . 1. A. M. - Full moon. Arose and went to the river and bathed. . . . I do not remember what I observed or thought in coming hither. . . . It is not easy to realize the serene joy of all the earth when the moon commences to shine unobstructedly, unless you have often been a traveller by night. . . . The moon has gone behind a large and black mass of clouds . . . the bats are flying about on the edge of the wood. . . . The moon appears at length . . . with a frozen light, ominous of her fate.

Aug. 15 May I love and revere myself above all the gods that men have ever invented. May I never let the vestal fire go out in my recesses.

Aug. 17. . . . I am unworthy of the least regard. . . . I am impure and worthless, and yet the world is gilded for my delight. . . . But I cannot thank the Giver; I cannot even whisper my thanks to those human friends I have.

Several times Thoreau asked Channing to walk with him in the moonlight, but decided correctly that the journey into the self could be done best alone. His comment on the moon as an original and worthy disciple of the sun suggests his tensions with Emerson. The world he confronts seems very far away[18] distant, disconnected with his personal ego. It is a world of magnificent archetypal simplicity, more primal than the daylight universe, and one that can be understood only symbolically or intuitively. The slow motion of the frogs "eructating" is like primeval time.

Thoreau moves through a variety of moods, exhibiting in turn humility and a sense of being divine, mourning the gap between the ideal person he wants to be and the actual person he is. He thinks

himself "impure and worthless" and smells the
excrements of human inhabitants. But the humble
animal he is seems somehow spiritualized in the
moonlight and integrated into a greater psychic
whole. He searches for himself; remembers his
youth; sees a mandala in "a phosphorescent arc on
the hillside," and watches the moon's "incessant
victory" over the black clouds. He identifies
himself with the moon, begins to distinguish a
wholeness of himself, to recover sanity, and the
lost child that he was. In the middle of the night
he travels, but cannot remember how, to bathe in the
sacred river of the interior world--hence comple-
menting his dawn baptism in Walden. He compensates
for his sense of worthlessness by cherishing himself
and by vowing to keep his "vestal fire" always
burning. He continues:

    Aug. 19 [1851]. I fear that the character
of my knowledge is from year to year becoming
more distinct and scientific.

    Sept. . . . Moonlight on Fair Haven Pond.
. . . This is my world now, with a dull whitish
mark curling northward through the forest
marking the outlet to the lake. . . . This
light and this hour take the civilization out
of the landscape. . . . The landscape seen from
the slightest elevation by moonlight is seen
remotely, and flattened, as it were, into mere
light and shade, open field and forest, like
the surface of the earth seen from the top of a
mountain.

    Sept. 7. We sometimes experience a mere
fullness of life, which does not find any
channels to flow into. . . . How to get the
most life. . . . That is my everyday business.
. . . I bathe at the north side Cliff, while
the moon shines round the end of the rock.
Two or three pines appear to stand in the
moonlit air on this side of the pond. . . . It
reminds me of placid lakes in the mid-noon of
Indian summer days, but yet more placid and
civilized, suggesting a higher cultivation, as
the wild ever does, which aeons of summer days
have gone to make. Like a summer day seen far
away. . . . It tells of a far-away, long-passed

civilization, of an antiquity superior to time, unappreciable by time. . . . A certain refinement and civilization in nature . . . increases with the wildness. The civilization that consists with wildness, the light that is in night. . . . The period of youth is past. . . . May my life be not destitute of its Indian summer, a season of fine and clear, mild weather in which I may prolong my hunting before the winter comes, when I may once more lie on the ground with faith, as in spring, and even with more serene confidence.

Sept. 9. . . . I come out thus into the moonlit night, where men are not, as if into a scenery anciently deserted by men. The life of men is like a dream. . . . Go forth and hear the crickets chirp at midnight. Hear if their dynasty is not an ancient one. . . . I go by the farmer's houses and barns, standing there in the dim light under the trees. . . . The fog . . . covers the meadows like a web. I hear the clock strike three.

Sept. 12. . . . That kind of life which, sleeping, we dream that we live awake, in our walks by night, we, waking, live, while our daily life appears as a dream.

Oct. 1. . . . The moon is not quite half full. . . . Looking west at this hour, the earth is an unvaried undistinguishable black in contrast with the twilight sky. It is as if you were walking in night up to your chin. The river is a dark mirror with bright points feebly fluctuating. . . . At 8 o'clock the fogs have begun, which, with the low half-moon shining on them, look like cob-webs or thin white veils spread over the earth. They are the dreams or visions of the meadow.

Oct. 5. Moon three-quarters full. . . . The moon gives not a creamy but white, cold light, through which you can see far distinctly. . . . Saw some fishermen kindling their fire for spearing by the riverside. It was a lurid, reddish blaze. . . . They appear as dusky, fuliginous figures, half enveloped in smoke. . . . A high bank of moonlit hills rises at a distance. . . . The bright sheen of the moon is constantly travelling with us.

Oct. 12. . . . I seem to be more constantly merged in nature. . . . I am getting used to my meanness.

Oct. 26. . . . My regret arose from the consciousness how little like a musical instrument my body was now.

Oct. 27. . . . The night is oracular.

Nov. 1. . . . I feel blessed. I love my life. I warm toward all nature.

Nov. 9. . . . Our life is not altogether a forgetting, but also, alas, to a great extent a remembering.

Nov. 12. . . . A still, cold night. The light of the rising moon in the east. Moonrise is a faint sunrise. . . . Absolutely no crickets to be heard now. . . . It is worth the while always to go to the waterside when there is but little light in the heavens and see the heavens and the stars reflected. . . . The reflection has the force of a great silent companion.

Nov. 18. . . . The man who is bent upon his work is frequently in the best attitude to observe what is irrelevant to his work. (Mem. Wordsworth's observations on relaxed attention.).

Dec. 13. . . . It seems an age since I took walks and wrote in my journal, and when shall I revisit the glimpses of the moon? To be able to see ourselves, not merely as others see us, but as we are.

Dec. 21. . . . I am under an awful necessity to be what I am.

Dec. 23. . . . I detect, just above the horizon, the narrowest imaginable white sickle of the new moon.

March 7. [1852] . . . Going through the high field beyond the lone graveyard, I see the track of a boy's sled before me, and his footsteps shining like silver between me and the moon. . . . What a man does abroad by night requires and implies more deliberate energy than what he is encouraged to do in the sunshine. He is more spiritual, less animal. . . . The moon, the stars, the trees, the snow, the sand when bare, - a monumental stillness, whose void must be supplied by thought. It extracts throught from the beholder, as the void under a cupping-glass raises a swelling.

March 15. . . . May I attain to a youth never attained!

March 17. . . . I am conscious of having, in my sleep, transcended the limits of the individual.

April 2. . . . Man is but the place where I stand. . . . It is not a chamber of mirrors which reflect me.

April 11. . . . For a month past life has been a thing incredible to me. None but the kind gods can make me sane. . . . I ask to be melted.

April 16. . . . Might I not write on sunshine as well as moonshine?

May 3. . . . The moon is full. The air is filled with a certain luminous, liquid, white light.

May 7. . . . I would fain see the sun as a moon, more weird.

June 14. . . . Walking much by moonlight, conversing with the moon, makes us, then, albinos.

Aug. 8. . . . I am conscious of the presence and criticism of a part of me which . . . is no more than it is you.

> Aug. 23. . . . I live so much in my
> habitual thoughts, a routine of thought, that I
> forget there is any outside to the globe, and
> am surprised when I behold it as now,--yonder
> hills and river in the moonlight, the monsters.
> Yet it is salutary to deal with the surface of
> things. What are these rivers and hills, these
> hieroglyphics which my eyes behold?

Thus Thoreau perceives, in September, 1851, the
moonlit landscape "flattened" and remote, like a
map; the world lies before him, in psychic distance,
reflecting with dull luster, the light, as it were,
of his diamond body, the moon. A year later he
wonders about the "hieroglyphics" of the shadowy
landscape, not knowing exactly what the message is
but confident that he is receiving curative information. He continues his ritual of bathing. The
remote, silver landscape suggests a civilization
superior to time, a "higher cultivation, as the wild
ever does;" or, according to Jung, the nocturnal
order of the Great Mother, the psychic residue of
the behavioral norms of ancient cultures, even
prehuman organic life, immutable and eternal, beyond
immediate consciousness.[19] From renewed contact
with this timeless order of dream-like nights,
Thoreau regained serenity and faith in himself. He
became used to his "meanness," saw the inconse-
quentiality of his culture's mores in respect to his
absolute identity.

In October, 1851, he wades up to his chin in
the dark instinctive life. He observes fishermen,
like archaic man, "dusky, fuliginous," partly
concealed by smoke, preparing their hunting ritual.
He feels depressed, and then, three weeks later,
"blessed." In November, the crickets are gone but
the reflection of the night sky in the water "has
the force of a great silent companion," perhaps like
that stillness "brooding like genius," a tutelary
figure symbolic of "the whole psyche, the larger and
more comprehensive identity that supplies the
strength that the personal ego lacks."[20] In
December he regrets that he has not seen the moon
for a great while, and follows this by wishing to
see himself again as he really is. In March, 1852,
he views a boy's footsteps in the snow, near a
graveyard, shining with numinosity "between me and
the moon," thereby connecting in a quarterity,

youth, death, himself, and the moon--envisioning in detached self-reflection the balanced eternality of beginning and end of finite things, like himself, the boy whose footsteps he saw. A week later he states outright that he wishes to "attain to a youth never attained!" and dreams of having "transcended the limits of the individual." In April he denies solipsism; and yet, nine days later, his mood fluxtuates, and he asks to "be melted," believing that only the "kind gods" can make him sane.

Thoreau's search for individuated wholeness went on. He continued to try to battle "past his personal and local historical limitations to the generally valid, normally human forms" of the higher cultivation of the collective unconscious.[21] He walked in moonlight at other times in his life, but only during these years of the early fifties, the crucial years of the revisions of Walden, he recorded clusters of magnificent moonlight scenes. In the darkness he drifted back into himself, altering the center of gravity of his total psyche away from the insoluable problems of the acrid world of ego-consciousness. He turned down the lights on the distracting drama of the daylight world, as it were, leaned back, listened to the healing advice of the universal mind, regained composure and energy to complete Walden.

The moon symbolized, as mandala, his yearning for harmonized wholeness; and, as his "real self," his detached observation of who he really was. His admissions at this time that he was the humblest man in town, that he was a scuttle full of dirt, that his youth was lost, his pronouncement that we should "speak simply of the necessary functions of human nature," are indications that he was recognizing sources of obsessive tension in his personal unconscious that made impossible a balanced overview of himself and his work, and that blocked creative flow. The sense of gradual release from these tensions, due to his midnight therapy, therefore, helped to give depth of vitality and glow to Walden. Walden in part is a celebration of his partial liberation from shadowy dungeons of himself. The crafted persona of his labored Journal complements and heightens the vibrant self of the Pond; the imp of moonlight, the sun-hero of consciousness.

Thoreau's moonlight journeys, consequently, were not only retreats for detachment and control but were part of his total search for rejuvenation. He had "to return to us, transfigured, and teach the lesson he had learned of life renewed."[22] The final phase of his rebirth was the completion of his "greater-than-personal" objective, the mythic vision of his "second naivete." Thus his "fall" from "naively sensuous" consciousness of nature, from "subjective to objective idealism," however overwhelming it may have seemed to him, may be interpreted as part of the rebirth pattern.[23] He rose out of the isolated innocence of privateness to a more rationally controlled perspective. He complained, July 16, 1851, "Methinks my present experience is nothing; my past experience is all in all. I think that no experience which I have to-day comes up to, or is comparable with, the experience of my boyhood" (II, 306). In October of the same year, he wrote, "I seem to be more constantly merged in nature; my intellectual life is more obedient to nature than formerly, but perchance less obedient to spirit. . . . I am getting used to my meanness, getting to accept my low estate. O if I could be discontented with myself! If I could feel anguish at each descent!" (III, 66).

But at the same time that he was lamenting his lost youth and mean estate, Thoreau was celebrating his heightened perception of nature. March 15, 1852, he exclaimed, "A mild spring day. . . . I lean over a rail to hear what is in the air, liquid with the bluebird's warble. My life partakes of infinity. . . . May I dare as I have never done! May I persevere as I have never done! . . . May I gird myself to be a hunter of the beautiful, that naught escape me! May I attain to a youth never attained!" (III, 350-51). He stated in 1851 that "the possibility of the future far exceeds the accomplishments of the past" (II, 229). Although Thoreau periodically lamented his lost innocence, he certainly would not have chosen to retreat into childhood and to lose the "philosophic mind." He did not in fact wish to become childish nor brutish; nor did his "fall" degenerate into the thin meaningless objectivity of Naturalism nor fixate him on the un-regainable past.

The years of the early fifties when Thoreau completed _Walden_ were the summer of his life. During this time he found a delicate, creative equipoise between intensity and serenity, intimacy and distance, consciousness and the unconscious, his ego and his shadow, sunlight and moonlight. His growing collection of facts during these years was a manifestation of his necessity to be less absorbed in himself, to be more detached from the unrecognized shadow "that tends to narrow consciousness to an acute preoccupation with self."[24] November 1, 1851, he cautioned, "See not with the eye of science, which is barren, nor of youthful poetry, which is impotent. . . . What was _enthusiasm_ in the young man must a become _temperment_ in the mature man. Without excitement, heat, or passion, he will survey the world which excited the youth and threw him off his balance" (III, 85-6). "How few valuable observations can we make in youth!" he observed in 1852. "What if there were united the susceptibility of youth with the discrimination of age?" (III, 378). His record of his fluxtuating moods is the record of his exploration of himself in his struggle to gain knowledge of and control over his total psyche. He had to recognize the shadows of his grown-up experience that clouded the brilliant memory of the myopic monism of the innocent child. To clothe Walden Pond, "one of the oldest scenes stamped" on his memory ("The Bean-Field") in an artistic form that would preserve it as testimony of divine inspiration, he had to make that "fabulous landscape" of his "infant dreams" more coherent and universal.

The images of youth that came to Thoreau at this time were not merely "vestigal" memories of his own childhood in his private New England past. They were images of archetypal youth. He wrote, January, 1853: "I thought of those summery hours when time is tinged with eternity,--runs into it and becomes one stuff with it. How much, how, perhaps, all, --that is the best in our experience in middle life may be resolved into the memory of our youth!" (IV, 460). The actuality of his own childhood shone with archaic luster. His own wonderful youth came back to him, again and again, transfigured as the childhood of all childhoods. He prayed "to attain to a youth never attained!" the youth of the wonderchild who leads the way to transcendence of psychic tensions and prophesizes rebirth.

207

These images of youth, therefore, scattered through the _Journal_ for the terrible years of moonlight journeys, embedded like seeds of light among entries of factual observation, of philosophic statement, of bitter depression, were the "personification of vital forces" "that represented the strongest, most ineluctable urge" of Thoreau to endure and to create _Walden_.[25] The fossiled images of his individual youth fused with the archetypal child; or, in Hindu terms, with the "real self," impersonal, central, interiority, "the Counter-pole of the world," and enabled him to record mythically his personal experiences in universal, "objective" terms.[26] He ascended from the collective unconscious of his moonlight walks to complete his second naivete, the sun-myth of the Pond.

During 1851 and 1852 Thoreau was more fully and intensely (not more contentedly) alive than he had ever been. He wrote at the end of August, 1851, that "I too am at the top of my condition for perceiving beauty" (II, 436); and a week later noted, "we sometimes experience a mere fullness of life, which does not find any channels to flow into" (II, 467). He was experiencing the rich agony of renewed creative force, of observing _Walden_ gradually taking convincing organic form. The dim landscape at night consisted in props for his dramatic retreat from the distracting world into the quiet of reflection, back to the refreshment of intuitive beginnings. His struggles for freedom from the shadows of ego-centricity, professional jealousies, changing friendships, middle-age, were projected onto the night. "You all alone," he wrote, August 5, 1851, "the moon all alone, overcoming with incessant victory whole squadrons of clouds" (II, 374). Since Thoreau believed that "whatever we see without is a symbol of something within, and that which is farthest off is a symbol of what is deepest within" (III, 201), such apocalyptic visions surely must have sub-consciously prophesized for him his own victory. He was careful to include in his essay on moonlight an extended discussion of the moon battling the clouds.

A survey particularly of the _Journal_ for the summer of 1851, as we have seen, reveals a very great range of moods, an astonishing ebb and flow of failure and despair shot through with recollections of youth and audacious, if not heroic, affirmations. We are amid the psychic dynamism of rebirth. Of course, precise meanings of many of these impressionistic passages cannot be tied down. Their literal content, we may surmise, was taken over by the autonomous aliveness of the archaic mind; and to try to reduce them completely to rational analysis would be to destroy their holiness and to make them, Emerson would say, skeletonal or "village" signs. They are moonlight messages from the deep psyche, shining with redemptive energy, and signifying the future transcendence of Thoreau's creative imagination over knotty tensions of the ego and private unconscious. They must be read imaginatively to be understood.

Thus Thoreau, in the early fifties, seeking instinctively healing and inspiration, journeyed mournful and self-accussing into the "Brahmic night" of himself. The intensity, the texture, the variation of mood, of the _Journal_ passages that record his journey, their thriving matrix of psychological states, suggests that the summer of 1851 marked, as it were, the climatic nadir of this journey, the critical moment when Thoreau determined his adequate status as a man and his destiny as an artist. Late in 1851 or early in 1852, he went back to version IV of _Walden_.

Since the record of his journey represents an important phase in his mythic rebirth, Thoreau would have enriched and clarified the theme of _Walden_ if he had inserted at least part of this record into the chapter, "Solitude." If he had done so, these dream-like passages--in which the moon represents, on the one hand, his real self brooding in detached genius, and on the other, a mandala revealed through regression into archaic levels of self--these passages would deepen the preceding world of "quiet desperation" and add numinosity to the subsequent chapter, "Spring." If he had done this, he would have left us a more complete record of his sun-myth; if he had added his moon-myth, he would have made mythical our universal cycles on a deeper psychic level. That he did not use these moon passages in _Walden_ is indicative, once again, of his failure to perceive, perhaps because of doctrine, that they were symbolic of profound unconscious activity that contributed to his rebirth.[27] In any case, he was aware that the darkness bore its fruit for him, and proved itself good, no less than the light. He recovered "the dream for the health of life," and lingered in manhood to remake his Edenic past into the enduring reality of myth.[28]

1 Sherman Paul, The Shores of America: Thoreau's Inward Exploration (Urbana: The University of Illinois Press, 1958), p. 57.

2 The Journal of Henry D. Thoreau, ed. Bradford Torrey and Francis H. Allen (1906; rpt. New York: Dover, 1962), II, 146. Hereafter Journal references will appear in the text. Emerson wrote in his Journal, October 27, 1851: "It would be hard to recall the rambles of last night's talk with Henry Thoreau. But we started over again, to sadness almost, the eternal loneliness" (The Journals of Ralph Waldo Emerson, ed. Edward Waldo Emerson and Waldo Emerson Forbes [Boston: Houghton Mifflin, 1910-1914], VIII, 260).

3 J. Lyndon Shanley, The Making of Walden with the Text of the First Version (University of Chicago Press, 1957), p. 57.

4 Shanley, p. 67.

5 Perry Miller, Consciousness in Concord: The Text of Thoreau's Hitherto "Lost Journal" (Boston: Houghton Mifflin, 1958), p. 35. Charles Anderson comments on "the literary use of which [Thoreau] put the illusion of roundness with which the world is pictured to the human eye. . . . He returns again and again to this particular phenomenon, stressing its illusory quality" (The Magic Circle of Walden [New York: Holt, Rinehart, Winston, 1968], p. 213). But if Thoreau thought this perspective merely "illusory" why did he repeatedly return to it? On the contrary, he felt that it was a fact of experience that was expressive of reality.

6 Henry Seidel Canby, Thoreau (Boston: Houghton Mifflin, 1939), p. 353.

7 He received Cholmondelay's gift of oriental books in 1855, but he was by this time, according to Walter Harding, "no longer vitally interested in reading them" (A Thoreau Handbook [New York University Press, 1959], p. 100).

[8] Shanley, p. 30.

[9] V. K. Chari, *Whitman in the Light of Vedantic Mysticism* (Lincoln: University of Nebraska Press, 1964), pp. 74-5.

[10] *The Writings of Henry David Thoreau*, ed. R. B. Sanborn (1906; rpt. New York: AMS Press, 1968), VI, 215.

[11] Geoffrey H. Hartman writes: "Unconsciousness remains an ambiguous term in the Romantic and Victorian periods, referring to a state distinctly other than consciousness or simply to unselfconsciousness. . . . In America, Thoreau uses the word as equivalent to vision." (*Romanticism and Consciousness*, ed. Harold Bloom [New York: Norton, 1970], pp. 55-6).

[12] See for a technical analysis of Thoreau as yogi, William Bysshe Stein, "Thoreau's *A Week* and OM Cosmology," *American Transcendental Quarterly* (1971), pp. 15-36.

[13] Jung writes also that the Yoga seeks "a consciousness without content," and quotes the *Hui Ming Ching* about detachment from the world "and a withdrawal . . . to an extramundane point:"

> A radiance surrounds the world of the spirit.
> We forget one another, still and pure, all
>   powerful and empty.
> Emptiness is illumed by the radiance of the
>   heart of heaven.
> The sea of smooth and mirrors the moon on its
>   surface.
> The clouds vanish in blue space.
> The mountains shine clear.
> Consciousness dissolves itself in contemplation.
> The disk of the moon floats alone in the sky.

(*Psyche & Symbol: A Selection from the Writings of C. G. Jung*, ed. Violet S. de Laszlo [New York: Doubleday, 1958], pp. 340 and 338).

[14] Jung, often hesitant to give the unconscious metaphysical status, held that the most powerful archetype is God, the dominant experience of which is that of a power greater than the human

will. In his last work, Answer to Job, he conceived
"God" to be a blind, unconscious deity who becomes
conscious   in   man's   evolutionary   struggle.   He
commented elsewhere that Hindu thought "equated the
subject of cognition with the subject of ontology in
general," and that "Even today Western man finds it
hard to see the psychological necessity for a
transcendental subject of cognition as the counter-
pole of the empirical universe, although the postu-
late for a world-confronting self, at least as a
point of reflection, is a logical necessity" (Psyche
& Symbol, p. 137). Combining the above ideas, one
may conclude that Jung, like Thoreau, Emerson, and
Hindu   thought,   held   that   ego-consciousness   is
grounded on an impersonal, universal unconsciousness
or perhaps supra-consciousness.

     See   Martin   Bickman,   The   Unsounded   Center:
Jungian   Studies   in   American   Romanticism   (Chapel
Hill: University of North Carolina, 1980) for
Jungian   analyses   of   the   work   of   Poe,   Emerson,
Whitman,   and   others   of   the   American   group.   My
analyses   of   Poe's   and   Emerson's   thought   in   the
preceeding chapters could be easily transposed into
Jungian terms.

     [15]   The   Collected   Works   of   C.   G.   Jung
(Princeton University Press, 1957), V. 17.

     [16]   "Moon   myths   .   .   .   always   indicate   the
dependence   of   consciousness   and   light   upon   the
nocturnal side of life, i.e., the unconscious" (Eric
Neumann, The Origin and History of Consciousness
[Princeton University Press, 1954], p. 340).

     [17] Neumann, p. 162.

     [18]   Maud   Bodkin,   in   considering   the   tragic
vision, writes: "The painful images within the
vision are at once intimately known and felt, and
also 'distanced' like the objects in a far stretching landscape, 'estranged by beauty' [she quotes
Nietzsche]. . . . To the impersonal, 'distanced,'
vision   corresponds,   in   Schopenhauer's   phrase,   'a
Will-free subject,' one indifferent to the aims and
fears of the ego" (Archetypal Patterns in Poetry
[New York: Vintage, 1958], pp. 20-21).

     [19] See Neumann, p. 171.

20 *Man and His Symbols*, ed. Carl G. Jung (New York: Dell, 1968), p. 101.

21 Joseph Campbell, *The Hero with a Thousand Faces* (New York: Meridian, 1956), pp. 19-20.

22 Campbell, p. 20.

23 Sherman Paul, p. 263.

24 Harold Bloom, p. 6.

25 *Psyche & Symbol*, pp. 135-36.

26 *Psyche & Symbol*, p. 136.

27 Richard Lebeaux, in his interesting Eriksonian analysis of "the development of Thoreau's identity," writes:

> The writing and seven years of revising *Walden* was Thoreau's way of assuring himself that he could continue to live in the sunlight of his Walden experience even after he had left the pond. The book emerged out of his desperate need to keep away the shadows of identity confusion, shame, and guilt--shades which continued to hover threateningly over him in the post-Walden years. . . . It thus became imperative for Thoreau to cling to his Walden identity--indeed, to create and believe in a persona who was more independent and purer than the real man who had lived by the pond (*Young Man Thoreau* [Amherst: University of Massachusetts Press, 1977], p. 215).

But the writing of *Walden* seems to me to have been more therapeutic than this passage suggests. I hold that Thoreau, during the years of revising *Walden*, became enough reconciled with "the shadows of identity" to releash sufficient unifying energy and to attain aesthetic distance to finish his great work; and that the moonlight passages in his *Journal* during these years are symbolic of his journey into himself for the ego's partial reconciliation with these shadows.

28 Harold Bloom, p. 21.

KATAHDIN AND THE "WILD"

> "I cannot spare my moonlight and my
> mountains for the best of man I am likely
> to get in exchange"[1]

> Thoreau

I

Thoreau travelled three times (1846, 1853,
1857) to the Maine woods to study the Indians and
the wilderness. He found the former poverty-
stricken and propagandized by Christians, and the
latter, thriving with dense timber, animals, birds,
"no-see-ums," and briars. He climbed Mt. Katahdin,
waded through difficult swamps, paddled on black
moonlit lakes, heard the loon, and hid from thunder-
storms under canoes. He learned to build a birch
canoe, to portage, to live like an Indian off the
land. He was told that "It is a common accident for
men camping in the woods to be killed by a falling
tree." And he himself once heard "come faintly
echoing or creeping from far through the moss-clad
aisles, a dull dry rushing sound, with a solid core
to it, yet as if half smothered under the grasp of
the luxuriant and fungus-like forest, like the
shutting of a door in some distant entry of the damp
and shaggy wilderness," thus incidentally confirming
the possibility of an almost unbelievable near-
catastrophe in Cooper's novel The Pioneers.[2]

Thoreau found humor in Maine. He was amused by
his Indian guide whistling "O Susanna," and observed
that moose look like "great frightened rabbits, with
their long ears and half inquisitive looks." He
found anger: he was furious at hunters killing
moose for mere sport, which "without making any
extra-ordinary exertion or running any risk yourself, is too much like going out by night to some
woodside pasture and shooting your neighbor's
horse." Beyond touches of humor, humane and eco-
logical outrage, Maine Woods abounds with Thoreau's
enduring interest in natural facts, in historic
events, and in people.

The book is mossy and moosey, and deceptively
plain in philosophy and symbolism. But Thoreau went

to Maine to meet the challenge of starkest "unhandselled" nature. He decided eventually that "The
wilderness is simple, almost to barrenness," a place
to be humanized by loggers and pioneers before poets
can live there permanently. While he was there,
however, he sought to look through and beyond the
symbolic lens of the harsh wilderness.

II

Thoreau climbed Mt. Katahdin in 1846 and found
on the summit "Vast, Titanic, inhuman nature. . . .
Matter, vast, terrific . . . the presence of a force
not bound to be kind to man." Howard Mumford Jones
feels that Thoreau received a "cosmic scare" from
the experience, and Matthiessen thinks that Thoreau
considered it an encounter with the "diabolic" in
nature.[3] Two other critics believe that Katahdin
invalidated Thoreau's life-long quest that "was
founded on the pantheistic belief that the universe
was congenial to human life and that human meaning
could therefore be found in nature. The stark,
inhuman nature Thoreau experienced at Katahdin thus
threatened his most basic premise" which he eventually solved by formulating "a distinction between
the mountains, which repelled his understanding, and
the plains which were receptive to his search for
ultimate reality."[4] This essay argues that
Thoreau did indeed find in Maine elements of creation that challenged his philosophy, but that he
incorporated in his thought forces "not bound to be
kind to man."

In his formally published work, in his _Journal_,
and in his letters, Thoreau mentioned mountains
frequently and invariably used them as standard
nineteenth-century symbols of infinity and inspiration. For example, he wrote in _Walden_, "by
standing on tiptoe I could catch a glimpse of some
of the peaks of the still bluer and more distant
mountain ranges in the north-west, those true blue
coins from heaven's own mint" ("Where I lived"). In
"Walking," he said that "there is something in the
mountain-air that feeds the spirit and inspires."
In 1852 he exclaimed "that blue mountain range in
the northwest horizon to Concord, . . how poor,
comparatively, should we be without it! . . . The

216

privilege of beholding it, as an ornament, a suggestion, a provocation, a heaven on earth." (IV, 264). In 1853 he noted that "I set out once more to climb the mountain of the earth; for my steps are symbolical steps, and in all my walking I have not reached the top of the earth yet" (V, 35). Mountains, he determined, "are stepping stones to heaven" (V, 141). To his friend, Harrison Blake, he stated in 1855 that "I was glad to hear the other day that Higginson and _____ were gone to Ktaadn; it must be so much better to go to than a Woman's Rights or Abolition Convention; better still, to the delectable primitive mounts within you, which you have dreamed of from your youth up, and seen, perhaps, in the horizon, but never climbed."[5] In 1856 Thoreau wrote to Blake, "As for the dispute about solitude and society, any compromise is impertinent. It is idling down on the plane [sic] at the base of a mountain, instead of climbing steadily to its top. Of course you will be glad of all the society you can get to go up with. Will you go to glory with me? is the burden of the song. . . . It is not that we love to be alone, but that we love to soar, and when we do soar, the company grows thinner and thinner till there is none at all. It is either the <u>Tribune</u> on the plain, a sermon on the mount, or a very private ecstacy still higher up."[6]

In 1857 Thoreau recorded a dream that he had repeatedly about a mountain in "the easterly part of our town (where no high hill actually is):"

> My way up used to lie through a dark and unfrequented wood at its base. . . . I steadily ascended . . . til I lost myself quite in the upper air and clouds, seeming to pass . . . into a superterranean grandeur and sublimity. What distinguishes that summit above the earthly line, is that it is unhandselled, awful, grand. It can never become familiar; you are lost the moment you set foot there. You know no path, but wander, thrilled. . . . There are ever two ways up: one is through the dark wood, the other through the sunny pasture. That is, I reach and discover the mountain only through the dark wood. . . . Why is it that in the lives of men we hear more of the dark wood than of the sunny pasture? . . . Though the

pleasure of ascending the mountain is largely
mixed with awe, my thoughts are purified and
sublimed by it, as if I had been translated (X,
142-4).

This dream mountain was not in itself alien to
Thoreau but grand, thrilling, purifying, awful, a
region similar to the "unhandselled savage nature"
Emerson referred to in "The American Scholar," out
of which Druids and Berserkers come "to destroy the
old and to build the new." The dark feature of the
dream is not the mountaintop but the unfrequented
and lonely route which Thoreau said he always chose.
This universal motif of working out of darkness into
light seems to express a conviction that he was
destined, by temperament and circumstance, to earn
his victories by fighting through partly self-
induced handicaps, literary and social neglect, to
eventual light and recognition.

He wrote in 1857, again to Blake:

It is a great satisfaction to find that
your oldest convictions are permanent. With
regard to essentials, I have never had occasion
to change my mind. The aspect of the world
varies from year to year, as the landscape is
differently clothed, but I find that the Truth
is still True, and I never regret any emphasis
which it may have inspired. Ktaadn is there
still, but much more surely my old conviction
is there, resting with more than mountain
breath and weight on the world, the source
still of fertilizing streams, and affording
glorious views from its summit, if I can get up
it again. As the mountains still stand on the
plain, and far more unchangeable and permanent,
--stand still grouped around, farther or nearer
to my maturer eye, the ideas which I have
entertained,--the everlasting teats from which
we draw our nourishment.[7]

The only evidence that Katahdin may have disturbed
Thoreau is in this letter in the sentence, "Ktaadn
is there still, but much more surely my old conviction is there." But on such tenuous grounds one
may not argue with any weight that Thoreau's entire
philosophy was at stake, especially since he immediately affirms his "old conviction."[8] And

this old conviction was essentially that matter is an expression of mind, not that mind is a product of matter. The letter as a whole implies at most that Katahdin may have represented for Thoreau some kind of problem, that he faced it, and that indeed his "maturer eye" had solved it.

But the letter needs further comment. In it he envisioned his ideals as mountains that were "everlasting teats" from which he gained spiritual nourishment. If he had pictured them as hanging down, they could be taken as Platonic Ideas mirrored by material mountains, balancing peak to peak, draining their spiritual nourishment onto the plain. Instead, he saw them rising from the breast of prone nature, continguous with, and superimposed upon, material mountains. In "Ktaadn" he remarked that "We sucked at the very teats of Nature's pine-clad bosom." He climbed the teats on which he nursed; they did not hang from a supernatural sky. And in <u>Walden</u> he said that his instinct told him that his "head is an organ for burrowing," and that with it he could burrow his way "through these hills" to reach the "richest vein."[9] Thoreau went up in spirit by doing down to matter.

He was a Fundamentalist of nature, sauntering through the holy land, touching the words of things, sucking on leaves and berries, getting in touch, by a kind of mystical osmosis, with the spirit that was at once within himself and behind nature. "There is no other land," he assures us; "there is no other life but this. . . . There is no world for the penitent and regretful" (XII, 159-60). Like Emerson, he believed that nature is the direct expression of universal mind with which his unconscious blended, and on which his personal consciousness was grounded. Nature, the language of his Greater Self, spoke of reality here and now, reality that "will never be more divine in the lapse of all the ages."

In sum, Thoreau believed that mountains represented the closest point that man can come to pure spirit. He distinguished them from the plain which stands for the ordinary routine of the practical understanding, the area of commodity, which few villagers leave. He chose to live in a "ravine" so that he could be as near as possible to

219

the source of inspiration day after day and still endure as a finite creature. His mountain symbolism reenforces the basic Transcendental premise that the Understanding has no business in the area of inspiration. Thoreau never wished to "reduce the mountain tops to the terms of his understanding on the plain."[10] He should not have expected to find the summit of Katahdin to be logically comprehensible.

III

And yet, Thoreau's cry upon Katahdin lingers, and one finds hard to deny that his whole Maine journey in 1846 was not different somehow from his other trips to the wilderness. But the uniqueness of his Maine experience seems one of degree not of category. He had had, and was to have, other experiences with natural forces that were indifferent to man. He and Harrison Blake, for example, ascended Monadnock, June, 1858, and Thoreau recorded that the top of that mountain "often reminded me of my walks on the beach, and suggested how much both depend for their sublimity on solitude and dreariness. In both cases we feel the presence of some vast, titanic power" (X, 473). Two years earlier Thoreau waded through a swamp near the Assabet and contemplated "wildness:"

> What's the need of visiting far-off mountains and bogs, if a half-hour's walk will carry me into such wildness and novelty? . . . Wading in the cold swamp braces me. . . . I see that all is not garden and cultivated field, that there are square rods in Middlesex County as purely primitive and wild as they were a thousand years ago . . . wild as a square rod on the moon, supposing it to be uninhabited. I believe almost in the personality of such planetary matter, feel something akin to reverence for it, can even worship it as terrene, titanic matter extant in my day (IX, 42-45).

Once Thoreau observed a "very large white ash tree . . . which was struck by lightning" and asked, "For what purpose? The ancients called it Jove's bolt, with which he punished the guilty, and we moderns understand it no better. There was displayed a Titanic force, some of that force which made and can unmake the world. The brute forces are not wholly tamed. Is this of the character of a wild beast, or is it guided by intelligence and mercy? If we trust our natural impressions, it is a manifestation of brutish force or vengeance, more or less tempered with justice. Yet it is our own consciousness of sin, probably, which suggests the idea of vengeance, and to a righteous man it would be merely sublime without being awful" (IV, 155-57). Such references by Thoreau to vast, titanic power in nature indicate that his experience on Katahdin was not new in kind; he had faced before the brute forces of nature and had found them sublime and awful.

Even in _Walden_ Thoreau did not omit implicit references to similar events, if not to Katahdin itself. In the chapter "Spring" he wrote, in speaking of the "wild," that "we must be refreshed by the sight of inexhaustible vigor, vast and titanic features, the sea-coast with its wrecks, the wilderness with its living and decaying trees. . . . We need to witness our own limits transgressed, and some life pastured freely where we never wander." These are some of the very terms Thoreau used for the summit of Katahdin. By the phrase "life pastured freely" he described those flocks and herds he had encountered on the "side-mountain" among the dark and silent rocks, herds that looked at him "with hard grey eyes, without a bleat or low." Moreover the phrase "the sea-coast with its wrecks" recalls Thoreau's journeys to Cape Cod where he observed the sodden hulks of drowned passengers of the ship _St. John_, and sought the remains of Margaret Fuller. Thoreau knew well wilderness that was not bound to be kind to man.[11]

Katahdin was exhilerating and shocking, but it did not deny in principle "the unity of confidence and exhortation he wished to display" in _Walden_.[12] He did not explicitly refer to Katahdin in that book because such a reference would have negated the book's geographic unity and defeated his organic principle that in every part of creation all modes of creation are found. The fields around Concord, the local hills through which he burrowed, the streams on which he sailed, contained in some degree all aspects of creation. In principle he had no "need of visiting far-off mountains and bogs" to find the refreshment of wildness and forces unkind to man. He found near home such forces in miniature: frozen toads, rotting horses, lightning bolts, forest fires. The violence in nature symbolized for him the indominable and super-abundant energy of creation. He "loved" to see nature, he stated in Walden, "so rife with life that myriads can be afforded to be sacrificed and suffered to prey on one another; that tender organizations can be so serenely squashed out of existence like pulp--tadpoles which herons gobble up, tortoises and toads run over in the road; and sometimes it has rained flesh and blood!" ("Spring"). Thoreau encountered in Maine simply on a larger scale what he had found already in his home territory.

IV

What startled Thoreau on top of Katahdin, what makes this mountain journey different from the others, was his encounter with the massiveness of Matter, of the winds, the mist, the ragged hodge-podge of giant boulders that make-up that unique summit. Such a display of Matter did indeed seem to decentralize his central perspective, to challenge his "old conviction," to create a dualism in which Spirit was the lesser half.

The matter to which I am bound has become so strange to me. I fear no spirits, ghosts, of which I am one--that my body might--but I fear bodies, I tremble to meet them. What is this Titan that has possession of me? Talk of mysteries! Think of our life in nature--daily to be shown matter, to come in contact with it--rocks, trees, wind on our cheeks! the solid earth! the actual world! the common sense! Contact! Contact! Who are we? Where are we?

Four years before his first visit to Katahdin, Thoreau had experienced the dualism of spirit and matter even more intensely. In 1842 his brother John died of lockjaw, and the terrible impact of this tragedy caused him to$_{13}$ suffer sympathetic symptoms of the same disease. In June, 1840, he noted that "I never feel that I am inspired unless my body is also" (I, 147). Six months later he advised, "we should strengthen and beautify, and industriously mould our bodies to be fit companions of the soul" (I, 176). But on February 11, 1842, five weeks after the death of John, he lamented that "there is nothing so strange to me as my own body" (I, 321). For Thoreau, the Not Me at once had more substantial reality than the Me, and was more intimately related to the Me, than it had and was for Emerson. That is, Thoreau was less a subjective idealist and identified more with nature as fact. He therefore lived in a less coherent universe than the older man for whom the spirit maintained a steady pressure of dominance, even when Waldo died. Emerson spoke of "the reverential withdrawing of nature before its God;" but on Katahdin Thoreau felt nature overwhelm its god. Yet it was only a momentary loss of true perspective. In the long run, Katahdin simply taught him once more that matter had to be treated with respect if he were to survive as a unity of form and content.[14]

Although Thoreau at John's death felt alienated from his body and felt like a ghost on Katahdin, there is, again, little or no evidence that either event, or any other assertion of matter, disrupted his faith in the ultimate preeminence of spirit. "Katahdin is there still, but much more surely my old conviction is there, resting with more than mountain breath and weight on the world, the source still of fertilizing streams, and affording glorious views from its summit, if I can get up it again." Thoreau's nagging problem about Katahdin, if he had one, was about the meaning of the mountain as symbol, not about whether or not it was a symbol. "Man is all in all," he said in 1856, "Nature nothing, but as she draws him out and reflects him" (IX, 121).

V

Thoreau's Maine experience in 1846 is an extreme example of what he called the "wild." And the "wild" in nature for him was the expression of the sheer energy of Being, beyond the relative good and evil of humanity.[15] "What a wilderness for a man to take alone!" he exclaimed in "Ktaadn." "It was Matter, vast, terrific--not his Mother Earth-- the home this, of Necessity and Fate." "The fates are wild," he said elsewhere, "for they will, and the Almighty is wild above all, as fate is" (IV, 482). Katahdin presented to Thoreau in no uncertain terms the pure power of Being underlying the ordinary life of the plain.

"When I would recreate myself," Thoreau wrote in "Walking," I seek the darkest wood, the thickest and most interminable and . . . most dismal swamp." The "wild" he thought is necessary for "resource and background," for disruption of the stultifying patterns of mental lethargy. "In literature it is only the wild that attracts us" ("Walking"). Thoreau's sojourn at the Pond was an attempt to gain pastoral balance between the primitive and cultural, matter and spirit, the energy of nature and the forming ability of the mind. He wrote in "Higher Laws" of "the generative energy, which, when we are loose, dissipates and makes us unclean, when we are continent invigorates and inspires us." Like the hard urge of bodily appetites, the undisciplined potency of Katahdin dissipated and made the soul seem alien. But when Thoreau disciplined it, made it "chaste" and "pure" in his imagination, it became creative inspiration. Hence he advocated living close to nature only when one intellectually guides the power that the language of nature elicits. "It is the marriage of the soul with Nature that makes the intellect fruitful, that gives birth to imagination" (II, 413). A James Collins is merely gross; and Katahdin stands at once for the "possibility that nature is unfriendly to humanity" and for the possibility that it is the preservation of the world.

Near the beginning of "Ktaadn," Thoreau comments on the "wholly uninhabited wilderness, stretching to Canada" where "one could no longer accuse institutions and society, but must confront the true source of evil." The "true source of evil?" He does not elaborate this idea, but it is just as challenging to his Transcendentalism as his experience of titanic matter. The statement seems to strike at the heart of his position that the origin of evil is the human will, especially the corporate will. Men are the originators and sustainers, as Emerson said, of the blank in their eye, not something beyond their powers from which they can be saved only by a personal god. But Thoreau accommodated even this idea of "evil" originating beyond the ego.

He was caught off-guard, not enough awake with infinite expectation, when he went north and suddenly confronted the startling expression of the Transcendental demonic or super-wild. As he climbed, he lost the equilibrium of form and content of the pastoral plain. He was utterly alone on the mountain top with "its hostile ranks of clouds . . . ever rising and falling with the winds' intensity," the initial stage of creation. He was perched at "the true source of evil" and the true source of good; or rather, perched beyond the relative good and evil of the plain, at the mystical peak of Becoming from which emanated downward this world's growth of multiplicity, a dispersion of forms, flowing through ravines, onto the plain, the moral area of the Understanding. Even "simple races, as savages," Thoreau wisely observed, "do not climb mountains,--their tops are sacred and mysterious tracts never visited by them." Katahdin was Thoreau's most stunning and ineffable encounter with the divine language of a-moral energy.

Thoreau was not naive nor dishonest with himself, as his *Journal* shows. He was no more disturbed that part of creation, that indeed the very ground of creation, was "unfriendly" to mankind than was Jonathan Edwards, a hundred years earlier, by the unknown god who, in defiance of sentimental humanity, displayed his power and glory by sustaining hell forever. Thoreau found in Maine sheer power of Being beyond relative value, beyond poor Indians, poor moose, beyond Walden and civilization. He found there on an immense scale the same abundance of energy that he loved to see in miniature in organic life around Concord, energy that made nature "so rife with life that . . . sometimes it has rained flesh and blood!" The material energy, the substantiality of Katahdin were in truth symbols of the intense power of impersonal (but non-material) Being to which Thoreau was not alien but akin.

Afterwards, Thoreau went back to Walden Pond to try to come to grips with what he found in Maine. As Transcendental Logos, as it were, he disciplined it by conceiving it a manifestation of the "wild." But he did not cultivate it; he wanted Katahdin still to defy his Understanding. Indeed, the original goal of the Transcendentalists was to escape from the pastoral plain with its Unitarian church, and to find immediate revelation beyond rational thought. "We want no completeness but inensity of life" (IX, 378), Thoreau insisted. He was careful to say that "at the same time that we are earnest to explore and learn all things, we require all things mysterious and unexplorable" ("Spring").

When Thoreau, in this same chapter, in speaking of the "wild," wrote that "we need to witness our own limits transgressed," he was denying Naturalism. He was stating that we are nothing in ourselves until we commit ourselves to an alignment with the Greater Self of which we are a part. "Not till we are lost," he exclaimed in "The Village," "in other words not till we have lost the world, do we begin to find ourselves, and realize where we are and the infinite extent of our relations." We must open ourselves to the wild areas of ourselves beyond self-consciousness, pastoral Mother Earth, humanity, to the hidden will, to the power of Being expressed by Katahdins of the Not Me, to the power the source of which, although beyond our comprehension, is inside ourselves, for "it is vain to dream of a wildness distant from ourselves."[16] We must commit ourselves, in Emerson's words, to that "deeper fact in the soul than Compensation, where the soul is not a compensation, but a life . . . the aboriginal abyss of real Being" ("Compensation").

VI

Bronson Alcott wrote in 1869 that "New England has produced little pastoral, idyllic--Thoreau hardly attaining to the music of humanity but chanting that of nature, loving the wild and savage even, with a sylvan rather than urbane affection." In contrast, Alcott said that he himself sought "the genius of the home and household . . . the charming

226

humanities[17] to complement the wild, untamed, impersonal."[17] Thoreau's sustained interest in the "wild," the "Indians," testifies that he was more eager for the evangelical power of Being than for social order. In "Civil Disobedience," his revolutionary tract on social action, he admitted in the final analysis that he "came into this world, not chiefly to make this a good place to live in, but to live in it, be it good or bad." He sought life, energy, not behavior patterned on social norms. The profoundest reform, he thought, "is the effort to throw off sleep." He craved reality, be it life or death, just so it was alive. He sought his "private ecstacy" in the power of self-existence grounded on God that "culminates in the present moment." And "God . . . has no moral philosophy, no ethics" (I, 359).

When Thoreau said, "whatever we see without is a symbol of something within" (III, 201), he did not mean that all "within" is mortal and humane. He was religious in the sense that he believed that salvation comes only when one abandons himself to a reality that is more than mankind. He travelled alone to find out if there is anything more than man that could save him, and believed that he found that there is. "Alone in distant woods or fields, I come to myself," he said. "I once more feel myself grandly related, and that cold and solitude are friends of mine. . . . This . . . wildness of nature is a kind of thoroughwort, or boneset, to my intellect" (IX, 208-9). "The best thought," he declared, "is not only without sombreness, but even without morality. The universe lies outspread in floods of white light to it. The moral aspect of nature is a jaundice reflected from man. . . . Occasionally we rise above the necessity of virtue into an unchangeable morning light, in which we have not to choose in a dilemma between right and wrong, but simply to live right on and breathe the circumambient air. There is no name for this life unless it be the very vitality of _vita_" (I, 265). With serene stoicism Thoreau believed that "the grandest picture in the world is the sunset sky. In your higher moods what man is there to meet? You are of necessity isolated. The mind that perceives clearly any natural beauty is that instant withdrawn from human society" (IV, 258). Thoreau and Emerson were lovers of nature not merely because they found nature some-

227

times friendly. They were such lovers because they found by way of nature that which is eternal, which underlies and transcends nature and humanity, and to which they belonged.

As we have seen, Frederic Hedge and others thought that the concept of an impersonal deity verged on atheism. They could not conceive, for example, how such a divinity could care for man. "The question is what we mean by 'He,' whether blind force or intelligent Will," Hedge stated. "It is that which fixes the dividing line between theism and atheism."[18] The two great Transcendentalists would have answered that the universal does not care for persons in the way a person cares for persons. Mankind is not subjected to the arbitrary will of a transcendent personal god; nor God to sentimental anthropomorphizing. The universal is not a particular, not a distinct and separate being apart from other beings; it is the morning light and sunset ground of all egos, beyond good and evil. Love and pity, although essential for communal welfare on the busy plain, are horizontal virtues, not vertical knowledge of God, not assured salvation. The answer they would have said to the question, Who cares for man? is that only God in man can save man by showing man, through nature, that man is in God; only "the aboriginal abyss of real Being" can save man, only "the very vitality of _vita_."

VII

Copleston describes a kind of "panpsychism" similar to Thoreau's notion of deity.

If . . . we can perfectly well add to the purely empirical study of the world-process a metaphysical picture which involves a teleological interpretation but which at the same time excludes as superfluous the concept of a transcendent Absolute, we must, I think, have recourse to the idea of an unconscious selection of means to an end. We must interpret the world on an analogy with the living organism, which can reasonably be regarded as displaying teleological activity and selecting means to a determinate end, though not by conscious and

228

deliberate choice. Probably we shall have to adopt some form of panpsychism. Infra-spirit-ual Nature will be looked on, for instance, as slumbering spirit, to borrow a phrase from Schelling. And humanity's developing scien-tific knowledge of the world can then be regarded as the world's knowledge of itself. Thus if we speak of the world-process as the Absolute, we have the picture of the Absolute coming to self-consciousness in and through man.[19]

Thoreau believed that "the unconsciousness of man is the consciousness of God, the end of the world" (I, 119). He asked, "Why, God, did you include me in your great scheme? Will you not make me a partner at last? Did it need there should be a conscious material?" (I, 327).[20] And I have argued in the fourth essay that Emerson held that the conscious-ness of man and God is the same. The two men differed perhaps in that Thoreau conceived of existence more in terms of an open-ended organic metaphor than Emerson, more like a growing but wise, old animal; and Emerson, more in terms of an "arrived" spirit. Thoreau lived more easily than Emerson with the proposition that the evolution of the world is not mainly by conscious and deliberate choice; he travelled the "wild," the mysterious, the unexplored. Emerson, on the other hand, undulated among public eloquence, nature walks, and withdrawal into the candle-lit study of the Over-Soul. What Emerson was to Unitarianism, Thoreau was to Emerson. Yet both men were "panpsychists," holding that the concept of a transcendental Absolute is superfluous. And of course both men would have added knowledge of the humanities to that of science in the world's developing knowledge of itself.

The ascending Becoming of Thoreau's Greater Self was a spiral curve: eternal becoming summer, fall, winter, spring; life unto death unto higher life. His Journal is filled with minute recordings of this Self in process. He faithfully measured its depth of snow, took its temperature, admired its contours, its sublimity, its delicacy, noted which of its flowers were blooming today. He was steadily examining the body and getting to know the psychic dimensions of the Eternal Organism which supported him, as ego, with energy and primordial wisdom.

When his greater body, Nature, called to him, he was driven to partake in its excitement. "The wind has fairly blown me out doors; the elements were so lively and active, and I so sympathized with him, and I could not sit while the wind went by" (II, 338). "What life! What society!" he exclaimed. "The cold is merely superficial; it is summer still at the core, far, far, within. It is in the cawing of the crow. . . . What a delicious sound! It is not merely crow cawing to crow, for it speaks to me too. I am part of one great creature with him; if he has voice, I have ears. . . . Ah, bless the Lord, O my soul! bless him for wildness, for crows" (VII, 112-13). In springtime Thoreau was estatic as the ancient organism of which he was a part awakened in the eternal ascension of Being.

VIII

As consciousness of the Great Creature of the world, Thoreau disciplined its primitive energy and listened to its instinctual wisdom. For there were these two aspects of the "wild:" energy and wisdom. In regard to this wisdom, he noted that "a certain refinement and civilization . . . increases with the wildness" (II, 477). "What we call wildness is a civilization other than our own" (XI, 450), that is, other than our superficial, constantly changing, ego-civilization. On his night journeys, the stars and moonlit landscapes hinted to him of "a higher civilization, as the wild ever does" (II, 476). The "wildness" of moonlit scenes were manifestations of ancient patterns of order of the universal mind, primitive though it may be, patterns which he instinctively used to help him gain control over himself as ego. On the other hand, the "wildness" of mountain scenery was a symbol of crude spiritual energy which, when disciplined, powered his creative apsiration toward higher levels of consciousness. In the "Conclusion" of <u>Walden</u>, he declared that "I did not wish to take a cabin passage, but rather to go before the mast and on the deck of the world, for there I could best see the moonlight amid the mountains." He preferred to ride on deck to avoid the acerbating confinement of ego-civilization, to be immediately in touch with the dim patterns of ancient organic orders as they stood in the eternal mind, and to be open to the aliveness of the future. During his moonlight excursions he journeyed back to the archetypal behavioral patterns of his Greater Self for help in controlling his limited condition; and on his trips to the mountains, he sought inspiration of the unlimited wild. He drew upon the content and form of the transcendental world in advancing the consciousness of God in himself.

[1] The Journal of Henry D. Thoreau, ed. Bradford Torrey and Francis H. Allen (1906; rpt. New York: Dover, 1962), VI, 415. Hereafter references to the Journal will be included in the text.

[2] In chapter twenty-two Judge Temple and his party are nearly killed by a falling tree in the deep forest.

[3] Howard Mumford Jones, "Thoreau and Human Nature," in The Thoreau Centennial, ed. Walter Harding (State University of New York Press, 1964), p. 85. F. O. Matthiessen, American Renaissance (New York: Oxford University Press, 1941), p. 163.

[4] John C. Blair and August Trowbridge, "Thoreau on Katahdin," American Quarterly, XII (1960), 508-17). Lawrence Buell concludes that "the only safe biographical conclusion one can draw from the episode is that Thoreau simply felt more at home in a semidomesticated nature than in the remote wilderness" (Literary Transcendentalism [New York: Cornell University Press, 1973], p. 180).

[5] The Writings of Henry David Thoreau, ed. F. B. Sanborn, (New York, 1906), VI, 260.

[6] Writings, VI, 281.

[7] Writings, VI, 316.

[8] Blair and Trowbridge's two strongest items of evidence for their argument, I believe, are Thoreau's statement in "Ktaadn" that the mountaintop pilfered him "of some of his divine faculty" and this sentence in his letter to Blake.

[9] Thoreau wrote: "So the mind develops from the first in two directions: upwards to expand in the light and air; and downwards avoiding the light to form the root. . . . One half of the mind's development must still be root, - in the embryonic state, in the womb of nature, more unborn than at first. . . . The growing man penetrates yet deeper by his roots into the womb of things" (II, 203).

[10] Blair and Trowbridge, p. 516.

[11] In "Cape Cod" Thoreau wrote:

> On the whole, it was not so impressive a
> scene as I might have expected. If I had
> found one body cast upon the beach in some
> lonely place, it would have affected me
> more. I sympathize rather with the winds
> and waves, as if to toss and mangle these
> poor human bodies was the order of the
> day. If this was the law of Nature, why
> waste any time in awe and pity? . . . Why
> care for these dead bodies? . . . I saw
> their empty hulks that came to land; but
> they themselves, meanwhile, were cast upon
> some shore yet further west, toward which
> we are all tending, and which we shall
> reach at last, it may be through storm and
> darkness. . . . It is hard to part with
> one's body, but, no doubt, it is easy
> enough to do without it when once it is
> gone. . . . The strongest wind cannot
> stagger a Spirit; it is a Spirit's breath.

[12] Blair and Trowbridge, p. 512.

[13] The Letters of Ralph Waldo Emerson, ed.
Ralph L. Rusk (Columbia University Press, 1939), II,
4. See Richard Lebeaux, Young Man Thoreau (University of Massachusetts Press, 1977), p. 172 and
passim, for an interesting interpretation of this
crucial event in Thoreau's life.

[14] Thoreau wrote to Blake: "I suppose that I
feel the same awe when on their summit that many do
on entering a church. . . . You must ascend a
mountain to learn your relation to matter, and so to
your own body, for It is at home there though you
are not" (The Correspondence of Henry David Thoreau,
ed. Walter Harding and Carl Bode [New York University Press, 1958], p. 497). The height of mountains
symbolized for Thoreau spiritual aspiration; their
physical massiveness emphasized the distinction
between spirit and matter and the apparent inferior-
ity of the former.

[15] Thoreau's Katahdin experience might be seen
as one of the "Aesthetic Sublime." Wordsworth, more

than any other of the great English Romantics, found in the vastness of mountains the terror and exultation of sublimity, and comes closer than any of the others in temperment to Thoreau. But if "the perfect expression of 'The Aesthetic of the Infinite'" is found in Wordsworth in his "transfer of Infinity and Eternity from a God of Power and a God of Benignity to Space, then to the grandeur and majesty of earth," Thoreau's journey on Katahdin is not really comparable to Wordsworth's experience in his trips through the Alps, described in the Prelude (Majorie Hope Nicolson, Mountain Gloom and Mountain Glory [1959; rpt. New York: Norton, 1963], p. 393). Thoreau did not find on Katahdin the self-conscious awe and reverence of deity, "the sweep of indefinite time or the sense of infinite space" which are "the shadows of divinity," to allow classification, without reservation, of his Katahdin experience as an example of the Aesthetic Sublime. He found there neither terror nor exultation; he was awe-struck and shocked.

William James wrote that "certain aspects of nature seem to have a peculiar power of awakening . . . mystical moods" in which the "larger God may then swallow up the smaller one." As an example of such a mood James quotes the following account: "I never lost the consciousness of the presence of God until I stood at the foot of the Horseshoe Falls, Niagara [sic]. Then I lost him in the immensity of what I saw. I also lost myself, feeling that I was an atom too small for the notice of Almighty God" (Varieties of Religious Experience [New York: Modern Library, n.d.], p. 393). This experience is similar to Thoreau's on Katahdin, but not quite; for one thing, it lacks his intuition of "the true source of evil."

Paul Tillich, considering the concept of the Trinity, states that the Father, "the first principle [of] the basis of the Godhead," is "the unapproachable intensity of his being . . . the power of being infinitely resisting nonbeing, giving the power of being to everything that is." "The second principle," Tillich continues, "is the mirror of the divine depth. . . . Without the second principle God is demonic, is characterized by absolute seclusion" (Systematic Theology [University of Chicago Press, 1951, vol. I, Part II, Chapter II,

Section B, pp. 235-52]). Here are terms within an accepted system that are somewhat analogous to the significant principles of Thoreau's Maine journey. Within himself or his cosmos, Thoreau had a "Father" or "wild" of Katahdin that symbolized power of Being beyond relative value, power that could be mirrored by him, as a particular "Son," and disciplined by his reason.

16 Quoted by George Whicher in _Walden Revisited_ (Chicago, 1945), p. 93.

17 _The Journals of Bronson Alcott_, ed. Odell Shepard (Boston: Little Brown, 1938), p. 397.

18 _Martin Luther_ (1888), p. 291.

19 Frederick C. Copleston, _Religion and Philosophy_ (New York: Harper, 1974), pp. 167-8.

20 Sherman Paul writes: "He [Thoreau] knew that the higher ends of the empirical self were self-consciousness, that the eternal self, the passive center, only acquired consciousness by observing the empirical self at work on the circumference" (Emerson's _Angle of Vision_ [Harvard University Press, 1952], p. 344).

Albert Camus writes in "The Myth of Sisyphus" about this world stripped of the illusions of religion.

> At the heart of all beauty lies something inhuman, and these hills, the softness of the sky, the outline of these trees at this very minute lose the illusory meaning with which he [man] had clothed them, henceforth more remote than a lost paradise. The primitive hostility of the world rises up to face us across millenia. For a second we cease to understand it because for centuries we have understood in it solely the images and designs that we have attributed to it beforehand. . . . The world evades us because it becomes itself again. . . . That denseness and that strangeness of the world is the absurd.

Camus discovers only moments of bright sun and physical pleasure in an indifferent, even hostile, nature. Indeed, he thinks that man's relation to nature is so absurd that man is "radically-different from the rest of creation. His consciousness as a human being seals him off from the world."[1] Two centuries earlier, Jonathan Edwards, choosing to live in a meaningful wilderness, found nature numinous with divine reality: "God's excellency, his wisdom, his purity and love, seemed to appear in every thing; in the sun, moon, and stars; in the clouds, and blue sky; in the grass, flowers, trees; in the water, and all nature." Later, after Edwards but before Camus, Emerson and Thoreau discarded the idea of a supernatural being, and conceived themselves in a world which they helped to make, which expressed their unique identities, and which was theirs.

Edwards and Channing were convinced that the Bible is God's gnostic message to mankind; and nature, his empirical message. Sunny days speak of his beneficence; cloudy days, of his will to test our spiritual credentials. But diseases, accidents, natural catastrophies, what do these words speak about? These are the words that orthodox theists have the most difficulty in interpreting. How can a

236

supposedly all-good, all-wise, all-powerful god say such terrible things to us? Their resolution of this problem is that these words are inscrutible to finite being, but that we must accept them with faith that God knows what he is doing. Camus, rejecting this hypothesis, designated random hostility of a materialistic world to be the cause of natural evil. Emerson and Thoreau, holding God to be impersonal and unconscious, and holding man to be the consciousness of God, fall mid-way between Edwards and Camus on this issue.

Unlike Camus but like Edwards, Emerson assumed that mankind and nature spring from a common metaphysical source, and that therefore there is ultimately a correspondence between the well-being of mankind and nature. And like Edwards, Emerson assumed that the principal cause of moral and natural evil is humanity's loss of contact with its and nature's divine source. Edwards designated the cause of this disconnection aggressive pride; and Emerson, loss of faith in a biblical god conceived in hostile terms. In either case, the consequences of the split from the divine ground are obvious. Men, sealing themselves off from deity and therefore from nature, are self-reflecting atoms of pride, lonely droplets of shame and incapacity. Their eccentricity rebounds upon them in terms of "spiders, snakes, pests, mad-houses, prisons, enemies." Our knowledge of nature is corrupt; bad art proliferates; and moral evil is rampant.

Emerson, like Edwards, Channing, and Hawthorne, believed that no man is perfect, that all men are ruined gods. He held, like them, that all men belong to a Whole of Truth, Beauty, and Goodness; and that consequently all men share responsibility for the experiences of each man: "The violations of the laws of nature [i.e., spirit] by our predecessors and our contemporaries are punished in us also" ("Heroism"). In this sense, Emerson accepted the notion of inherited evil. But unlike Edwards, he denied that the salvation of mankind depends upon the mercy and forgiveness of a supernatural personal god. Mankind alone, responsible for its corruption but filled with immanent deity, progressively determines its own destiny, and raises the divine consciousness.

Thus unlike Edwards and Camus, Emerson thought that natural evils are neither due to chance in a materialistic world nor sustained by a supernatural person. The furiousness of nature, hurricanes, earthquakes, diseases, like those which killed Ellen Tucker, Charles Emerson, John Thoreau, Waldo Emerson ("Oh that beautiful boy"), Margaret Fuller, are the result of mankind's failure to align himself with the powers and the laws of its own universal unconscious. These spiritual laws, like the laws of matter (to the knowledge of which Newton a mere century before had helped give new religious significance),$_2$ transcend local concerns; they are impersonal.^{2} Thus men suffer, whether apparently innocent or guilty, according to impersonal spiritual law. The responsibility for their suffering lies not with a conscious god but with mankind as a Whole; man "has wronged himself;" all men are responsible for the death of Waldo. In truth all men are Waldo himself, because all men belong to that Unity "which abolishes time and space," in which "every man's particular being is contained," and which "make one with all."

Emerson did not linger among ruins to ask mercy and forgiveness. By positing God to be the universal unconscious, he avoided at once the alienation of consciousness and matter, and the pitfalls of anthropomorphism. He saved man from an absurd relation to nature, and saved God from consciously permitting the terrible suffering of mankind.

But commenting on Emerson is like commenting on life itself: he is different when viewed from different angles. And the foregoing explication of his implicit thought on natural evil is too neat, too Edwardsean in its symmetry, to characterize adequately the stance of this great Romantic. It gives too much responsibility to consciousness and mankind, too little to the thrust of instinctual (spiritual) power.

In "Fate" Emerson faced directly the problem of natural evil. He spoke first of our physical and psychological limitations, of the "tyrannous Circumstance." He then described, in effect, how strong, gifted, lucky men, like himself, use tragedies and disasters as challenges toward greater spiritual power; and how the growth of mankind as a species

238

takes place by the strong learning from the futile efforts of the weak. But he does not treat the problem of compensation for those who are not lucky enough to have the strength and skill to overcome the tyranny of circumstance. He does not consider the possibility of ultimate failure for individuals or for mankind. The buoyancy of his faith, his tremendous sense of his own power and accomplishment, compels him irresistibly upward from the murky bottom of actual experience. He is almost as terrifying as Edwards who damned the majority of mankind. Of course Emerson may be right. Of course, for him, the sentiments of compassion belong to persons, and the Soul knows no persons. Of course the Reason may see that Waldo's death served "a universal end," although Emerson himself had a hard time seeing it so. But if Waldo's death was "a spur and a valuable hint" to Emerson, what was it to Waldo, Lidian, Thoreau? Of course, since there is no personal immortality, Waldo does not suffer; he no longer exists. "Life only avails, not the having lived." Of course mind never dies, and we are all Waldo now. But would Emerson have said that he himself would have been a lesser genius if Waldo had lived? The smile on the face of his "Beautiful Necessity" is not nice. And we feel that his pronouncement that natural evil is "good in the making" is methodically pressed upon us by someone who was once as desperate as we.

(Of the major writers considered in this book, I choose only Hawthorne as the one who had sufficient compassion for the eccentric and downtrodden; and even he could have had a more working compassion.)

Although Emerson would have admitted that knowledge of evil may deepen our knowledge of humanity, he stated that grief taught him nothing about God; it gave him no insight into that "vast affirmative" that underlies the world of finitudes, of relations, of humanity, of common morality. For the Over-Soul swallows all relations and is the opposite of evil which is its absence. It is that Unity of Form and Content, Emerson informs us at the end of "Fate," "which rudely or softly educates him to the perception that there are no contingencies; that Law rules throughout existence; a Law which is

not intelligent but intelligence;--not personal nor
impersonal--it disdains words and passes understanding; it dissolves persons." This description
is consistent with the concept of God as universal
unconscious mind; whether or not it satisfies the
religious craving of the reader, is another question. The Over-Soul is that power of Being which
allowed Emerson to shed like scales the foolishness
of sin, the _ignis_ _fatuus_ of disease, the terrible
invasion of the accidental, the sentimental appeal
of impotent philanthropies. It is that joy he spoke
of, in 1859, "which did not let me sit in my chair,
which brings me bolt upright to my feet, and sends
me striding around my room, like a tiger in his
cage."[3] One could do worse than to descend from
an optimism to a pessimism such as this.

FOOTNOTES

[1] Said by John Cruickshank in his _Albert Camus_ (New York: Oxford University Press, 1959), p. 52.

[2] Carl Becker writes that the eighteenth century came to presume that "the mind of God could be made out with greater precision by studying the mechanism of his created universe than by meditating on the words of his inspired prophets" (_The Declaration of Independence_ [1922; rpt. New York: Vintage-Random House, 1942], p. 39).

[3] _The Journals of Ralph Waldo Emerson_, ed. Edward Waldo Emerson and Waldo Emerson Frobes. 10 vols. Centenary Edition (Boston: Houghton Mifflin, 1910-1914), IX, 221.

INDEX

Abbot, F. E., 110.
Alcott, Bronson, 77, 94, 95, 100-104, 105, 118, 163, 166, 174, 175, 225.
Allen, Gay Wilson, 119.
Allen, V. G., 12-13, 115.
Anderson, Charles, 70, 210.
Anderson, Sherwood, 195.

Bartol, A. C., 104, 105, 106, 109, 115.
Becker, Carl, 240.
Bellows, Henry, 126.
Bercovitch, Sacvan, 32, 90.
Berkeley, George, 70.
Bhagavadgita, 187.
Blake, Harrison, 185, 216, 217, 219, 232.
Brook Farm, 77, 158.
Brownson, Orestes, 94.
Bryant, William Cullen, 129.
Buell, Lawrence, 65, 91, 231.
Burke, Kenneth, 138.
Butler, Joseph, 27, 125.

Camus, Albert, 235, 236, 237.
Caponigri, Robert, 66.
Carpenter, F.I., 115.
Centrality of Self, 69-75, 107, 183.
Channing, Ellery, 167, 195, 198.
Channing, William, Ellery, Sr., xi, xii, 13, 31, 57, 61-65, 67, 69, 75, 76, 77, 78, 83, 85, 89, 95, 96, 97, 98, 100, 101, 103-104, 112, 114, 125-137, 141-150, 155, 166, 167, 170, 235, 236.
        "Father of Spirits," 125-128, 130, 131, 141-150.
        "God Revealed in the Universe and in Humanity," 128.
        "Likeness to God," 63, 126, 128, 129.
        "The Moral Argument Against Calvinism," 31, 85, 127.
        "Self-Culture," 64.
        Treatise on Man, 61-62, 64, 90.
        "Unitarian Christianity," 127.
Channing, William Henry, 167, 179.
Chari, V. K., 185.

243

Newton, 26, 36, 144.
Norton, Andrews, 95, 111, 112.

Original Sin, 21, 25, 28, 151.

Packer, B. L., 138.
Pantheism, 13, 15, 25, 34, 44, 62, 63, 95, 96, 107,
    108, 109, 129, 136, 215.
Parker, Theodore, xi, 94, 95, 104-105, 109, 110,
112, 166, 167.
Pater, Walter, 61.
Paterson, Robert Leet, 85.
Peabody, Elizabeth, 61, 77, 106, 167, 176.
Personal Identity, xii, 21-29, 61-84.
Persons, Stowe, 121, 122.
Poe, Edgar Allan, ix, x, 33-60, 88.
    "Annabel Lee," 51.
    A. Gordon Pym, 37.
    "Bereniece," 41.
    "The Black Cat," 40.
    "The Chapter of Suggestions," 58.
    "The City in the Sea," 40.
    "The Colloquy of Monos and Una," 42, 43, 44,
        46, 49, 57.
    "The Conversation of Eiros and Charmion," 40,
        43.
    "A Descent into the Malestrom," 50.
    "The Domain of Arnheim," 51.
    Eureka, ix, 33, 34, 35, 38, 43, 45, 46, 48, 53,
        55.
    "The Fall of the House of Usher," 39, 40.
    "How to Write a Backwood Article," 44.
    "The Imp of the Perverse," 40.
    "The Island of the Fay," 51.
    "Ligeia," 49, 58.
    "The Man of the Crowd," 41, 48.
    "Mesmeric Revelation," 34, 42, 43, 46, 47.
    "Morella," 44, 58.
    "MS Found in a Bottle," 50.
    "Philosophy of Composition," 55.
    "The Pit and the Pendulum," 41, 50.
    "The Poetic Principle," 49, 51.
    "The Power of Words," 43.
    "The Tell-Tale Heart," 40.
    "To One in Paradise," 51.
    "William Wilson," 56.